An Ethic of Mutual Respect

Bruce Morito

An Ethic of Mutual Respect
The Covenant Chain and
Aboriginal-Crown Relations

UBCPress · Vancouver · Toronto

21 20 19 18 17 16 15 14 13 12   5 4 3 2 1

Printed in Canada on FSC-certified ancient-forest-free paper
(100% post-consumer recycled) that is processed chlorine- and acid-free.

Library and Archives Canada Cataloguing in Publication

Morito, Bruce
   An ethic of mutual respect : the Covenant Chain and aboriginal-crown relations / Bruce Morito.

Includes bibliographical references and index.
Also issued in electronic format.
ISBN 978-0-7748-2244-2 (cloth); ISBN 978-0-7748-2245-9 (pbk)

   1. Indians of North America – Government relations – To 1789. 2. Iroquois Indians – Government relations – To 1789. 3. Indians of North America – Government relations – Moral and ethical aspects. 4. Iroquois Indians – Government relations – Moral and ethical aspects. I. Title.

E91.M67 2012	970.004'97	C2012-904146-7

Canadä

UBC Press gratefully acknowledges the financial support for our publishing program of the Government of Canada (through the Canada Book Fund), the Canada Council for the Arts, and the British Columbia Arts Council.

This book has been published with the help of a grant from the Canadian Federation for the Humanities and Social Sciences, through the Awards to Scholarly Publications Program, using funds provided by the Social Sciences and Humanities Research Council of Canada.

UBC Press
The University of British Columbia
2029 West Mall
Vancouver, BC V6T 1Z2
www.ubcpress.ca

Contents

Preface and Acknowledgments

Is it possible for culturally divergent peoples, Aboriginal and western European, to have a mutually recognized, respectful relationship? This became a central question in my attempt to understand the struggle between the Chippewas of Nawash-Saugeen, who occupy the shores of the Bruce Peninsula on Georgian Bay, and the province of Ontario over Aboriginal fishing and treaty rights. Following the province's defeat in the courts – owing, in part, to the court's recognition of treaty rights and an imperial proclamation of 1847 by Queen Victoria – it continued to assert jurisdictional control over the management of recreational fisheries.[1] Management practices such as stocking Pacific salmon conflicted with the community's commitment to protect indigenous (and commercial) species, especially lake trout and white fish. The Nawash view this commitment as part and parcel of treaty and Aboriginal rights.I am grateful to the Chippewas of Nawash for explaining and allowing me to witness their conflicts with the Crown, at both the provincial and federal levels, and for allowing me to participate in discussions of these rights. The experience not only widened my appreciation of issues concerning justice and crosscultural understanding, it also deepened my understanding of the value of examining these issues from a philosophical or ethical perspective.

Will Kymlicka's conceptualization of multiculturalism and liberal democratic principles formed the initial framework for this study, but interactions with friends and colleagues eventually led me to seek an alternative framework.[2] "We are not just one cultural group among others!" I was told. "Aboriginal rights are not just about being protected against arbitrary discrimination. They are rights by virtue of our being here first." Even more radically, they argued, "There is no word in our language for *right;* we have responsibilities toward the land and one another." Despite Kymlicka's efforts to address at least some of these concerns (e.g., to maintain a distinction between Aboriginal and other minority rights), I found myself looking to Aboriginal peoples' historical treaty relationship with the Crown for clues to explain their dissatisfaction with the liberal framework. I was told *medicine* was a word I needed to understand, because it was more central to Aboriginal conceptions of treaties and justice than was *right*. The tension between individual and collective rights added to the confusion. These complexities played a part in my examination of what it means to respect a people. Respect, I learned, involves understanding a people's way of framing concern: in other words, their worldview and related systems of values, normative commitments, and knowledge acquisition.

Some believe it is impossible to develop true respect since it involves overcoming fundamental cultural barriers, including differing ontologies, as anthropologists John Clammer, Sylvie Poirier, and Eric Schwimmer argue. Traditional Aboriginal perspectives were shaped by such fundamentally different metaphysical, epistemological, and axiological assumptions that it is either impossible or extremely difficult for non-Aboriginal people to understand Aboriginal peoples' normative positions or viewpoints.[3] Indeed, many Aboriginal people have told me that they view and experience the world differently when they switch from their own language to English. If two peoples do not share the same conceptions and perceptions of time, place, existence, knowledge, and language, then developing a moral framework of mutual respect and understanding may well be impossible. All we can do is find the political and legal means to negotiate compromises, approximations of mutual respect.

Yet a mutual demonstration of respect continues to be important among Aboriginal people. Elders (old people) have consistently used terms such as *mnaadenmowin* (respect, in Anishnaabemowin, the Ojibway language) to explain what they view as the central problem of intercultural relations. Since respect (respect for the law, respect for individual autonomy, respect for cultural differences, and so on) is, in essence, a moral expectation, it became a key point of reference for my analysis of the differences between cultural perspectives. Darlene Johnston (Anishnaabe), my colleague and a legal scholar, often told me that, if I was to understand what I was seeking to understand, I would need to go back to the beginning. "Back to the beginning," I found out, meant examining the relationship from its point of inception. Because of her, I began the historical research on which this book is based. I want to thank Patricia Kennedy of Library and Archives Canada for helping me along this path. She quickly grasped what I was seeking to do and not only helped train me in the use of the archive's referencing system but also planted seeds that would grow into the methodology I used to identify ethical factors in the historical record. Patricia noted how important it was to examine records from various perspectives (including the financial) and pointed out a number of primary and secondary sources that stimulated new ideas about how I could approach the data. I also wish to thank Valerie-Ann Lutz at the American Philosophical Society Library, Philadelphia, for similar reasons. After listening patiently to me as I explained what I was trying to do, she brought me material I would never have imagined examining and showed me how I might use the finding aids to greater effect.

I also wish to extend my gratitude to Eric Johnston, who on more than one occasion said to me, "We need to go back to the wampum." Although I had little understanding of wampum when he made these comments, I knew wampum was important, not only to the Anishnaabek but also to the Haudenosaunee (Iroquois). I was already somewhat familiar with the Six Nations wampum reclamation or repatriation efforts in southern Ontario. Eric's statement helped give my archival research focus and, as it turned out, a surprise. I initially conducted a keyword search to extract whatever ethical significance I could from the way the historical record described wampum. I expected to find only fragments of data pertaining to wampum, but I instead found a rich set of descriptions of wampum use. Wampum were described not only as cultural artifacts but as intercultural legal and political devices as well. This latter aspect of wampum use is central to my interpretation of the Covenant Chain as an intercultural ethic.

The writings of Olive Dickason and Bruce Trigger also prepared me to revise my assumptions about Aboriginal peoples and North American history; however, it was not until I actually read the records of the Department of Indian Affairs that I was faced with the full significance of what taking a revisionist historical perspective implied.[4] The experience forced me to shift both my perspective and method because they were based on an assumption – that Aboriginal peoples were victimized by irresistible colonial forces – that conflicted so much with what I was reading that it was impossible to make sense of the material.

I am also grateful to those who have asked me to contribute to analysis of the problem of crosscultural understanding and mutual respect. I wish to thank CIDA/Environment Canada for allowing me to help critique initial drafts of *Guidelines for Environmental Assessments and Traditional Knowledge*.[5] I also wish to acknowledge the work of scholars in related fields who have influenced my view of how successful intercultural relations can be formed. For example, Nancy Turner, an ethnobotanist at the University of Victoria, has worked with the Nuu-chah-nulth on Vancouver Island to foster a shift away from demands for finality and closure to bring about a more mutually respectful relationship. Her work brings Western scientific descriptions of the flora and fauna of the Carmanah Valley together with Nuu-chah-nulth knowledge to provide a mutually informed database. It attempts to create a crosscultural dialogue in the interest of finding common ground in the arena of natural resource management.[6]

In 2001, Aboriginal people and academics came together to discuss the question of Aboriginal rights at "Aboriginal Voices and Aboriginal Rights," a conference held in Winnipeg on 22-25 June. Elders, who were asked to respond to the academics' talks, often gave their responses in Anishnaabe-mowin (the language of the Anishnaabek), in part to drive home the point that the terms of reference used in discussing Aboriginal rights were not entirely in keeping with Aboriginal peoples' perspectives and practices. Each day of the conference began with a pipe and smudge ceremony, the Anish-naabek's way of clearing the mind and heart to speak honest and true words. The conference took place at the beginning of my archival research, and it was not long before I was reading about the same practices in historical records. Even some modern academics' impatience with these ceremonies was reflected in the record, which helped me identify divergent attitudes among Europeans and their Aboriginal interlocutors. I continue to benefit from discussions with Sandra Tomsons and Lorraine Brundige (now Mayer), the conference organizers, on these matters.

I am especially thankful to Aboriginal friends and colleagues who have helped me to understand their side of the story. The people to whom I owe thanks are too numerous to list, so I name only those who intentionally taught me about Aboriginal ways or informed the research for this book. They are, in an arbitrary order, as follows: Winona Arriaga, Ross Waukey, Ralph Akiwenzie, John Borrows, Butch Elliot, Paul Jones, Rick Hill, Amos Key, Frank Calder, Raymond Skye, Mary Druke-Becker, Linda Bull, Maria Campbell, Paul Chartrand, Taiaiake Alfred, Lorraine Mayer, and Sandra Tomsons. Others who have indirectly, but not unintentionally, instructed me are Joyce Johnston, Isabelle Millette, Elijah Harper (sitting around a campfire), Alex Akiwenzie, and Keith Conn.

I wish to thank the Social Sciences and Humanities Research Council for financial support to conduct the archival and other research for this project. Additional research would not have been possible without travel support from the Alberta Law Foundation. The Athabasca University Academic Research Fund enabled me to conduct initial exploratory research, while Athabasca University's Office of the President provided release time to complete the book in the form of a President's Award for Research and Scholarly Excellence. I wish also to thank my research assistants, who proved adept at reading historical documentation from a philosophical perspective. They are Katherine Duthie, Kirk Michaelian, Aryne Sheppard, and Louise Vigeant. I also wish to thank Jim Gough and Jill Hunter for reading and offering comments on parts of earlier drafts.

There are many people who prodded, helped, and corrected me as I researched and wrote this book. But I especially wish to thank Paul Jones, who inspired me more than I can describe and exposed me to many cultural practices and community issues over the years. The motivation to keep struggling with the issues I address here and elsewhere would have diminished greatly were it not for him. I also wish to thank Amos Key of the

Woodland Cultural Centre on the Six Nations Reserve in Brantford, Ontario, who opened the centre's archives to me. It was there that I met Raymond Skye, whose work on cultural reclamation and the wampum tradition helped me get a handle on wampum protocol. Any mistakes or misrepresentations are, of course, the result of my own shortcomings.

A Note on Terminology

In an attempt to maintain as much clarity as possible, I use *Haudenosaunee* (Iroquois) interchangeably with *Five Nations* and *Six Nations*. Until the early 1700s, the Iroquois Confederacy included the Mohawk (Kanien'kehaka), Oneida, Onondaga, Cayuga, and Seneca. The Tuscarora later (at some point between 1713 and 1724) joined as the sixth nation. Although there is at least one reference to the Seven Nations (which included these Six Nations and the Waganhaas, associated mostly with the Ottawa) in 1723, the term *Seven Nations* is reserved for a more northern confederacy. Various spellings and their referents are indicated in the text. When referring to Iroquoian-speaking people (e.g., Huron, Erie, Cherokee, and Susquehanna), the term *Iroquoian-speaking* or *Iroquoian* is used. The term *Iroquois* is restricted to the Five or Six Nations, and it refers in particular to how the French identified them. *Algonquian-speaking* or *Algonquian* is likewise used to refer to those peoples whose language had an Algonquian root. *Algonquin* or *Algonkin* refers to a nation that resided near the Ottawa River. Algonquians include those who consider themselves Anishnaabek (Ojibwa, Chippewa, Ottawa, Mississauga, Potawatomi), Abenaki, Miq'maq, Penobscot, Wampanoag, Delaware (Lenni Lenape), Shawnee, Miami (Twightwees), and Cree, among others. It also includes those whom the British referred to as "Waganhaas" or "Waganhase." References to this nation are most closely connected to the Ottawa, Mississauga, and perhaps the Fox.

The names *Haudenosaunee* and *Anishnaabek* are never used in historical records, which makes using the term *Anishnaabek* difficult. Today, the term refers to the confederacy among Ottawa, Chippewa (Ojibwa), and Potawatomi, although some people suggest it refers to all Algonquian-speaking people. In 1764, however, the three-nation confederacy was referred to as the Three Fires Confederacy. Prior to that year, the British seemingly used the term *Waganhaes* or *Waganhaas* to refer to this confederacy, although it was also used to refer to a variety of Algonquian people, as noted above.

Moreover, it is not clear that these terms referred to distinct peoples or nations. For the sake of clarity, I restrict use of the term *Anishnaabek* to the Three Fires Confederacy and refer to other Algonquian-speaking peoples by using other terms or names for confederacies (e.g., Illinois Confederacy, Eastern Confederacy, or Abenaki Confederacy).

The terms *Indian, Aboriginal,* and *First Nation,* although often treated as synonyms, have distinctive meanings, and the meaning of each term has evolved over time. In the United States, *Indian* is used in the way Canadian scholars today use *Aboriginal people,* albeit with some qualifications. In Canada, *Aboriginal* refers to people who identify as First Nations, Metis, and Inuit. This work focuses exclusively on First Nations, although I avoid using this term, since it is not historically appropriate. In the seventeenth and eighteenth centuries, the British used *Indian. Reservation* is used in connection to the United States, whereas *reserve* is used in connection to Canada. When I refer to the period before the unification of parliaments (1707), I use the term *English;* after that date, I use *British* and *English* for the most part interchangeably.

My decision not to use formal titles is not intended to offend anyone or to demonstrate disrespect for any nation, society, or group. Certain groups, for instance, refer to William Johnson as "Sir William" to recognize his baronetcy. I refer to him as Johnson or William Johnson not only for convenience but also to avoid recognizing his title while not doing so for others, such as Aboriginal *sachems* (paramount chiefs). Sachems had Aboriginal names and titles that were not used in the historical records, except on rare occasions. I do, however, use titles such as "governor" or "general" to indicate the political or military significance of the person. It is clear that Aboriginal peoples recognized the importance of certain positions and responded accordingly. Likewise, I indicate when the Aboriginal people being discussed had sachem status. Sachems represented their communities but did not have the same authority as their English and French counterparts.

An Ethic of Mutual Respect

Introduction

This book aims to inform current debates about the nature of mutual respect in intercultural relationships by showing that there was once a mutually recognized, respectful relationship between the British Crown and the Aboriginal peoples of North America. This ethic of respect, captured in what was known as the Covenant Chain – the treaty relationship that evolved between the English Crown (and to some extent the Dutch) and the Aboriginal nations with whom it formed alliances in the seventeenth and eighteenth centuries – derived moral force from the way in which it was grounded in human community, a sense of tradition, and other conditions that typically remain hidden when we analyze moral life (see Chapter 1 for a more complete description of this early treaty relationship). If we were to recognize the relevance of the Covenant Chain's ethic today, thinking about Aboriginal rights would shift away from an intense focus on legal and policy instruments toward a consideration of alternative foundations more attuned to those hidden aspects of human relationships. This book has three connected but distinct aims: (1) to demonstrate that there was in fact an ethic that operated in the historical relationship between the Crown and Aboriginal peoples; (2) to identify the core elements of this ethic and then thematize them to demonstrate coherence (that is, to show that this ethic was not merely a cobbled together set of moral sensibilities); and (3) to show that the ethic is neither historically nor culturally bound (that is, it has the potential to be universalized).

To examine the relationship between the Crown and Aboriginal peoples through an ethical lens – especially in light of the existence of Indian-hating colonists, Indian killers, assimilation programs, and genocidal practices – seems pointless, if not outright insulting, to some audiences. European colonists, some have argued, only demonstrated respect for Aboriginal peoples when prudence overcame otherwise persistent assumptions and feelings of superiority. Only when faced with Aboriginal peoples' military prowess did Europeans show respect – a fear-based, calculated respect. Some

Aboriginal people express incredulity at the suggestion that Europeans ever demonstrated anything but contempt for them; the historical record of massacres, warfare, broken treaties, and dispossession that followed contact makes the search for an ethic of mutual respect seem utterly futile. To those who have struggled to have Aboriginal people and their concerns recognized by the dominant society through a long and combative series of court challenges, the search for an ethic of mutual respect could appear as an affront. Indeed, some insist that only the instrument of law has any chance of making a difference for Aboriginal people and that the idea of a mutually recognized respectful relationship is an empty concept.

This book, as a result, adopts an incremental approach by examining the process by which normative elements emerged in the Covenant Chain relationship. This relationship, in turn, reveals the existence and operation of ethical sensibilities, values, and principles. The forces that shaped these norms, moreover, were not reducible or limited to economic, military, and other nonmoral values; rather, moral sensibilities and norms came to govern the relationship as it evolved.[1] By understanding the conditions from which such an intercultural ethic emerged, and by recognizing that similar conditions could exist today, it is possible to develop a more formal theoretical framework to shape the relationship between the Crown and Aboriginal people today.

Before explaining my approach, I must first explain what students of this historical relationship may view as a serious omission. Since the Iroquois were central to the Covenant Chain, many would argue that an analysis of the Two Row Wampum (Guswentah) should be a major focus of this book. Robert Williams Jr., a legal scholar, and many Aboriginal people argue that the existence of Guswentah supports the thesis that the "West had to listen seriously to indigenous tribal visions of how different peoples might live together in relationships of trust, solidarity and respect."[2] I found, however, no references to Guswentah in the historical records for this period. This does not mean that Guswentah did not exist or was ineffective. The wampum described might, in fact, have been Guswentah. But my approach is to analyze the evidence found in the historical written record.

On Perspective and Historiography

A critique of historiography is useful, because it helps to identify the underlying assumptions that have shaped descriptions of Aboriginal people by historians and others. In the eighteenth and nineteenth centuries, historians were influenced by thinkers such as Jean-Jacques Rousseau who helped shape the idea of Aboriginal people as noble (or ignoble) savages, which, in turn, fostered the attitude that Aboriginal people had no voice, because their cultures were grounded in primitive worldviews. These concepts obviated the need to regard Aboriginal people as moral agents in their own right. As revisionist scholars argue, these ideas enjoy little evidentiary support from the historical record.[3] Yet they became effective devices for justifying assimilation practices in North America, a phenomenon illustrated amply in the person of Duncan Campbell Scott, a Canadian poet and deputy superintendent of Indian affairs from 1913 to 1932.[4] In explaining the emergence of this attitude, anthropologists and ethnohistorians Wilcomb Washburn and Bruce Trigger describe how Aboriginal people increasingly became politically marginalized, how representations of their perspective were ignored, and how the so-called Indian personality was constructed to justify this behaviour. Assumptions about the Indian's lack of civility supported the view that Aboriginal cultures could not be respected, at least not in any moral sense. Attributions of savagery justified the exclusion of Aboriginal people from political and legal arenas, and from the moral community as well. This marginalization helped entrench attitudes about European cultural superiority and an unwillingness to reflect critically on Aboriginal people and their cultures.[5] This construction and marginalization, in turn, helped deflect concerns about encroachments on Aboriginal land and assimilation practices by enabling the proponents of such practices to deny that considerations of justice had any relevance to those who were being displaced and marginalized.

Washburn and Trigger explain how it is that we continue to live with the legacy of these conceptions and practices and how we continue to harbour some of the prejudices according to which they were formulated. In the twentieth century, much North American popular culture sought to reestablish respect for Aboriginal people by reinstating the idea of the Noble Savage (as exemplified by Archie Belaney, otherwise known as Grey Owl, Ernest Thompson Seton, and elements of the North American counter-culture and environmental movements). And it is not entirely clear that our formal institutions are free of such ideas.[6] The question remains, how deeply has dichotomous and misrepresentative thinking become entrenched in our institutional and moral frameworks? Furthermore, how deeply has this kind of thinking affected our understanding of the relationship between Aboriginal people and the Crown?

By contrasting these misrepresentations and false assumptions with the historical context of the relationship between the Crown and Aboriginal peoples, as represented in the records pertinent to the Covenant Chain relationship, and by attending to the complexities of the relationship, I attempt to bring into relief the moral factors that shaped the relationship. This approach clears the ground of preconceived expectations of what an ethical approach to the relationship should look like. A critique of the work of Francis Parkman, a central nineteenth-century historian, illustrates how I attempt to avoid importing false assumptions into my reading of the historical record. Many records of the colonial period on which revisionists and I draw were collected by Edmund O'Callaghan and published between 1853 and 1887. Parkman, who is probably best known for *The Oregon Trail: Sketches of Prairie and Rocky Mountain Life* and his descriptions of North American Indians, wrote during the same period. He had acquired volumes of records from Europe for his research and had access to the O'Callaghan records. Parkman did not utilize these sources to analyze Aboriginal people's contribution to history, however; his focus was almost entirely on what we today call anthropologically interesting information.[7] He characterized Aboriginal people as uncivilized savages.[8] Typically, Parkman focused on wars, trade, religion, and anthropological and sociological curiosities. He even described the ceremonial and decorative use of wampum within the communities (Huron especially).[9] But there is no account, at least in Samuel Morison's edition of his work, of how wampum was used in the treaty relationship. The overall focus of his account is periodic encounters between the British and French and Aboriginal people, who are treated as worthy of little more than a footnote in a larger political and economic history. That Parkman makes nothing of the many dialogical elements of council meetings is noteworthy in light of just how numerous they are in the records.

Washburn and Trigger note how Parkman and other historians of the time must have read the record from the standpoint of ideological commitment. But there seems to be more involved because, when the records are examined in detail, the question still remains, how could these historians, even if they were ideologues, pass over so much evidence without even attempting to explain it away? The answer becomes clearer if we consider how the dominant narrative served various purposes, from supporting doctrines such as Manifest Destiny in the United States to justifying assimilation policies in Canada. Acknowledging Aboriginal people as agents, negotiators, and the like would have threatened the Crown's economic and political ambitions by rendering them vulnerable to reflective social forces.

Washburn and Trigger also explain how moral agency was denied to Aboriginal people.[10] Bernard Sheehan and Francis Jennings, historians who wrote during the 1960s and 1970s, adopted a determinist stance when interpreting history.[11] James Axtell, a central historian on Indian-European relations, explains that these historians viewed history as a "process in which personality was submerged in the sweep of inexorable, inevitable, and impersonal social and cultural forces. Focusing on the individual, both as a historical actor and as a moral one, was unnecessary, if not improper."[12] Washburn and Trigger advance this explanation when they describe the controversy over whether Aboriginal people actually contributed to the making of North American history.[13] They discuss the thesis of inevitability, whether Aboriginal people's conquest was, as the dominant narrative would have it, a product of their semi-civilized state.[14] They explain how anthropology, as it developed in the nineteenth century, came to be shaped in part by Social Darwinism, a deterministic evolutionary framework.[15] At a time when Aboriginal populations were experiencing massive declines, Social Darwinism helped shape the belief that the extinction of Aboriginal cultures was inevitable. This "scientifically" supported simplification of both the "Indian personality" and Indian-Crown relations lent deterministic ideologies coherence and plausibility, engendering a systemic resistance to reading the historical record in all of its complexity by the twentieth century. It would have taken courage for historians of the day to read the record against this tide.

I use this skeptical, deterministic rendering of history as a foil against which to formulate observations concerning the record. My approach is not simply to replace this deterministic framework with one based on the assumption that Aboriginal people were full moral agents, as we would assume today. Rather than imposing an alternative frame of reference, I reframe the moral context in which the Covenant Chain evolved in light of the ways in which ethical factors appear in the historical record. Chapters 1 and 2 counter traditional biases and point out what the record says or implies about moral factors. They disclose the complexity of the Covenant Chain relationship and how that complexity evolved. I use the term *evolution* to describe the process, even though it is commonly used to refer to a deterministic process – the advancement of society from a primitive to a more civilized state, a process fuelled by the competition for survival (in which the fittest survive). Georges Sioui, a Wendat-Huron historian and philosopher, views this term as particularly ruinous for Aboriginal people, because it suggests that the undermining of Aboriginal cultures and systems has been the inevitable outcome of progress.[16] The term is suitable for my purposes, however, because the process of developing an intercultural ethic, as reflected in the Covenant Chain, involved adaptive responses to conditions that compelled them to behave and think in new ways. In addition, the normative conditions that came to affect the relationship emerged in the course of adaptation. These conditions did not, in other words, exist prior to the adaptive response. My use of *evolution*, then, is premised on the idea of adaptation to conditions over which adaptees have little initial control (or even awareness) and on the idea of emergent properties. However, my definition of the term also allows for human agency.

To answer the question, how did the moral economy operate? I pay close attention to speech and interactive patterns as they appear in historical documents. For example, the historical record includes references to the presentation of wampum belts or strings that wipe tears from eyes and purify hearts, often with little or no explanation. Such presentations are described in such a way that they appear to be nothing more than punctuation marks, not materially significant to the discourse. For someone intent on mining textual records for information on political or military events or data on the finances of the day, much of this detail appears gratuitous and irrelevant. But to follow the record from the early 1600s to the mid-1700s is to observe clerks becoming increasingly attentive to the presence of belts and their details. They begin transcribing speeches and noting details, such as the presentation of "a belt" or "a belt with seven rows." These details disappear from the record after the War of 1812, when Aboriginal military and economic force declined. The difference between eras suggests that speech and interactive patterns can serve as indicators of how the moral economy operated. Noting these differences establishes a comparative context that highlights what in the relationship came to be ignored, suppressed, and indeed lost.

What was going on during meetings in the seventeenth and eighteenth centuries when wampum formed the basis for speech and interactions, and how did wampum acquire intercultural significance, which was lost after the demise of the Covenant Chain? One possible way to approach these questions is to observe how wampum presentations and the language in which they were couched became integral to business meetings. By doing so, the significance of peculiar phenomena come to light and demand interpretation. Responding to this demand, in turn, discloses the complexity of how these meetings were conducted. Unravelling this complexity by using presupposition analysis shows that even business meetings cannot be described in accordance with the dominant nineteenth- and twentieth-century historiography. Since I do not use upstreaming techniques – that is, I do not interpret the past in terms of current meanings and practices – however, I have had to find an alternative way to determine what, exactly, wampum use presupposed.[17]

The writings of Umeek (Richard Atleo) – academic, author, and hereditary chief of the Nuu-chah-nulth – offer a path forward. Umeek explains that the Nuu-chah-nulth have a high-context language: "Each Nuu-chah-nulth word may be associated with a world, or cultural and historical context, that is commonly understood."[18] When a word is used or a reference is made, say, in an origin story, the audience automatically draws a number of associations, possibly inferentially. That is, the word and its context have a logical relation, not merely an associative one. The Covenant Chain's communicative devices, I argue, must have presupposed a high-context language, since the treaty protocols incorporated origin stories, ceremonial practices, and most importantly, wampum protocol. Once the British became familiar with Aboriginal protocol and practices, they adopted origin stories and associated means of communication as elements in a shared high-context language, and wampum was central to the communicative framework of the Covenant Chain (Chapters 1-3).

Adopting the notion of a high-context language into the explanatory framework, then, becomes an instrument to draw out the complexity of the relationship from the text alone. Gilbert Ryle and Clifford Geertz's notion of rich description helps describe this instrument.[19] Geertz's work on cultural interpretation is an attempt to take into account the complexities of real world situations while trying to capture (conceptualize) cultural practices as clearly and precisely as possible (a simplification process). The tension between acknowledging complexity and needing to simplify leads Geertz to use the term *rich descriptor* to satisfy this double-edged demand: "Our double task is to uncover the conceptual structures that inform our subjects' acts, the 'said' of discourse, and to construct a system of analysis in whose terms what is generic to those structures, what belongs to them because they are what they are, will stand out against the other determinants of human behavior."[20] Geertz draws on Ryle's seminal work on the distinction between the twitching of an eye (a thin description) and winking (a thick description). Twitching is involuntary (it may be the result of a physiological condition), whereas winking is a voluntary act of communication, however phenomenologically indistinguishable it may be from twitching.[21] Being able to distinguish between a wink and a twitch is critical, because interpreting someone's twitch as a wink can be disastrous to personal and professional relationships.

To continue the analogy, to know what a Beethoven quartet is, one must understand what music is, what significance music has for a society, what distinguishes a Beethoven from a Mozart score, and so on. Individual noises made by instruments, however identical to the notes in the quartet, would not count as a Beethoven quartet without this interpretive background. When we use a thick descriptor, then, we assume a social, interpretive context of shared meanings that cannot be reduced to a set of behaviours, or even to an idea (as if meaning resides exclusively in individual minds). We assume a set of intangible factors. The relationship between the score, an understanding what music is, and what significance music has for a society is not based solely on accidental (associative) connections but rather on the conceptual (logical) connections between these intangible factors. To understand the difference, one must also understand the social meaning and context of the acts, both of which are intangible. In cases where rich descriptors are used for purposes of communication, we can conclude that the people who use them appropriately presuppose a rich array of supporting and contributing intangible factors. When these presuppositions are identified and analyzed, they must be framed in such a way so as not to ignore or diminish the importance of these intangibles.

Geertz argues that we can never completely recover or capture the context, since what we are attempting to do when we try to capture the context in language is capture its meaning – not its nature.[22] The event itself was, or is, a dynamic flow of events, whereas the attempt to capture its meaning in a description is an attempt to transform the event into something fixed. The description, however rich, never completely matches the event. On the one hand, we use concepts to thematize what we are trying to understand; by doing so, we attempt to fix meaning so that our concepts are clear and unambiguous. On the other hand, our concepts become increasingly vague as we become more familiar with the context. Although we know to what these concepts refer, we also know that their significance will not be fully or even adequately understood by those with whom we wish to communicate, if they are not familiar with the context. Similarly, an explanatory scheme that depends on the presupposition of an operation of intangibles will suffer from an inability to fully articulate what is operative in the situation to be explained. Accordingly, to frame the Covenant Chain's ethic of respect, I attempt to familiarize the reader with its context by moving from a description of the general historical context (Chapter 1) to the treaty relationship (Chapter 2) and then to a discussion of how individuals operated and related to one another (Chapter 3). Establishing context in this way forms a background against which an explanation of how and why various moral elements of the moral economy, including the intangible ones, emerges.

Since the concept of moral agency is central to my argument, it is important to provide some indication of how it works. Geertz's conceptions of culture and the role of intangibles help explain how moral agency is conceived, even if it is not fully explicable. *Culture,* to Geertz, refers to the webs of significance that human beings spin. Although analysis of these webs does not belong to experimental science, it does belong to an "interpretive search of meaning."[23] Furthermore, since interpretation – the communicative effect of rich descriptors – brings about and directs actions, the meaning these actions communicate is causally relevant. If a person does not understand or cannot interpret what a wink means, that wink will not produce the intended response. Hence, meaning, interpretation, and modes of understanding must be figured into the causal explanation of events; in particular, they must be factored into the explanation of how moral agents, acting in accordance with the moral economy, affect historical outcomes. In Chapters 1 through 3, I describe the historical relationship between the Crown and Aboriginal peoples with an eye to disclosing how approaches to communication developed and how the meaning of those communications pointed to the intangible forces that operated in the moral economy.

A Historical-Philosophical Approach
Since this book is written from a philosophical perspective and with contemporary debates in mind, ethicists may well criticize my approach on a number of fronts, the apparent leap from descriptive to prescriptive ethics, for instance. Some may view appealing to a description of an actual ethic

as a basis for how we ought to practise ethics as fallacious. Some may also argue that the job of description is better left to sociologists, not philosophers. In either case, the analysis of a historical ethic can have no prescriptive force. According to this view, the move from Chapter 3 (description) to Chapter 4 (prescription) is illegitimate, as is the claim that my re-examination of the Covenant Chain is relevant to contemporary discussions of Aboriginal rights. For various reasons, which will become more apparent in Chapter 4, I must assume that the dichotomy between descriptive and prescriptive ethics is given too much weight in moral theory. Since this and other thorny philosophical problems (e.g., agent causality) are beyond the scope of this study, I utilize the work of thinkers such as Jürgen Habermas throughout this book and Charles Taylor in Chapter 4 to frame ethics in such a way as to make the connection between description and prescription and the conceptualizing of moral agency at least intelligible. A full defence of the ethic remains for another time.

In response to those skeptics and determinists who deny that ethics can have explanatory significance because moral principles, beliefs, and so on have no causal force and cannot, therefore, shape historical outcomes, I must again point to a possible defence strategy rather than provide the defence itself. This defence strategy would begin by appealing to thinkers such as Donald Davidson and John Searle to establish the possibility of agent causality.[24] It would then proceed to reframe the concept of causality and, in turn, agency in light of how complexity affects fundamental metaphysical assumptions. A full articulation of the resulting ethical theory would not only support my approach, it would also prove more philosophically satisfying than most theories that have dominated Western thought. For the skeptic, how the ethic is shaped throughout this book can be viewed as an indication of how a full articulation would proceed.

The Peculiarity of the Records of Indian Affairs

In 1928, American historian Lawrence C. Wroth made the following comment about the richness of colonial government records in his classic essay "The Indian Treaty as Literature":

I am not ... concerned here with the self-interest of both sides that the Treaties reveal but with their importance as a neglected literary type that arose without conscious artistic design from the conflict of two distinct civilizations on the same soil – a type in which one reads the passion, the greed, and the love of life of hard-living men brought into close relationship without parallel conditions in the history of either race to guide its conduct. In it are displayed certain raw emotions: on the part of the Indians the fear of extinction, the desire to keep what the hand holds, the love of life, of ease and security. Seething in the same pot with these were the white man's passion to acquire and till the land, to build, to fill the left hand with more and more of the stuff that the right hand has grasped. All this is in the Indian Treaties, and in dramatic form. I wish that some teacher of history had poured for me this strong wine instead of the tea from Boston harbor with which the genuine thirst of my youth was insufficiently slaked, or that some teacher of literature had given me to read these vivid, picturesque records instead of saying that the colonial period had nothing to show of literary production except dull sermons, political tracts, prosy essays, and poems of invincible mediocrity.[25]

Ethnologist William Fenton, who began studying the Iroquois in the 1930s, joined Wroth in paving the way for a new and more probing reading of colonial records by paying close attention to their peculiar forms of expression. He noted that the American treaty record constituted a literary form in itself.[26] On a collection of thirteen important treaties published by Benjamin Franklin, he remarked, "Here was a new form of literature that was native American, as straightforward as a play, replete with homegrown metaphors, and with a certain style that found immediate appeal."[27] More recently, legal scholars Robert Williams Jr., Paul Williams, and Mark Walters, among others, have also paid attention to the peculiarities of government records to shed new light on the nature of treaties.[28] Michael Pomedli, a philosopher and long-time student of issues concerning Aboriginal people, goes so far as to say that these records indicate that the treaty partners went beyond acting out their mercenary interests and entered into human fellowship.[29] Robert Williams Jr. sees them as entry points to reinterpret the dominant American historical narrative.[30] Despite being written in European languages for purposes set by European agencies, treaties, Pomedli observes, have an "overarching format and context not of European fashioning."[31]

   Reading more like a narrative than a set of codifications, the early treaty record captures the puzzlement the British experienced in their interactions with Aboriginal peoples. Compared to traveller accounts, which were designed to either titillate European readers or use Indianness for purposes of cultural self-critique, early treaty records are matter-of-fact. Descriptions of interactions with sachems and warriors, of Aboriginal ceremonial behaviour and wampum protocol are similar to the notes of new university students who write down everything they hear because they cannot yet discern what is important. It is at times obvious that clerks struggled to describe what they saw and heard. That editing took place is undeniable – explanatory marginal notes are sometimes inserted in preliminary and even final drafts of reports. But on the whole, from about the 1670s to the 1770s, and to a lesser extent up to and including the War of 1812, the narrative character of the records conveys a tone of what today would be called anthropological curiosity. Clerks attempted to capture as much as might be significant to interpreting Aboriginal people's behaviours and speeches. The documents include evidence of codified laws, but they also include abundant and seemingly superfluous descriptions of people wiping away tears, presenting belts of varying numbers of rows, and burying hatchets in underground pits. What early historians dismissed as extraneous details were, in fact, part of official documentation read by superiors, including the Lords of Trade in London. These extraneous elements were read with philological care.

The dominant view is that the documents pertaining to the Covenant Chain were principally records of treaties designed to enable all parties to look after their own interests and pursue their own goals.[32] This description fails to answer a number of philological or philosophical questions. What did it mean when two distinct peoples used wampum to wipe away each other's tears, when they made their hearts pure and their throats clear in order to speak true words? What did it mean when the treaty agreement was contained in belts? Why did clerks not simply use shorthand to capture the legal significance of this behaviour? Engaging with the primary documents as they present themselves – rather than simply mining them for evidence to support a predetermined theory – reveals a world of intercultural and dialogical relations that stands in contrast to that presented in mainstream historical narratives, a world that reflects a robust moral economy.

Certain warnings about dealing with European historical documents require attention. Peter Nabakov, an anthropologist and ethnologist, for instance, argues that western European and Aboriginal ideas of history diverge markedly, even though, in certain contexts, they are compatible. Nabakov addresses concepts as fundamental to the meaning of history as time, worldview, and memory to illustrate the problems associated with the idea of history itself and, more importantly, with dismissing Aboriginal understandings of it.[33] A truly crosscultural account would include evidence from both historical traditions.

The problems associated with trying to develop such a comparative crosscultural approach are insurmountable, however, because western Europeans and Aboriginal peoples had radically different backgrounds in the period under consideration. There are numerous examples to support this view. When General W.H. Harrison of the US army invited Tecumseh to sit on a chair in 1810, the Shawnee leader rejected the offer and responded, "the sun is my father and the earth is my mother; she gives me nourishment and I repose upon her bosom."[34] Something as simple as an invitation to sit on a chair can reveal cultural incompatibilities. Historian Georges Sioui argues that the Aboriginal perspective commits Aboriginal people to respect the land and its order, as established by the Great Mystery.[35] In my book *Thinking Ecologically*, I describe the differences between the two cultures in relation to metaphysical, epistemological, and axiological shifts that occurred throughout Western history. From Plato through to the Enlightenment, the idea that human rational agents were separate from and superior to other beings became entrenched. Western Europeans came to believe that they gave other beings value by "mixing their labour with them" or by taking an interest in them. In this worldview, the nonhuman world, for all intents and purposes, was valueless until human agents took an active interest in it. The stark contrast between Aboriginal and European meta-ethical beliefs became a rationale for demonizing Aboriginal cosmologies and ethical orientations, their fundamental cultural commitments. Indeed, many environmentalists appeal to the same contrast between cultures to advance their critique of Western culture and to advocate for a radically different set of cultural beliefs and norms.[36]

These and observations by John Clammer, Sylvie Poirier, and Eric Schwimmer (see the Preface) leave little hope that a comparative analysis of culturally defined moral frameworks would yield a mutually recognized ethic. The best we could hope for is the discovery of common principles or values that operated, or were used to negotiate compromises, in certain contexts. We could not be sure that the interface between the two ethics could be universalized; that is, we could not guarantee that these two cultures would not interpret these principles or values differently in a different context, producing different actions. Using Nabakov's method, whatever commonality we could discover would be accidental and heavily context dependent. In Chapters 2 and 3, I in fact show that the initial commonalities that brought the British and their Aboriginal allies together masked underlying differences that threatened to pull them apart. These differences ran deep, to the point where they prevented the two sides from agreeing on what constitutes justice or even what it meant to be reasonable.

My approach is to begin by describing the actual relationship that enabled the Crown and Aboriginal people to cooperate, argue, and communicate effectively over a long period of time. I then analyze the conditions that made this common ground possible, acceptable, and highly valued on both sides. The descriptions of the relationship yield patterns of interaction in which both parties engaged in debates about justice, lawfulness, truth, worthiness, and the like; both sides made certain that their perspectives were represented and that articulations of a common ground were consistent with their cultural beliefs and values. This common ground was not established through a comparative analysis of each other's culture but was developed, perhaps paradoxically, through conflict and dealing with misunderstandings.

Even though I rely on British records, written by the British for British purposes, the peculiarity of these records and my method of reading and analyzing them make it impossible to deny the presence of Aboriginal voices.

British agents and clerks took Aboriginal speech patterns and ways of communicating seriously and wrote about them in ways that had to be acceptable to their Aboriginal interlocutors. Because the British wanted to maintain military and trade alliances, especially against the French, the records they kept of councils and treaties had to be reliable as proof of agreements and interactions. More importantly, to be effective, their system of record keeping had to be compatible with that of their Aboriginal allies. That the British replaced the peculiar genre of the early colonial record with a more typical bureaucratic form after the War of 1812, when the Aboriginal allies' military strength was all but destroyed, indicates that the Crown would have abandoned this form of record taking earlier, if it had been possible to do so.

Many scholars, including some of the Aboriginal scholars already mentioned, believe the historical record can provide an acceptable, though indirect, representation of the Aboriginal voice. It is not that they, or I, think that the record alone is sufficient to represent Aboriginal perspectives. But the manner in which Aboriginal voices come through offers a valuable and unique way of incorporating their point of view into the historical narrative. The practices characteristic of the Covenant Chain relationship were principally of Aboriginal origin and both the British and the French adopted them as their diplomatic framework.[37] Record keeping was, therefore, a concerted attempt to convey what Aboriginal people said and how they said it. The voices that come through are certainly not defined purely in accordance with British sensibilities and frames of reference. The Covenant Chain was a culturally hybrid institution, and its language and records were hybrid constructions. Aboriginal practices and protocols informed council meetings, and Aboriginal metaphors and linguistic devices often dominated the pages of council meeting records, even when clerks did not fully understand their meaning. Finally, the record indicates whether Aboriginal people were dissatisfied or satisfied with the British record keepers. It is possible, then, to determine the conditions that led to mutual satisfaction. Doing so, in turn, allows for an analysis of the conditions that enabled the Aboriginal voice to be adequately represented.

Indeed, the records tell of the forces that led the British to try to keep an adequately representative record of events and alliances. Peter Wraxall, secretary to William Johnson, who was superintendent of Indian affairs in the north, noted that Aboriginal people demanded that their voice be properly represented. In July 1724, a scribe noted that the Indians were often influenced in their speech by members of the Commission for Indian Affairs at Albany, whom Wraxall took to be a group of scoundrels and immoral profiteers.[38] Moreover, he cast doubt on the translations of some Indian speeches by noting that some translators were of suspicious character, men who could barely pass competency tests.[39] At times, clerks were even instructed by

Aboriginal speakers to listen well and write down exactly what was said. That clerks recorded these instructions reinforces the claim that significant forces were at play to ensure adequate representation of Aboriginal voices. Examining the differences between the records kept by competent versus incompetent agents can, as a result, help sort the records that adequately represent Aboriginal voices and those that do not. The voice that emerges, when the focus is on the more competent agents, seems like raw data because of an apparent lack of filtering devices.

Even if a complete Aboriginal record of events existed, either in oral or visual form, this indirect way of identifying and representing Aboriginal voices would still be useful and, in a certain way, vital. For instance, Aboriginal record keepers might not have described crucial parts of a process or event because they took them for granted, their communicative skills might have been limited by translation difficulties, or they might have been prevented from recording something for strategic reasons. British clerks recorded what was necessary, or seemed necessary, to avoid failures in communication, which could result in dissolution of the treaty relationship. As a result, they would not take much for granted until they were confident that they could. They were not constrained by cultural censoring forces and likely recorded details that culturally constrained recorders might have been more hesitant to record. The utilitarian motive of British agents, I argue, made more information about the nature of the communicative context evident than might otherwise have been the case.

Differences between the two cultures that led to conflicts over treaty interpretation likewise reveal a common ground that would remain hidden if analysis of the Covenant Chain were based on a comparative approach. As John Borrows, an Anishnaabe legal scholar, demonstrates in his examination of the *Delgamuukw* (1997) case, certain factors become evident when conflicts arise. They arose in *Delgamuukw* because Aboriginal oral history and practices were denied recognition and legitimacy.[40] In 1991, Chief Justice MacEachern of the BC Supreme Court denied Gitskan and Wet'suwet'en claims to title on the grounds that Aboriginal rights depend on the good will of the sovereign and could be extinguished unilaterally. They had nothing to do with oral tradition. The decision made it clear that colonial attitudes toward Aboriginal peoples' oral traditions were being propagated by the courts. Borrows, however, argues that Aboriginal people should see something positive in this attitude. Just as Canada's much-reviled Indian Act had protected Aboriginal people from Prime Minister Trudeau's attempt to make them full citizens of Canada (thereby losing their distinctness) in the 1970s,[41] MacEachern's assertion that the courts had a mandate to protect lawfulness, and his assumption that his assertion was universally and self-evidently legitimate, could be viewed as the result of comparing European and Aboriginal legal traditions and finding no common understanding. But if we examine the conflict itself, Borrows argues, a different perspective on the decision is possible.

In the aftermath of the conflict, Aboriginal people more clearly realized that without recourse to oral tradition, no treaty discourse could be conducted in a way that would enable First Nations to speak from their perspectives. Understanding the implications, Aboriginal people asked, who gave the courts, or the Crown for that matter, the right to assert sovereignty unilaterally? Who gave the Crown the right to unilaterally extinguish another people's rights and declare them to be without law? Increasing numbers of non-Aboriginal people subsequently began to see the arbitrariness of the court's assumptions and assertions, creating a context in which the search for a mutually acceptable common ground is now widely accepted. The Supreme Court of Canada eventually did recognize oral tradition as a legitimate body of evidence, setting the stage for discussions about the Crown-Aboriginal relationship at deeper levels.[42]

Just as the BC Crown denied the legitimacy of Aboriginal perspectives in *Delgamuukw* and asserted its own legitimacy, so too did the governor of New York in 1730. But the Crown, more quickly than in the *Delgamuukw* case, had to acknowledge the legitimacy of Aboriginal systems of law because its Aboriginal allies could and did challenge the governor's assertions, setting the stage for both parties to recognize a deeper level of mutual understanding. What Borrows's argument and the discussion of seventeenth- and eighteenth-century record keeping tell us is that what can appear to be irresolvable conflicts and misunderstandings can also reveal underlying beliefs, assumptions, and even truths when both sides are prepared to continue in a critical dialogue that takes them beyond their pre-established cultural beliefs.

Cautions and Opportunities

Since my analysis depends, in a peculiar sense, on the reliability of the historical record, some comment on unreliable texts is in order. Early records from Albany (1677-1722) are sketchy, at best. They were either lost or destroyed and no longer exist in their original form. Peter Wraxall, however, possessed a version, while Robert Livingston, clerk of Albany, held another.[43] An index of these earliest records has also survived. It summarizes the early records, but in some cases the records appear to be complete replications.[44]

We know that these records were familiar to the British Board of Trade. Wraxall, for instance, transcribed his version to convince the board that Colonel William Johnson should replace the Board of Commissioners (Commission for Indian Affairs) as sole superintendent of Indian Affairs in 1755.[45] Wraxall's somewhat politicized transcriptions are fairly reliable, since they agree with the index, the Livingston records, and the records of other colonies. These records, however, sometimes contain conflicting accounts of events. A case in point involves Edward Cornbury, the governor of New York, and his inability to attend a meeting with the Five Nations sachems in 1707. He had to reschedule a planned meeting for July for 12 September. The meeting, in the end, did not take place until 29 September. In Wraxall's account, the sachems immediately and gladly accepted the governor's judgment on how best to deal with the affairs they were to discuss. In the index, however, the sachems adjourned for a day to discuss the matter among themselves. They then agreed to let the government take care of the matter.

Historian Francis Jennings exposes more serious inconsistencies that can be explained only if it is assumed that a great deal of unrecorded backroom politics took place. For instance, according to one set of records, Tanaghrisson and Scarouady, chiefs of the Six Nations and Mingos (former Seneca and Cayuga who settled in Ohio), respectively, both refused to allow the British to build forts in the Ohio Valley. According to other records, the chiefs allowed such forts and settlements to be built. To explain this discrepancy, Jennings attempts to reconstruct the negotiation process and speculates that it must have included backroom ("in the woods") dealings.[46] The reconstruction helped to determine which account was closer to the truth, because it brought to light angry retorts by Delaware and Shawnee, who were also present at the negotiations. Their complaints suggest they were left out of a critical decision-making event, Jennings argues.

Rather than focusing on records of discrete events to reconstruct the historical narrative, I deal with factual inconsistencies by focusing on patterns of behaviour and speech. I also use disputes over claims of fact to achieve my purposes. For example, in a series of meetings with the Board of Commissioners at Albany between October 1729 and April 1730, the Oneida accused the Virginia Indians of attacking them and taking prisoners. They asked the governor of New York, James Montgomerie, to write to the governor of Virginia to ask the Virginia Indians to return the prisoners. They accused the Virginia Indians of treachery. They had, the Oneida accused, offered a treaty of peace and then attacked the Oneida when their guard was down. After a delay of several months and two letters from Montgomerie to Governor William Gooch, the commission received word from Montgomerie that Gooch had replied. Gooch had expressed incredulity at the Oneida's claim. The Indians who remained in Virginia, he claimed, were too few in number and too fragmented to muster the numbers the Oneida claimed had attacked them. Gooch countered that it was the Catawbas of the Carolinas (some four hundred miles away) who had taken the prisoners, but only after the Oneida had attacked one of their defenceless villages. The Oneida ignored Gooch's alternative version of events, as did the commissioners at Albany.[47] In these records, the historical relationship between the Crown and Aboriginal peoples unfolds as a drama, in which claim and counterclaim, accusation and counteraccusation, much like in Jennings's case, make it difficult to rely on the record to discern matters of fact. But they do expose moral indignation and the extent to which both sides were subject to the moral economy and their willingness to exploit it.

Disputes over treaty obligations offer significant clues to sort out fact from fiction with respect to the moral economy. During the Seven Years' War (1756-63), for instance, William Johnson was under great pressure from his commander-in-chief, John Campbell, 4th Earl of Loudoun, to rally the Iroquois to take up the hatchet against the French. The western Iroquois (the five nations west of the Mohawk) stalled and admitted they feared reprisal from the Mississauga, who had driven them out of Ontario in the late seventeenth century. Johnson pressed the western Iroquois by accusing them of allowing the Covenant Chain to rust and of endangering the relationship completely (allowing it to be "absolutely broke between us"). The Onondaga replied that there were times when they and the Seneca had been being attacked by the French "while you English sat still and smoked your pipes."[48] These accusations, claims, and counterclaims reveal much about how treaty negotiations took place. Lord Montcalm, commander of the French forces during the war, for instance, argued that he had been helpless to prevent his Indian allies from taking English scalps following victories at Oswego and Fort William Henry. In his response to the demand for capitulation from the English commanders, Loudoun and Daniel Webb, he defended himself against their accusations of dishonour by proclaiming that he had risked his own life trying to prevent the massacre, telling his Aboriginal allies, "Since you are rebellious Children who break the promise you have given your Father and who [do] not listen to his voice, kill him [Montcalm] first."[49] The English did not buy into his explanation, and the truth is not known. But this controversy, like the others, shows how disputes over what actually happened can express how certain moral values came into play. Inconsistencies and uncertainties in the record actually aid in the task of disclosing the existence of a moral economy.

1

The Historical Context

The revisionist narrative of the encounter between Europeans and indigenous people in North America today rejects the once received view that Aboriginal people were passive victims of imperialist forces. Thanks to the work of scholars such as Francis Jennings, William Fenton, James Merrell, and Richard White, Aboriginal people are now seen as active agents in the making of North American history. This revisionist view dominates Francis Jennings's Covenant Chain trilogy (*The Invasion of America* [1975], *The Ambiguous Iroquois Empire* [1984], and *Empire of Fortune* [1988]), Stephen Webb's *1676: The End of American Independence,* Alan Trelease's *Indian Affairs in Colonial New York,* James Merrell's *Into the American Woods,* and Richard White's *The Middle Ground.*[1] I agree with their main argument, but I go beyond it. Even these scholars tend to overlook some of the richness contained in the historical record, especially government documents from New York, Pennsylvania, and other colonies, sources that reveal a moral economy at work in the evolution of Aboriginal-European interactions from the seventeenth to the nineteenth centuries.

The terms *Covenant Chain, Silver Covenant Chain,* and *Chain of Friendship* refer roughly to the same type of treaty relationship, although distinctions can be drawn between the Silver Covenant Chain, which allied New York with the Six Nations, and the Covenant Chain or Chain of Friendship, which allied the colony of Pennsylvania with the Six Nations, the Delaware, and the Shawnee. I focus mostly on New York, for reasons that will become evident. Politically, the various colonies and Aboriginal nations that had covenant chain relationships were distinct. Francis Jennings views the Pennsylvania Chain, for example, as completely separate from the Iroquois Covenant Chain. He refers to Governor Patrick Gordon's description of the Delaware-Crown relationship as a "Strong Chain of Friendship," whose beginning can be traced to 1682, when William Penn, founder of the colony, made a separate treaty with the Delaware.[2] The Covenant Chain can be described in a variety of ways – from a loose confederation of allied peoples

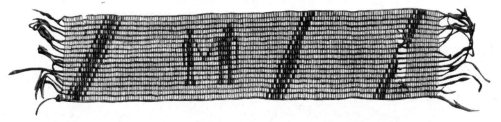

Wampum belt presented to William Penn by the Lenni Lenape at the Great Treaty ceremony of 1862. From Speck's, *The Penn Wampum Belts* (1925).

(who came and went from the alliance throughout its tenure) to a fellowship bound by familial ties – depending on which political arrangement one examines.[3] Despite these political, temporal, and geographical differences, the concept of the Covenant Chain employed by various Aboriginal groups and colonies did not vary widely. For example, the treaty recorded on the Great Treaty Wampum Belt or Penn Belt shows a portly William Penn holding the hand of a skinny Aboriginal person in the tradition of linking hands, the same symbolic representation of unity and solidarity that characterized the Silver Covenant Chain of New York. In light of these similarities, I treat the Covenant Chain as a treaty framework in which early peace and friendship relationships were formed. This framework was known to and, at various times, accepted by all Aboriginal peoples east of the Mississippi in British North America.

The Covenant Chain was a distinctive type of intercultural arrangement, quite different from the relationship that the Spanish, for instance, had with the indigenous people they encountered. It also differed from the relationships that the British had with indigenous people of other colonies (e.g., Australia), even though some representatives and settlers tried to treat them as identical. Each rendition of the chain embodied a relationship governed by similar or even identical ceremonial protocols, the use of wampum, acts of condolence, the wiping away of tears, and the like. Indeed, similar (sometimes seemingly identical) protocols were used between the French and their allies, the Algonquian and Huron. In other words, the term *Covenant Chain* describes a distinctive crosscultural, transnational political relationship.

The Covenant Chain was not the product of a golden age of Crown-Aboriginal relations. The treaty relationship was established in the context of war, intrigue, hard-edged and often illicit trading practices, and an array of related conflicts. Nor was it a relationship in which Europeans viewed Aboriginal people as noble savages. When the English and French encountered Aboriginal people, they were clearly not a people living in Rousseau's Golden Age of Humanity.[4] Aboriginal people were not savages whose purpose was to remain in the "veritable prime of the world"; they neither lived in

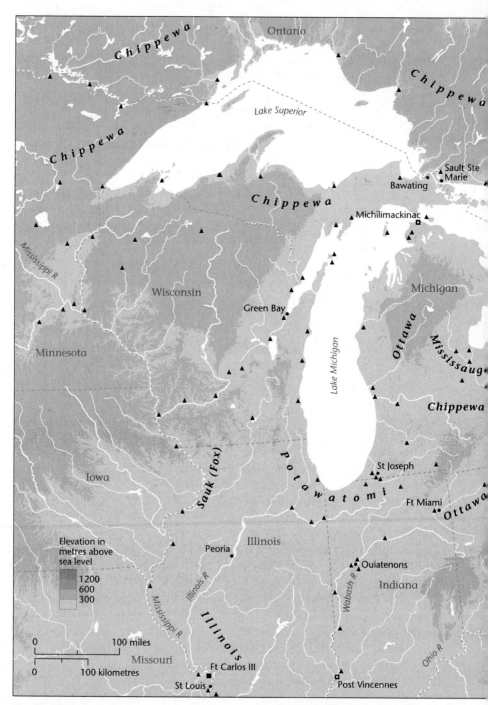

The Six Nations and other nations involved in the Covenant Chain (or relevant to its discussion) in the 1760s. Locations of the nations are approximate, and

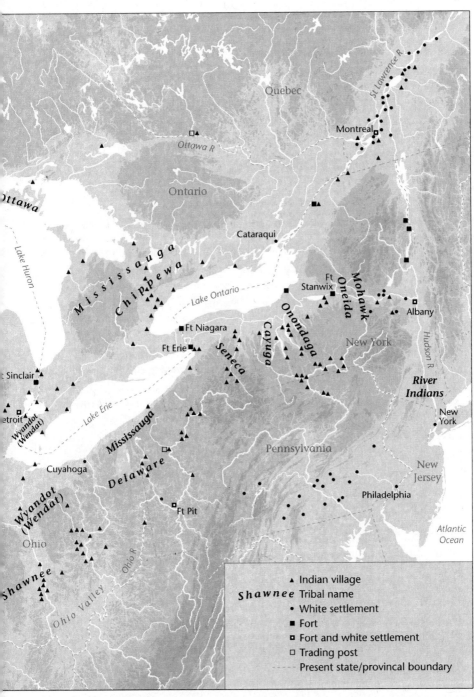

some of the areas were under dispute or not clearly documented in historical or tribal records.

a primitive state, "free, good and happy ... according to their nature," nor lacked knowledge of good and evil or law and morality.[5] Historical records indicate that the English were quite aware of the function of law and morality in Aboriginal communities. Colonists constantly negotiated fair trade deals and mutually satisfactory solutions to various conflicts. The historical relationship was affected by a network of forces and influences, which, when considered together, make explanations of Aboriginal systems and their interactions with those of Europeans a complex business. The world in which the Covenant Chain developed was neither ideal (a world in which colonists encountered noble savages) nor the opposite (a world in which colonists encountered ignoble savages). It was a world in which the Covenant Chain evolved from a strict trade relationship to one that incorporated military alliances and political arrangements to resolve conflicts. It was not a terribly romantic world.

Aboriginal nations that joined the Covenant Chain used council meetings to negotiate trade and military agreements with the British, declare war against their enemies, sue for peace, complain about the price of goods, judge what should be done about murders, leverage various principles and beliefs to gain military support, and accuse their European allies of breaching agreements or of defrauding them of land. The Haudenosaunee often accused the English of breaking covenant, typically by failing to send troops in the war against the French and their Indian allies. In *The History and Culture of Iroquois Diplomacy,* Francis Jennings and his colleagues list a number of treaty councils and conferences in which these complaints were aired.[6] The Haudenosaunee also defended themselves against British accusations of breaking treaty agreements, disloyalty, and failure to uphold military commitments. Although both sides used language that conveyed confidence in the viability of the covenant, neither side during the tenure of the Covenant Chain was immune to such accusations. Any attempt to identify an ethic or moral economy in this relationship must, then, take into account the centrality of conflict.

Conflict and Conflict Resolution

One case in particular illustrates how conflict and conflict resolution defined the Covenant Chain relationship and suggests how the moral economy began to take shape. In 1684, the governor of New York, Thomas Dongan, was informed by the governor of Virginia, Baron Howard of Effingham, that the Five Nations had killed two hundred cattle and about six English settlers on their return from warring with southern Indians. An initial violation of the covenant had occurred seven years earlier, in 1677. The incident therefore constituted an ongoing breach of the Covenant Chain, which Effingham took to be sufficient reason to issue an ultimatum (at a council meeting in Albany in July 1684). He prefaced his ultimatum by emphasizing that the Five Nations had promised to keep the covenant on numerous occasions.[7]

He added that Maryland and Virginia would have destroyed the Five Nations in retaliation but for the intervention of Edmund Andros, governor of New York, through Colonel Henry Coursey. Ever since, he continued, they have "broake the Covenant chain which you Promist our Agent Col. Kendall should be both strong and bright." Effingham went further, claiming that the Five Nations had deceived English folks by using white flags of truce to gain entrance to forts and, after being fed, raiding the forts, killing its inhabitants, and taking prisoners. After these prefatory remarks, he presented an ultimatum – to cease hostilities or be destroyed. Dongan, in apparent desperation, sent out his interpreter, Arnout Viele, to the Five Nations to tell them that he would not consider their actions a breach of the Covenant Chain, but only if they changed their warpath and stayed away from Maryland and Virginia.[8] During a council meeting arranged by Andros to prevent war from breaking out, the Mohawk intervened on behalf of the other four nations. In a peculiar manner, they claimed their own innocence but accepted blame on behalf of their brother nations.[9] After several days of treating, they renewed and polished the Chain, which required an unusual amount of gift giving (in the form of beaver, otter, and wampum).

This case is one of the earliest records that illustrate both the routine pattern of accusation, counter-accusation, shrewd negotiation, mediation, and resolution that typified the relationship and the distinctive way in which conflict resolution was managed. The pattern established itself at the beginning of the official relationship (arguably, 1677 in New York). Council meetings, even at the early stage, were nothing like what one would expect were Aboriginal people the idyllic noble savages of Rousseau's imagination. In one respect, the meetings were like proceedings at a court of law between interlocutors willing and able to sue, negotiate, and construct narratives in an attempt to gain legal advantage.

Not only were Aboriginal people not Rousseau's noble savages, they were also not the ignoble savages imagined by Hobbes or modern historians. As much as the English and others would have liked to treat Aboriginal peoples as such, and to assert their cultural superiority by calling them savages, they had to engage with Aboriginal people much as they would with one another. They had to argue, justify their actions, rebut their interlocutor's claims, and negotiate resolutions to conflicts. At the same time, the Effingham case shows that they, at times, had to attenuate their senses of justice to bring about a resolution to conflict. They did so by recognizing the Haudenosaunee's conflict resolution system, according to which the four western Haudenosaunee nations allowed the Mohawk (the easternmost nation) to speak for all five nations. The Mohawk could extend the plea of guilty on behalf of the four western nations, but at the same time, by playing a dual role, they could also claim to be an innocent party (they had not, after all, been involved in the raids on New England and Virginia). The Mohawk could at once represent their brother nations and reprimand them for violating the treaty. Similarly, New York played a mediating role for the other colonies. However strange the system appeared, the English well understood that it enabled councils to acquire the character of a crosscultural legal institution, including the appointment of official adjudicators to mediate disputes. This piece of diplomacy or legal instrumentation might have been a clever political manoeuvre, but it was, all the same, a manoeuvre that integrated diverse formal conflict resolution systems and protocols.

The treaty relationship was entered into not by noble or ignoble savages but by people who well understood the process of negotiation and litigation. The Covenant Chain forum was one in which discourse was driven by the need for justification; Aboriginal people were not constantly duped by Crown officials, assuaged by gifts (often described as trinkets in the popular historiography), or cheated because they did not know any better. In fact, the British used illicit means such as alcohol to undermine Aboriginal people's reasoning abilities and cheat them of land. Indeed, the use of illicit means itself became a source of conflict.

Origins

Origin stories tell not only how the Covenant Chain relationship came about but also what it became, as it evolved into an institutional arrangement that involved trade and military alliances. In 1755, William Johnson, British superintendent of Indian affairs for the northern colonies from 1756 until his death in 1774, described the origin and evolution of the Covenant Chain as follows:

Behold Brethren these great books, 4 folio volumes of the records of Indian Affairs which lay upon the table before the Colonel. They are records of the many Solemn Treaties and the various Transactions which have passed between your Forefathers and your Brethren the English, also between you here present & us your Brethren now living. You well know and these Books now testify that it is now almost 100 years since your Forefathers & ours became known to each other. That upon your first acquaintance we shook hands & finding we should be useful to one another entered into a Covenant of Brotherly Love & mutual Friendship. And tho' we were at first only ties [sic] together by a Rope, yet lest this rope grow rotten & break we ties ourselves together by an Iron Chain. Lest time or accident might rust & destroy this Chain of Iron, we afterwards made one of Silver, the strength and brightness of which would subject it to no decay. The ends of this Silver Chain we fix't to the Immovable Mountains, and this in so firm a manner that no Mortal enemy might be able to remove it. All this my Brethren you know to be Truth. You know also that this Covenant Chain of Love and

Friendship was the Dread & Envy of all your Enemies & ours, that by keeping it bright & unbroken we have never spilt in anger one drop of each other's blood to this day. You well know also that from the beginning to this time we have almost every year, strengthened & brightened this Covenant Chain in the most public & solemn manner. You know that we became as one body, one blood & one people. The same King our common Father that your enemies were ours that whom you took into your alliance & allowed to put their hands into this Covenant Chain as Brethren, we have always considered and treated as such.

If you will now stand by & uphold the Covenant Chain of your Forefathers; if you will continue to be dutiful & faithful Children of the Great King of England your Father; if you will be true Brothers to the English, and neither enter into any under handed agreements with the French, or any Treaties with them against your Brethren the English, if you will do this with sincerity & keep it truly & honestly.

I am now ready with this Belt in the Great King your Father's name, to renew, to make more strong & bright than ever, the Covenant Chain of Love and Friendship between all the English upon this Continent & you're the Confederate Nations here present, all your Allies and dependents and that it now be agreed between us, that those who are Friends or Enemies to the English shall be considered such by the Confederate Nations their Allies & Dependents, & that your Friends and Enemies shall be ours.

Here the Union Belt was given.[10]

The general features of this origin story are corroborated many times by the Haudenosaunee and other nations.

Earlier, at the Treaty of Lancaster (1744), Canasatego (a Haudenosaunee speaker) also recounted the covenant's origins:

We saw what sort of People they were, we were so pleased with them, that we tied their Ship to the Bushes on the Shore; and afterwards, liking them still better the longer they stayed with us, and thinking the Bushes to [sic] slender, we removed the rope, and tied it to the Trees; and as the Trees were liable to be blown down by high winds, or to decay of themselves, we from the Affection we bore them, again removed the Rope, and tied it to a strong and big Rock *(here the Interpreter said, They mean the Oneida country)* and not content with this, for its further Security, we removed the Rope to the big Mountain *(here the Interpreter says they mean the Onandago country)* and there we tied it very fast, and rolled Wampum about it; to make it still more secure, we stood upon the Wampum, and sat down upon it, to defend it, and to prevent any Hurt coming to it, and did our best Endeavors that it might remain uninjured for ever. During all this Time the New-comers, the *Dutch,* acknowledged our Right to the Lands, and solicited us, from Time to Time, to grant them parts of our Country, and to enter into League and Covenant with us, and to become one People with us.[11]

This rendition, which describes a council meeting convened to resolve a dispute over land, clearly indicates how the Dutch were involved in the Covenant Chain and how trade, alliances, and land transactions were elements in the treaty relationship. Bonds formed and evolved because they brought mutual benefits to the members of the alliance.

The records indicate that Johnson had also appealed to the origin story during a three-day council at Onondaga, on 25 April 1748, to which he had been sent by his superior, Governor George Clinton. At the time – during the penultimate war with the French to gain dominance in North America (King George's War, 1744-48) – Johnson wrote often to governors and military commanders to request that they send troops to aid the Six Nations in the war against the French. The colonies constantly failed to satisfy these requests. Their lack of support for the Haudenosaunee was noted by the Board of Trade and Plantations. In its instructions to the colonies, Jennings notes, the board emphasized the importance of the Six Nations to English interests and that their disillusionment could well result in the destruction of British interests in America.[12] Meanwhile, the governor of Canada was sending wampum belts to request that the Six Nations come talk (treat) with him. After being reminded of this at a council meeting by the Onondaga speaker, Ganughsadeagh, Johnson spoke the following:

It may seem strange to you that a Foreigner should know this, But I tell you how I found out some of the old Writings of our Forefathers which was thought to have been lost and in this old valuable Record I find, that our first Friendship Commenced at the Arrival of the first great Canoe or Vessel at Albany, at which you were much surprized but finding what it contained pleased you so much, being Things for your Purpose, as our People convinced you of by shewing you the use of them, that you all Resolved to take the greatest care of that Vessel that nothing should hurt her Whereupon it was agreed to tye her fast with a great Rope to one of the largest Nut Trees on the Bank of the River But on further Consideration in a fuller meeting it was thought safest Fearing the Wind should blow down that Tree to make a long Rope and tye her fast at Onondaga which was accordingly done and the Rope put under your feet That if anything hurt or touched said Vessel by the shaking of the Rope you might know it, and then agreed to rise all as one and see what the Matter was and whoever hurt the Vessel was to suffer. After this was agreed on and done you made an offer to the Governour to enter into a Band of Friendship with him and his People which he was so pleased at that he told you he would find a strong Silver Chain which would never break slip or Rust to bind you and him forever in Brothership together and your Warriors and Ours should be one Heart, one Head, one Blood &ca. and that what happened to the one happened to the other. After this firm agreement was made our Forefathers finding it was good and foreseeing the many Advantages both sides would reap of it, Ordered that if ever that Silver Chain should turn the least Rusty, offer to slip or break, that it should be immediately brightened up again, and not let it slip or break on any account for then you and we were both dead.[13]

Johnson mentions a multiplicity of reasons, besides conflict resolution, for forming the relationship, but the focus is mutual interest in forming trade and military alliances.

Origin narratives almost always include a description of growth and transformation (e.g., from a rope to an iron chain to a silver chain). These descriptions represent the Covenant Chain's evolutionary character. Members viewed the Chain as having evolved from a purely economic trading arrangement into a military alliance and political arrangement. Utility had been the principal motive for initiating the relationship (symbolized by a rope and articulated in the phrase "finding one another useful"). At the same time, origin stories also mention that the relationship transformed into something considerably more robust. Both sides consistently claimed never to have violated the relationship and, in return, demanded loyalty and protection from the other. As in the Lancaster Treaty, which was held to settle a land dispute, both sides also used the forum to argue over matters of land ownership and justice.[14] Hence, despite its utilitarian basis, the partnership had evolved into a conflict resolution forum characterized by justice, familial loyalty, fairness, and lawfulness, and the parties drew attention to this evolution when they emphasized that the relationship was no longer bound by a rope or even an iron chain but by a silver chain. The silver chain also symbolized their alliance against a common enemy – the French and their Aboriginal allies.

Origin stories were recorded as far back as 1691 (probably earlier) at Albany, one of two council fires. The other was at Onondaga. Council fires were official places where treaties were negotiated and conflicts handled. References to a datable starting point in origin stories indicate that the idea of the Covenant Chain took hold some time in the 1600s between the Dutch and Aboriginal people, but the Silver Covenant Chain (a clearly English-Haudenosaunee version) was established in the wake of the so-called King Philip's War (1675-76). The date of the Chain's origin suggests its formal political nature and its legal function. Treaty council records from April through September 1677 indicate that the Silver Covenant Chain was formally shaped and ratified during this period.[15] For instance, at the 20 July council meeting with the Onondaga, the Onondaga spokesman says, "Bot wee desyre now ane absolut Covenant of Peace wch we shall bind wth a chayn for the Sealing of ye Same and doe give ane band of Therten deep."[16] On 6 August, the Mohawk (called "Maquasse") likewise say, "& wee are one, and one hart and one head, for the Covenant that is betwixt ye Govr: Genll: and us is Inviolable yea so strong yt if ye very Thunder should upon ye Covenant Chayn it wold not break it in Sunder."[17]

The dominant view regarding the formal inception of the Covenant Chain places it somewhere in the mid- to late seventeenth century. It undeniably existed by 1677 and included New York, the dominant colony; New England, a reluctant (because forced) member; and Virginia on the British side. The Aboriginal side comprised the Five Nations, the River Indians, and nations within the borders of the signatory colonies. In 1701, the River Indians claimed that the Covenant Chain had been established ninety years earlier between the Mahicans and Dutch.[18] During that period, however, Dutch traders, who operated from a ship, met Mahican traders only occasionally and by chance – hardly a tight relationship. Fort Orange had not yet been built, and there are no reliable records of treaties. Nevertheless, the River Indians clearly felt something was at stake in making such a claim.

Differing views on inception dates among contemporary scholars suggest that different peoples, including Europeans, vied for recognition as members of the Chain. Origin stories consistently trace the trade relationship back to the Dutch, and some associate its beginnings with a questionable treaty known as the Treaty of Tawagonshi (1613).[19] Jennings, in *The Ambiguous Iroquois Empire,* declares this to be false, because, if made at all, the treaty would have been made between suspicious traders on board a ship and Mahicans, not Haudenosaunee.[20] If the claim were true, the Mahican-Dutch relationship would constitute the origin of the Chain, and the relationship between the Five Nations and the English would be derivative. Algonquian peoples, not Iroquoian peoples, would be the original partners of the Chain. Perhaps this is why the River Indians (some, if not most, of whom were Mahican) claimed to be original members of the Chain.

Other scholars have waded into the fray. Gunther Michelson argues in favour of an earlier origin date and traces it back to 1618.[21] Although the relationship's evolution into an iron chain can be traced to September of 1659, Michelson claims that 1664 is a more reasonable inception date.[22] Daniel Richter, by contrast, argues that the origin should be traced back to 1400, when the Great League of Peace among the Haudenosaunee was formed.[23] He is prepared, however, to accept 1665-67 as the official inception period of the Silver Covenant Chain, since it is the era when the Mohawk cemented Anglo-Iroquois relations in the face of French encroachment.[24] Others, such as Jennings and colleagues, trace the Chain's origins to 1643 or 1645, a period when an iron chain was forged between the Dutch and Mohawk.[25]

Disagreements over dates among scholars suggest that different nations either made agreements or gestured toward making agreements in a manner that motivated record keepers to take note. There were, it would appear, advantages to be gained over competitors by entering into a chain relationship and being able to claim a historical connection to the Covenant Chain. That the original members' descendants made reference to these earlier dates suggests that it mattered who was first or who was considered a long-standing member. There seems to have been some controversy in the early days over who belonged to the Chain and when they came to belong. By 1677, then, a considerable amount of competition for inclusion in the Chain had occurred, and competing parties had come to recognize the political, economic, and military value of being identified as a member of this intercultural arrangement. Whether and how nations could identify with the Chain became a serious matter.

The 1677 records say nothing explicit about the Chain's inception date, but later ones make clear that the Covenant Chain was already in place. Peter Wraxall's *An Abridgment of the Indian Affairs* – along with the Commission for Indian Affairs' "Schedule of propositions made by the Indians and answers given by the Commission at Albany, 1677-1719," to which it is connected – begin in 1678.[26] *The Livingston Indian Records* cover 1666-1723 but do not include a Tinontougen council with the Five Nations, where initial negotiations must have been carried out, since a reference is made to it at a council in 1688, according to the "Schedule of propositions." The schedule, moreover, lists visits by various members of the Five Nations in 1678, during which they renewed the Covenant Chain. The New York colonial documents also contain records that imply a date of 1677; for example, at a council held on 1 August 1678, a Mohawk (*Maquae* or *Maquasse*) sachem says, "Brethren the Covenant that was made here last year betwixt Major Pynchon & us in the Presence of yr Govr Genll is as fast firm & Inviolable as ever it was ... The Governor Genll & you of N. England & we are one in one triple Allyance wth another."[27] At the same time, another negotiation was being conducted with the newly formed River Indians (24 April 1677). The Mahicans, among others, agreed to act as props and to consider the governor general "father." In return, the Commission for Indian Affairs promised protection from their enemies, if the River Indians promised the same in return.[28]

These gaps in the dates are puzzling, but there may be a simple explanation – lost records. Nevertheless, it is clear that parties other than the Five Nations and the colony of New York recognized an official, datable silver chain and referred to its inception during later council meetings. What is important is that all parties understood that the Silver Covenant Chain had a formally recognized history, challenges to which had political significance. Origin stories were not simply myths or idealized representations of how the relationship began, myths constructed to teach some lesson. Nor were they religious in nature, handed down from a prophet who received them from a divine being. They were descriptions or interpretations of the actual course of events, of the evolution of a relationship from an informal and loose alliance to a formal political and legal relationship with established diplomatic centres. The story of this evolution was held in memory (as well as in English and Dutch documents) and handed down from one generation to the next. Diplomatic centres such as Onondaga and Albany were not merely symbolic centres, they functioned much like capital cities, as places where official diplomatic relations were negotiated. In other words, both sides recognized the Covenant Chain as an institution, not simply as a haphazard, accidental arrangement.

The evolution of the language used to describe the relationship – from rope to iron chain to silver chain – suggests an evolution of intercultural sensibilities, or the development of a shared culture, insofar as a formal institutional arrangement presupposes a shared purpose, common values, and a shared understanding of what it takes to establish and maintain orderly relations. In light of the demand for loyalty in military relations, the language of unity (e.g., one heart, one mind, one body) is indicative of a common interest in fostering a robust common identity. Associating origins with forefathers also suggests that members connected the dates of founding events to the idea of debts owed to ancestors, a link that tied members to a common memory and ancestral background.

The English viewed the official inception of the relationship as legitimating a code of law. At the treaty council between Edmund Andros and the Five Nations in 1677, a number of legal articles were articulated.[29] These articles were later used to ensure compliance with agreements. The central article states that if a crime was committed against the English, the Five Nations would bring the perpetrator to trial at Albany. Article 2 reads as follows: "In the event that any wrongdoing is committed by Dutch, English or Indian, if they complain to the Governor at New Yorke, or to the officer in Chiefe at Albany, if the person so offending can be discovered, that person shall receive condigne Punishment and all due satisfaccon shall be given."[30] In these records, treaty articles are numbered and written in English legal style.

These codifications might not have figured into the relationship as its main institutional expression, but they did continue to be relevant. During William Johnson's era, for instance, treaties retained their codified character: "Article 3rd – no friendship with His Majesty's Enemies or maintain any intercourse with those promoting war or trouble but will oppose them and treat them as common enemies and that they may never listen to any idle stories of any Whitemen or Indians who may spread." In this treaty, the partners agreed that all hostilities toward the Huron would cease and that all past offences would be forgiven. The said Indians would enjoy all their original rights and privileges, "as also be indulged with a free, fair and open Trade agreeable to such regulations as His Majesty shall direct." The agreement was signed by William Johnson and four chiefs of the Huron: Adinghquanouron (totem signature, turtle), Chohahagaytan (deer lying on back), Ariaghtatehade (sideways man?), and Tyyaghtah (turtle). They also agreed to maintain solidarity against the French.[31]

Here is an example of how the Six Nations (in this case, the Oneida) formulated the code in response to a murder of one of their sachems by a British soldier: "[I]t has been concluded by the antient [sic] covenant between Our ancestors that if any such accidents happen'd that it should be reconciled and forgiven & that it may be thrown in a great Pitt which is the Earth whereto is a Great Strong door whereon is a large Rock which can't be mov'd, wherein all such things are burry'd in Oblivion therefore we desire that the Soldier may be Releas'd."[32]

In another case, the Five Nations had claimed jurisdiction over the western frontier around Detroit on the grounds that they had conquered it during the Beaver Wars of the mid- to late 1600s. But by 1700, the French, with their Far Indian allies (Algonquians), were building forts in the territory, completely ignoring Five Nations claims. At the Canagariachio treaty council in Albany (1701), the English used the Five Nations jurisdictional claim to argue that the Haudenosaunee were the rightful proprietors of the territory. When the Five Nations asked the English for protection against the Far Indians at this council, the English had nineteen (or twenty) sachems sign over control of the 3,200-square-mile tract of land.[33] The English believed that the sachems had signed over ownership the land; the sachems, by contrast, claimed that they had only put it under English protection. The disagreement stemmed from ambiguity in the treaty, but it is clear that the dispute was, nevertheless, about jurisdiction and proprietorship. In other words, it was a legal dispute.

Treaty councils were places where the allies could argue over the interpretation of treaty agreements. However these conflicts were resolved, their existence indicates that the initial economic and military treaty relationship had evolved into an institution that could appropriate the right of members to claim ownership of certain military and economic functions unilaterally. Similarly, the Covenant Chain council appropriated the right of members to engage in direct trade with nations outside the agreement. When member nations gave the council the right to address disputes over land, trade relations, and military commitments, they in effect allowed interculturally negotiated legal and political principles to order and define an increasing number of dimensions of their relationship. The language of evolution – from a rope to an iron chain to a silver chain – therefore also represents a shift toward institutional control and recognition of the legitimacy of institutional mediation. The institutionalization process began to influence identity formation among the members of the Chain and the development of normative intercultural sensibilities. The legal character of the English-Haudenosaunee relationship, moreover, was not unique. The French-Algonquian alliance also demonstrated a propensity toward legally formalized treaties, as evidenced in "Articles of treaty of peace proposed by six ambassadors from the Iroquois to the French," signed on 13 December 1665. In these records, treaty articles were numbered and written in legalese.[34]

The idea of codification was not free of ambiguity, however, as is suggested by conflicts over interpretation. Moreover, the language of unity and reconciliation was more often than not Aboriginal in origin. Resolving conflicts and bringing justice to those who violated the law were typically accomplished by giving presents and symbolically throwing hatchets (expressions and instruments of enmity) into bottomless pits or underground streams, which would carry them away forever. Sometimes, these acts were acts of forgiveness, which was, for a time, emphasized more than punishment. At other times, every option – from threats of military abandonment and the cessation of trade to shame and public humiliation – was used to ensure compliance with the terms of the treaty agreement. Governor Effingham's controversy with the Five Nations is a case in point. Acting as mediators, the Mohawk addressed the other four nations in the following way: "[Y]ou are stupid Brutish and have no understanding that has broken the covenant chain." After claiming that they, the Mohawk, had always kept their covenant with Virginia, Maryland, and Boston, they stated, "therefore we must stamp understanding in you ... shame for your disobedience." They then presented belts of wampum.[35] Use of public humiliation is recorded on many occasions as part of the process of exacting justice. On more than one occasion, the British also used humiliation to ensure that their Aboriginal allies complied. At a council with the Six Nations, for example, Governor George Clarke said that, given the sincerity and solemnity with which the sachems had spoken and made promises the previous day, they (the British) have "wiped off the Stain that would otherwise have Remained upon you and would have Pointed you out to the World as a faithless People and haveing thus Retrieved your honour and Shaken off the fetters that the French by your own folly had begun to put upon you I open my arms to [missing word] you and imbrace you wit joy & affection equall to that [missing word]."[36] Thus, despite the ambiguity of what it meant to codify the agreement, it is clear that members referred to the codes as set down in official records (wampum belts and written documents) when they made demands for justice.

At a council held on 15-28 August 1694, after a procession in which representatives of the Five Nations entered two by two, singing songs of peace,

Sidekanactie, the speaker, told the origin story of the Covenant Chain and emphasized its evolution: "In the Days of Old, when the Christians came first to this River, we made a Covenant with them, first with the Bark of a Tree, afterwards it was renewed with a twisted Withe; but in the process of time, lest it should decay and rot, the Covenant was fastened with a Chain of Iron, which ever since has been called the Covenant Chain, and the end of it was made fast at Onnondage, which is the centre of the five Nations."[37] The origin story uses different metaphors than others, but it is clear that it emphasizes the course of events that eventually resulted in an official, geopolitically defined diplomatic relationship. Despite the use of codified law, the political aspects of the treaty relationship were treated as central. In other words, the historical foundations and evolution of the relationship seemed to matter as much, if not more than, the actual substance of treaty agreements. The emphasis on historical embeddedness indicates that datability was important, principally because it defined the relationship as a tradition that members could be expected to honour and uphold.

In Johnson's account, the origin of the relationship is traced back to a rope, which was not of British making. It was Dutch in origin, but the British incorporated the agreement as part of their historical relationship with the Six Nations. Johnson did not negate the Dutch agreement; he claimed that the British had transformed it into something more robust. In so doing, he used the Dutch relationship and origin story to draw attention to the continuity of the Chain and its character as a long-standing way of conducting affairs. Indeed, reinforcing this sense of tradition was far more important during council meetings than was upholding the legal aspects of the agreement. Origin stories were constructed and used to renew the relationship and to remind one another about how they had kept the Chain inviolable. They were then used to recall the substance of the agreements. Origin stories emphasized the purpose of the relationship rather than its explicit ordering principles.

In reminding members of the relationship's link to tradition and its evolved nature, origin stories also reminded them that bonds created by debts of gratitude (to ancestors and each other) and a sense of belonging had transformed into bonds of solidarity and unity. Origin stories helped foster an understanding that the utilitarian reasons for forming the relationship had changed into ties based on trust, honour, family, and the like. Images of linked arms on wampum belts represented the idea of belonging, a sense that unity had been accomplished through other than utilitarian means. To belong to the tradition was to belong to a system of ties (as brothers, fathers, children) that were replete with opportunities, rights, and responsibilities. Thus, even though advantages had been defined originally in terms of trade and military interests, all ties came to be defined by familial obligations.

Because the origin stories are supported by historical evidence, the stories, in turn, reveal how and why the evolutionary character of the relationship mattered. Once the Covenant Chain became a military relationship, the alliance depended heavily on trust. When military alliances are connected to economic ones, the result is not merely additive; rather, it is transformative. Terminating the military aspect of an alliance also threatens its economic foundation. Members cannot simply return to the original economic partnership as if the military one never existed. They cannot return to a relationship in which trust and betrayal are irrelevant. They cannot do so because prior to establishing a trust-based relationship, betrayal cannot be a factor; after the severing of a relationship, however, it almost always becomes a factor. Consequently, as the military function of the Covenant Chain developed it transformed the trade relationship and the expectations associated with it. Military alliance became a means of protecting the trade relationship, and trade became a way to cement military alliances.

By the time of its official inception, the Covenant Chain relationship had become a multifaceted institutional arrangement for ordering economic, military, and legal activities. Insofar as these activities influenced one another, the institutional arrangement was a product of complexification rather than complication. Complication is a property of externally related factors, whereas complexification is a property of internally related factors. Externally related factors are neither mutually supportive nor necessary; they are accidentally related. Take, for instance, the relationship between a vehicle and a stereo. Failing to install a stereo makes no difference to the core function of the vehicle or its identity as a mode of transportation, whereas failing to install an appropriate drivetrain makes a fundamental difference to the vehicle's functionality and identity (it can no longer count as a mode of transportation). Adding a stereo makes designing and manufacturing a vehicle more complicated because more devices need to be added, but it is optional. Adding a drivetrain is not optional because the vehicle would not be a vehicle without one. Moreover, altering a stereo component (e.g., upgrading it) does not change the core function of the vehicle (unless it draws too much power or is too large for the vehicle), whereas altering a drivetrain can have wide-ranging implications for the design of the vehicle, from the engine to differentials. The relationship between the economic, military, and legal functions of the Covenant Chain was, like the drivetrain is to the vehicle, internal. By 1677, one function could not be eliminated or altered significantly without affecting the others.

Thus, in order to explain how the Chain's economic, military, and legal functions became interdependent, an analysis of these functions must include an understanding of their interdependence as part of a larger process. The process involves various components that develop incrementally. As the parties share experiences and gain collective memories, precedents are set and new functions emerge as parts of a comprehensive system. Contrary to dominant historiographic biases, the Covenant Chain emerged as two peoples found each other useful and then learned that they needed to develop an institutional identity to order and protect their common interests and values. This identity, in turn, transformed their interests and values as an intercultural identity was formed.

War

Wars revealed just what was at stake for members of the Covenant Chain and for those who were affected by the arrangement. Wars brought values and expectations into bolder relief as they shaped the Covenant Chain relationship. The constant threat of war and an array of related conflicts were among the most discussed items at council meetings. It may even be appropriate to describe the period of the Covenant Chain as one of war broken by brief interludes of peace. Indeed, the Covenant Chain, originally a Dutch-Mahican and Dutch-Mohawk relationship, was born during the Dutch-English (and Iroquois-Algonquian) conflict. The British adopted the idea of a chain (the Dutch Iron Chain) and transformed it into a silver chain after finally defeating the Dutch in the New York area. For this reason, the silver version of the Covenant Chain was associated with military superiority. France and Britain were constantly at war or engaged in other forms of conflict. Spain was the other main competitor for dominance on the continent, and Sweden and Russia played minor military roles. But France and Britain were the primary warring powers allied with Aboriginal peoples in the geographical region of the Covenant Chain. Iroquoians were pitted against Iroquoians (Five Nations versus Huron, Cherokee, and Susquehanna). Haudenosaunee were at war with Algonquians, who also engaged in internecine warfare. From north of Florida to Lake Nipissing (south of Hudson Bay) and from the East Coast to approximately the Mississippi River, Aboriginal people juggled alliances with the French and British and conflicts with their own enemies and competitors in the fur trade. Few, if any, groups lived in peace by staying neutral. All were forced to some degree to ally with other Aboriginal nations or with a European power while the French and British attempted to extend alliances with the Six Nations and Algonquian confederacies. Despite the presence of advocates for nonviolent negotiation such as the Quakers, war raged, forcing even these pacifist Pennsylvanians to eventually agree to a standing army.

During this period, necessity, urgency, and desperation sharpened suspicions of enemies and expectations of allies. Major Aboriginal military powers moved in and out of alliances with the French and English in a process of sorting out and securing territories and trade relations. The Haudenosaunee, in particular, used a system of props (conquered nations) to act as buffers between themselves and hostile nations to the south.[38] Props or tributary nations accepted a lesser status as nephews, or sometimes children, to their uncles, the Five or Six Nations. Props could be called upon to war against enemies such as the southern Catawbas and Cherokees when they raided the Six Nations. The Haudenosaunee system had the character of an empire; some called it the Rome of the Western world.[39] Other confederacies and nations operated under different structures and preferred to maintain looser alliances. The Haudenosaunee and British often identified these alliances as "the Far Indians." Today, one alliance is referred to as the Three Fires Confederacy, which allied with the Dionondades or Wyandot, also known as the Huron (an Iroquoian nation). Other alliances were called or led by the Miami, Fox, and Illinois. *Eastern Indians* referred to an alliance of Abenaki or Penobscot confederacies. These confederacies were composed mostly of Algonquian-speaking peoples, traditional enemies of the Haudenosaunee.

From 1585, when England warred with Granganimeo in Virginia, to Champlain's initial conflict with the Mohawk in the early 1600s, to the War of 1812, war was a central feature of relations in the territory, which were heavily influenced and dominated by the Haudenosaunee. When the Dutch encountered the Mahicans on the upper Hudson, they found themselves amidst a war between the Mahicans and Mohawk over control of the Lake Champlain route (the Mahican Channel) to the St. Lawrence River. William Warren describes the Chippewa-Ojibway history of warfare with the Sioux nations.[40] Historian Richard White describes the situation among the Western Algonquians, where the Miami, Fox, Illinois, and Three Fires Confederacies negotiated various alliances against the Sioux and Haudenosaunee.[41] At times, conflicts among the Algonquians were so unresolvable that the French were able to adopt the role of mediator in what White calls the Pays d'en Haut, or upper Great Lakes region, partly because the role was foisted upon them by the Algonquians.[42] In this context, the idea of treaty cannot be disassociated from that of military alliance. The notion of alliance was central to origin stories and the unity about which they spoke. The effect of negotiating in such a context was an emphasis on mutual protection as the primary treaty obligation.

Although the British and French were always interested in allying with various Aboriginal groups, the main competition in the early days was for alliance with the Six Nations. Not only were the Six Nations a dominant military confederacy, but during much of the colonial period they also lived between the French and English territories, on land south of Lake Ontario and the St. Lawrence River. As allies, they served as a valuable buffer between the European enemies; as enemies, they were a formidable spearhead that could turn the tide of war. Allying with the English and Dutch also proved to be immensely beneficial to the Haudenosaunee, at least for a time. A series of victories – against the Mahicans in the Hudson River area in the mid-1620s (Dutch allies), against the Huron Confederacy in southern Ontario in 1649 (aided by Dutch firearms), and against the Susquehannock in the 1670s (with the aid of the English commander, Edmund Andros) – realigned the balance of power among Aboriginal groups in favour of the Haudenosaunee. When New York gained dominance in the New England colonies, the Haudenosaunee–New York alliance brought benefits to each side that neither could have gained alone. The other colonies were none too pleased with this outcome. For instance, Connecticut had once claimed jurisdiction over the Susquehanna River because of its alliance with the Susquehannock. It claimed a much smaller area after the Susquehannock were defeated.

New York's advantage was, in part, the consequence of a stroke of diplomatic genius. After King Philip's War, the New England colonies wanted to leave relations with the Mohawk and other Five Nations neutral to allow for open treaty relations in the future. Andros exploited the opportunity and established the Silver Covenant Chain with the Five Nations, putting New York at a permanent advantage over New England.[43] (Chapter 3 details this development in a way that draws out more of the ramifications of committing to a relationship of mutual protection.) The tension between New York and Pennsylvania also involved the Haudenosaunee, since both colonies jealously competed to win them over as allies. Moreover, establishing Pennsylvania as a proprietary colony in 1681 required the amputation of New York, an act that allowed the Aboriginal peoples of Pennsylvania (the Delaware and Shawnee) to fall under the "protection" of the new jurisdiction. Because the Delaware and Shawnee served as props to the Haudenosaunee, the amputation made Pennsylvania, not New York, their primary partner. Exacerbating the situation, in 1722, Thomas Penn, son of founder William Penn, lit a second council fire with the Six Nations at Philadelphia. The second council fire posed a threat to Albany, and its subsequent exploitation by Thomas, in what is known as the "Walking Purchase" (by all counts, an illicit appropriation of Delaware land), helped precipitate the wars in which the Delaware and Shawnee wreaked havoc on the Pennsylvania frontier. This intricate web of military and political alignments eventually played a significant role in the establishment of colonial and state boundaries.

On the other side of the yet-to-be-established international border, the French, owing to the less-than-prudent actions of Samuel de Champlain, had provoked a century-long conflict with the Haudenosaunee. The French and their Aboriginal allies came close to eliminating the Haudenosaunee altogether near the end of the seventeenth and the beginning of the eighteenth centuries. Haudenosaunee appeals to the British to help protect them against these "Far Indians" or "Waganhaas" were common. After the Beaver Wars in the mid- to late 1600s, when the Haudenosaunee conquered much of southern Ontario and dismantled the Huron Confederacy, the Haudenosaunee enjoyed a period of military dominance throughout the lower Great

Lakes region. But as Leroy Eid points out, raids by the Far Indians forced them to abandon Ontario by 1698-99.[44]

Although both sides attempted to broker a peace, treaty arrangements did not last long. As early as 1645, the Haudenosaunee linked arms with the French, Huron, and Algonquians near Montreal.[45] But soon afterward, in 1649, after receiving four hundred arms from the Dutch, they destroyed the Huron Confederacy. Subsequent raids led by French military leaders Lieutenant Marquis de Tracy (1666) and Governor Joseph Antoine de la Barre (1682) razed Haudenosaunee villages and crops. Acts of reprisal, in turn, resulted in many dead French settlers in the Montreal area. The Great Peace of Montreal of 1701, led by Louis-Hector de Callière, governor of New France from 1699 to 1703, was a monumental effort to bring the entire Great Lakes–St. Lawrence region to peace. Almost all of the region's Aboriginal peoples signed the treaty. This treaty proved to be quite significant in terms of its comprehensive inclusion of Aboriginal nations. An observer could claim that, compared to the Beaver Wars, the period from 1701 to the outbreak of King George's War in the 1740s was one of peace. But it was an unstable peace, at best. Skirmishes, declarations of war, and military invasions continued to be planned and implemented, even though all-out war was avoided. During Queen Anne's War (1703-13), the Five Nations often travelled to Canada to treat with Governor Philippe de Rigaud de Vaudreuil, and they at one point even asked him to punish the Ottawa (France's allies) for raiding the Five Nations on their western flank.

Wars were fought either to appropriate or protect territory, to gain economic advantage, to exact revenge, and to punish wrongdoers. Alliances shifted somewhat. French, English, Iroquoian, and Algonquian alike attempted to expand, control, and stabilize trade routes, partly by trying to win over each other's allies. The British sent emissaries, as did the Haudenosaunee, into Far Indian country to establish relations with the Waganhaas, Ottawa, Mississauga, Miami, Illinois, Dionondades (Huron), and others. Several records show that some "Canadian Indians" (Waganhaas, probably Ottawa) entered the Covenant Chain on 5 August 1684 and on 14 July 1701 made a treaty with seven nations (castles) of the Dowanganhaas.[46] The "Wississachoos" (likely Mississauga) entered the Chain on 31 January 1707-08,[47] as did the "Uttawawas" (Ottawa), who treated at Onondaga on 4-5 June 1710.[48] The following was reported by Schuyler and Banker, two messengers for Albany:

> When we came into the Castle we were sent for into the Genr Assembly, Where we found 3 Wagenhaes or Uttawawas singing the Song of Joy. They had long Stone Pipes in their hands & under the Pipes hung Feathers as big as Eagles Wings. When they left off singing well we filled the Pipes & let them smoak, when they had done, They filled the Pipes & let us to Smoak

– this is the token of Friendship ... One of the 5 Nations then stood up &
spoke, "Bretheren we being now to speak of Peace I desire that we may lay
aside all heart burnings against each other & behave with that Meekness
wch becomes Bretheren."

The Seneca reported what they said the next day:

"Go with us to your brother Corlaer, The Doors stand open for you, The
Beds are made for you from the Senecas Country to the Habitation of Corlaer,
the Path is secure & there is no Ill in our Country." Then the Wagenhaes
spoke to the Whole House & said. "Bretheren here I am, you have told me
the Doors stood open, the Beds made, yr Pots boiled & the Path was secure
from the Sennecas Country to the Habitation of Corlaer. Let it be so." and
gave a Belt of Wampum.

At a remarkable conference in 1723 – after the Tuscarora had joined the
Five Nations, making the Haudenosaunee the Six Nations – the Mississauga
even declared themselves the seventh nation.[49] What followed from these
alliances is uncertain, but many years later each side could refer back to the
treaties to claim that they were renewing the Covenant Chain (see Chapter
3). It is unclear what it meant for the Canadian nations to come under the
Chain because unlike other nations, such as the Mahicans and River Indians,
they did not become props of the Haudenosaunee and addressed the
Haudenosaunee as "brother" during council meetings. They entered the
Chain as equal partners and, as will be seen, eventually became the dominant partner. Nowhere have I found evidence that they fought alongside one
another. The lack of clarity regarding the status of the Canadian nations
indicates the great complexity of the Covenant Chain. This complexity,
however, cannot be unravelled much further.

The peace in this period might also have been the result of disease and
war reducing the numbers of Aboriginal people and nations in the eastern
region. Assimilation of defeated nations reduced the number of nations who
could be recognized as brothers. The Wampanoag, for example, were defeated
and removed from their territories during King Philip's War. They were
absorbed into the River Indians, who became props of the Haudenosaunee.
The Susquehannock were also adopted into the Seneca and Mohawk
nations.

War, the threat of it and attempts to negotiate peace, introduced new
levels of complexity to the treaty relationship, and this complexity, in turn,
complicated the context of mutual understanding, values, and expectations
that underpinned the Chain.

Religion played a significant role in shaping conflicts, alliances, and the
evolution of Covenant Chain. For instance, French efforts to court the Six

Nations were most effective when the Jesuits were involved. By living among and converting the Haudenosaunee to Christianity, the Jesuits often successfully turned members of the Haudenosaunee against the British. They convinced many Haudenosaunee to move to Montreal to live in Christian villages such as Kahnawake (often spelled more like *Caughnawaga* in the records). Kahnawake warriors then began to raid New England in alliance with the French and their Algonquian-speaking allies. The British, in response, put constant pressure on Haudenosaunee sachems to bring their brethren back from Canada. Therefore, the ways in which religious interests were recognized – about which more will be said shortly – added to the ways in which alliances and treaties were understood.

But perhaps the most interesting aspect of the treaty relationship's complexity is how trade shaped it. It is interesting because trade relations are generally considered more straightforward and hard-nosed. But the trade relationship of the Covenant Chain cannot be described in this way. The "Canadian Indians," most notably the Ottawa and Mississauga, began turning to the British for trade, since their goods were cheaper and of better quality than those offered in Montreal. Owing to their advanced manufacturing technologies and dominance of the sea, the British could undercut French trade and lure Far Indians into their sphere. The Ottawa and others often complained about how much more expensive it was to trade in Montreal than in Albany. In fact, during much of the conflict with France, Albany continued to trade with Montreal, because Montreal merchants profitted handsomely by doing so. The practice was virtually impossible to stop.

Arthur Buffinton emphasizes the importance of the trade relationship to the history of New York.[50] Partly because of their long-standing practice of not going out to Aboriginal communities to trade, and partly because they did not want to upset the Five Nations, who served as middlemen, Albany merchants remained politically neutral and focused on trade. As British settlement expanded westward, however, Albany could not remain neutral without compromising British security. Its so-called neutrality, consequently, attracted heavy criticism from Robert Livingston, secretary to the Commission for Indian Affairs. His concern was over the success of France's strategy to use the Jesuits and *coureurs de bois*, itinerant and unlicensed fur traders, to take trade to the Aboriginal communities. The political and military advantage gained by the French made Albany's policy of neutrality seem traitorous. When Dongan became New York's governor in 1683, he understood the importance of taking trade to his Aboriginal allies and suggested that forts be built on the shores of Lake Ontario (at Niagara, in particular) and that trade relations be opened with the western nations. This policy, however, threatened Albany's position as the centre of trade in the west.[51]

The twist in the story is that although the Grand Banks fishery was of greater economic significance, the English paid far more attention to the fur trade.[52] A communication between Thomas Butler, military officer at Oswego, and William Johnson on 29 May 1751 indicates why this was the case.[53] In it, Butler complains that the Oswego trading post had received only one Ottawa canoe ("Atowawa cannoe") all year, probably because the French were intercepting them at Fort Niagara and offering better prices. It was rumoured that the governor of Canada had commanded traders at Niagara to "sell goods cheap" to undercut the British. If the British lost their trading supremacy over the French, they also risked losing what military advantage they had. Two years earlier, during a so-called period of peace, Johnson wrote to his uncle Peter Warren about Britain's precarious situation:

> [B]esides my Situation among the Indians, & Integrity to them, made those poor Savages Seek to me, so that I have a Superior Interest with them, which Sort of Interest is the most advantagious to this Province, and to all the Neighbouring, & requires their Chiefest Policy to Cultivate, and Maintain. It is that Interest with ye. Indians that makes, our Neighbours the French an over match as we have woefully known this War.[54]

Johnson then acknowledged that neither the English nor the French were a military match for the Indians. He noted that the French were creating yet another threat through their agent "Jean Care" (i.e., Louis-Thomas Chabert de Joncaire), who was gaining influence in Seneca communities in concert with the Jesuits. Although Johnson's letter writing was an obvious attempt to make his worth to the British Crown clear to his influential uncle, it also indicated how devastating France's alliance with the Far Indians could be to British interests. During King George's War, the French came close to removing the English from what is now upper New York State area. Maintaining and creating alliances with Aboriginal people was, consequently, viewed as absolutely critical, and maintaining a trade advantage became a means to maintain a military advantage.

This inversion of the means-end relationship was connected to the influence that Joncaire and the Jesuits were having in the Algonquian communities. Religion and interracial marriage brought other factors (e.g., family loyalty, spiritual well-being) into the equation. Johnson and others began to realize that these French agents were affecting the network of forces that determined both military and economic advantage. As religious and familial factors were introduced into the relationship, terms of reference for negotiating treaties became even more complex. In 1700, during a particularly vulnerable period for the Five Nations, for instance, Robert Livingston sent a report to Governor Bellomont that expressed his views on Indian affairs.[55] In it, he stressed the advantage that the French had over the English as the Jesuits drew Mohawk and other Five Nations to the French side. The number of "praying Indians" who had left the Mohawk Valley to go to Canada, as reported by David Schuyler, had increased from 80 to 350 since the last war. A Jesuit, in an argument with Schuyler, claimed that warriors were arriving in Canada each day. Clearly, religious values were having an impact on the war effort. Livingston recommended resettling the Mohawk, Oneida, and Onondaga closer to Albany so that ministers could more easily preach to them.[56]

The report by David Schuyler, prominent Albany merchant and alderman, is revealing. It describes a debate between himself and a Jesuit. He sought confirmation from an Aboriginal witness who was familiar with the situation that his version of Christianity, the Protestant, was superior to the Catholic. The Jesuit argued that the Catholic version was superior because one could commit a murder and be absolved through confession. Schuyler seems to have lost that argument in the Aboriginal witness's eyes. Schuyler then stated, "There seemed to be no other reason for this exodus than 'the ardent desire of the Indians of the Five Nations to be instructed in the Christian Faith; the want of ministers to instruct them therein [at their own villages] being the apparent cause of their every day going over more and more to the French.'"[57] Without ministers, it would be impossible to keep the Five Nations within the Covenant Chain. Subsequent generations of governors and their agents also promised to send ministers to the communities, but they sometimes did so without having any ministers to send. Demands for religious instruction at times reached emergency levels.

The point here is that the historical record indicates that even what may appear to have been a straightforward trade relationship, from the point of view of many, if not all, Aboriginal people, involved satisfying a complex set of values, many of which were highlighted by the war context. People's sense of meaning, destiny, and identity, sometimes over and above their desire for military dominance and trade goods, were at stake. Although the British often tried to exploit Aboriginal people's desire for religious instruction by arguing that Protestantism was superior to Catholicism, they also scrambled to make empty promises to satisfy these demands. That the British could not satisfy religious demands gave the French a military advantage, despite their economic weakness. This turn of events and the concern that agents such as Livingston expressed suggests that the English were quite aware of the complexity of values that they needed to recognize and satisfy if they were to maintain alliances.

Owing to the plurality of demands on them, the English had to develop an understanding of their partners' cognitive and motivational complexes in order to respond appropriately and effectively. They had to develop a more complex and robust shared lifeworld than a straightforward trade relationship would allow.[58] A shared lifeworld based on a mutual understanding of the feelings and concerns that grounded each side's worldview, interests, and expectations had to be developed and communicated. Developing a system of communication to exploit and satisfy religious demands required the British to develop an intercultural, intersubjective world of "spiritual" values.

The French, more so than the English, were aware of the need to establish a robust intersubjective world with their allies. Their persistence, through alliances mediated by the Jesuits and coureurs des bois (called by the British "bush interlopers"), resulted in many Six Nations villages hosting not only priests but also French traders, a constant source of complaint by the British to the Six Nations. Joncaire – or one of the three men identified by the British as him – was a particularly notable problem because he (or they) had managed to negotiate the building of trading posts and military garrisons in Seneca territory. The British complained that these "Jean Couers" had intermarried and lived with the Seneca. Like Johnson was to the French (see Chapter 3), the Joncaires were among the most significant threats to the British because they had become insiders who could invoke loyalty and familial obligations to influence their allies against Britain.

Familial ties played a role when the British tried to stop raids on the New England colonies by the eastern nations (the Abenaki Confederacy). At one point, the governor of New York and commissioners called on the Six Nations to punish the Abenaki.[59] The Six Nations did not enter into battle against them but instead sent diplomatic commands to cease hostilities. These commands were ignored. Although it could be argued that the Six Nations' reluctance to fight the Abenaki was in recognition of their superior military power, the more plausible explanation is that the Eastern Confederacy was sometimes joined by Kahnawake Mohawk, whom the Six Nations were either reluctant to fight or refused to fight because they were brethren.[60]

Internecine conflicts reveal how familial relations, in the form of rivalries, affected the treaty-making process. Traditional rivalries precipitated wars of revenge. The Six Nations continually raided to the south and west, threatening Virginia and Carolina. The Catawba and Cherokee of the region were considered traditional enemies, even though they too were allied with the British. These raids proved to be unnerving for the southern colonies and Virginia. On the western front, they warred with the Miami, Dionondades, Fox, Ottawa, and their French and Aboriginal allies. War with the southern nations was more complex, because it also involved English-sponsored settlers and British allies (the Cherokee). At first, conflicts with settlers, as in New England, took the form of damaging crops and killing livestock. Later, skirmishes took place and war eventually ensued, making heroes of so-called

Indian killers (e.g., Virginia's Nathaniel Bacon) in the eyes of the settlers. In this case, war had little to do with gaining economic advantage or establishing trade relations; it reflected culturally entrenched traditions and warrior values: revenge, honour, and political order. Inter-Iroquoian and inter-Algonquian wars were more feud-like than all-out wars. The Six Nations' warpath down the Appalachians was not used to conquer the Cherokee or appropriate Cherokee land; raiding parties were too small for that. It gave warriors an opportunity to prove their mettle. The Six Nations, it appears, never sent major war expeditions to Cherokee or Catawba territories to appropriate land, as they did in Huron territory; revenge or pride was the primary motivation. If Richard White is right about the Ottawa war against the Fox, the Algonquians sometimes engaged in internecine warfare to punish those who threatened to undermine the political order of the nations.[61] For this reason, the French-Algonquian treaty-making process placed the French in the position of mediator. This role was established in the early relationship with Champlain.[62]

Warring and treating was also a way to protect territory. As in King Philip's Algonquian "uprising" in New England, southern Indians attempted to defend their lands against settler encroachments, which had resulted in the displacement of the Tuscarora. War in the south often included raids against settlers. War in the northeast continued after King Philip's War over territory, but it was more in response to advancing settlement, rampant by the early 1700s, rather than military threats. The French used this fact to convince their allies and, periodically, some members of the Six Nations that English settlers would overrun their territories unless New England was raided in a timely fashion. Wars, in these cases, were retaliatory and motivated by anger at having been displaced. They were wars of survival.

The plurality of reasons for war further reveals the complex motivations and values that operated in the treaty relationship. War was a way to establish and protect political and economic interests as well as military hierarchies. As previously noted, the Haudenosaunee appear to some historians as the Romans of the New World, but like the treaty relationship itself, the situation was more ambiguous than that. As the apt title of Francis Jennings's *The Ambiguous Iroquois Empire* suggests, there is plenty of ambiguity even in the idea of Five or Six Nations dominance. Earlier, the term *prop* was used to describe the so-called conquered or tributary nations that lived between the Haudenosaunee and their enemies. By definition, a prop was a nephew or child of the father nation and was to be obedient. They were considered dependants, but this designation was not always accurate. One of the most ambiguous props was the Delaware nation.[63] In 1742 (some claim as early as 1726),[64] after the Delaware failed to comply with the Six Nations' demand to rise up against the English, the Six Nations reduced them to "women." This designation implied that the Delaware could not speak for themselves at council meetings and were reliant on the Six Nations to treat for them. They were, at the same time, to help the Six Nations defend their interests and territory. This put the Delaware at a disadvantage during treaty negotiations with William Penn's corrupt sons (Thomas, in particular) in the infamous Walking Purchase. Penn apparently manipulated a Delaware sachem into signing an agreement and then interpreted it in favour of the English. Penn cheated the Delaware of their land by exploiting Six Nations influence.

In later records, it appears that the Delaware, led by Teedyuscung, were actually controlled by the Iroquois under Shikallemy, an Oneida sachem. But these Delaware were only the eastern branch of the nation, a minority. The majority had emigrated from their homelands to the Ohio Valley and became closely allied with the Shawnee. According to Conrad Weiser, an emissary and interpreter between Philadelphia and Aboriginal groups, the Delaware and Shawnee had emigrated from the Philadelphia area as early as 1724 (thirty years prior to the Albany Congress where he explained what had happened to create the Ohio situation) to establish an independent homeland.[65] These Ohio groups never accepted the Six Nations' right to govern Delaware interests and ignored every command. They, in fact, became the major military force in the final French and Indian War against Pennsylvania. The extent to which claims of control and jurisdiction over props can be substantiated remains uncertain, but the consequence of imposing the treaty system on the Delaware and Shawnee was that it allowed the British to exploit the Six Nations' dominance to give certain actions the appearance of legitimacy, which, in turn, provoked Delaware-Shawnee anger and resentment in the French and Indian War. The darker side of the treaty relationship reveals that both sides were quite prepared and capable of manipulating received systems of diplomacy and justice to their own ends. Perceptions of justice and legitimacy mattered, albeit in a negative manner, making the treaty relationship a diplomatic forum for both sides to gain power without shedding blood.

Owing to the complexity of treaty relations, it was quite easy to commit diplomatic blunders. Europeans came to realize that treating with the wrong nation could seriously undermine alliances. Weiser, for instance, resisted treating directly with the Delaware because to do so was to fail to recognize the Six Nations' right to treat on their behalf, however tenuous their status might have been. It was the only way he saw of retaining peace and stability in the region.

As the eighteenth century unfolded, raids on colonies gradually declined as more nations were brought into the Covenant Chain to "rest under the Great Tree of Peace." This image was a central metaphor used in Covenant Chain council meetings. For instance, Governor Cosby used it in 1733 as follows: "[W]hereof you are by way Similitude Like a great tree of Peace we [illegible] on this tree, that its branches may spread and its roots may Run down in the Earth that no Storm may hurt, & wish your Excellency a good voyage home."[66] Lawrence Claessen (sometimes spelled *Claasse* or *Claesse*) used it in 1737 in this way: "[N]o other place to treat with Us but at Albany, where the tree of Peace was planted and reaches unto Heaven whose branches have sheltered ourselves, whose roots spread itself East and West throughout this [island?] that no Storm can hurt Us."[67] Being brought into the Chain was to be protected by the Great Tree of Peace. The Great Tree of Peace symbolized, in part, a commitment to nonviolent conflict resolution in the interest of establishing social, political, and economic stability. In light of the need to develop robust treaty relations and the number of factors that had to be taken into account to achieve this end, the Covenant Chain took on the form of an internecine legal arrangement, that is, an arrangement designed for resolving internal conflicts.

This type of conflict resolution forum differs from those employed to settle disputes between parties considered foreign. They draw on different kinds of capacities and potentials for human-to-human engagement and understanding than do conflicts between foreign parties. As these kinds of forums evolve, they form new concepts and types of communication to capture the new dimensions of relationships. In the case of the Covenant Chain, initial trade relationships were seen as being based on fairness in exchange. But as the relationship evolved and as a shared lifeworld became more evident, the language of mutual protection and peace became more dominant. Trade became a means of mutual protection and maintaining peace. Communicative actions became norm-directed (e.g., based on justice) and richer as strategic actions intended to ensure the best trade deal became less dominant. Metaphor and recitations of origin stories came into use to entrench a sense of mutual obligation. Even if not used sincerely, this emerging language oriented interlocutors toward becoming more dependent on and confident in deeper and more robust kinds of commitments.

By the mid-1700s, the French and English had engaged in their final conflict over who would control the region. The beginning of the last French and Indian War saw the British suffering numerous defeats. One of the few victories, if it can be called that, was in 1755 at Crown Point, along the route between Albany and Montreal, where British troops were under the command of William Johnson. General Edward Braddock's expedition to Fort Duquesne had resulted in an ambush and massacre, while Washington had failed to take Fort Le Boeuf. He had, in fact, surrendered to the French at Great Meadows. These outcomes created a state of panic in the British colonies. When Johnson fought the French to a stalemate at Crown Point, his nondefeat was treated as a victory by his superiors in an attempt to bolster morale. He was subsequently made a baronet. Commanders-in-chiefs and governors began to rely heavily on Johnson's connections with the Six

Nations. Indeed, finding and establishing someone with the ability to mobilize Aboriginal people's military strength occupied much of the Crown's attention.

The shared lifeworld necessary for communication was a world of shared values, as was expressed when people recognized members of the culture as honourable, fair, or just. Johnson became indispensable to the Crown because his reputation enabled him to mobilize Six Nations warriors. He danced the war dance with warriors, fought alongside them, and was given the title *sachem* (today, we use the somewhat inadequate term *chief*). His "marriage" (the need for quotes is explained in Chapter 3) to Molly Brant made him a Mohawk insider. Johnson's role reveals that the shared lifeworld that developed involved forces that governed not only political and economic alliances but also personal relationships (Chapter 3). Johnson, much like Joncaire was to the British, became a thorn in the side of the French.

The last French and Indian War, part of the larger Seven Years' War of 1756-63, ended with the Conquest of New France and the Treaty of Paris. The French surrendered Canada to the British Crown, and French Canadians came under British rule. With victory, the British worked to bring the "Far Western Nations" (Ottawa, Potawatomi, Mississauga, and so on) more solidly into the Covenant Chain through treaties at Detroit (1761), Niagara (1764), and Oswego (1766). These treaties formed an independent wing of the Covenant Chain.[68] In an attempt to end hostilities, the treaty arrangement established territorial lines. In 1763, for instance, George III issued the Royal Proclamation, which established the Appalachian Mountains as a rough divide between settlers and Indian Territory.[69] No land could be purchased for settlement from Aboriginal people without the Crown's authorization. The proclamation was, in part, a response to Aboriginal peoples' demands for an independent territory free of settlers. Within five years, however, in 1768, British agents (Johnson was a central figure) renegotiated the terms of the Royal Proclamation in the Fort Stanwix Treaty, which set the line farther west.

As a result, the defeat of the French failed to bring an end to conflict. Aboriginal peoples renewed demands for an independent territory, and the Algonquian tribes, Huron and Mingos from Detroit through the Ohio Valley, continued to resist the British. A principal reason for their discontent was British betrayal. Rather than leaving the territory after victory over the French, as was promised during the war, the British sent more troops to occupy the formerly controlled French forts and failed to prevent settlers from moving into the region en masse. Not only did their actions demonstrate what the French had always claimed – that the English were concerned only with taking Indian land – they also violated Britain's explicit promise to withdraw from forts in the Ohio region.[70] Jon Parmenter points out that the

English continued to claim that they had no interest in Aboriginal lands.[71] For instance, while brokering a peace alliance in 1758 at Fort Pitt, Lieutenant Colonel Henry Bouquet asserted that the English had no designs on Aboriginal hunting lands and wanted only a healthy trade. In 1759, at the same place, George Croghan, Johnson's agent for the west nations, further promised to respect Aboriginal people's territorial integrity. The duplicity that western Aboriginal people saw in the British had much to do with Pontiac's (an Ottawa war sachem's) success in mobilizing the western nations against the British. He focused their resentment and wreaked havoc on English forts, taking all but three (Detroit, Niagara, and Pitt) in the region. Although Pontiac failed to remove the British, he at least forced a return to the middle ground, the hybrid, crosscultural system of trade and alliance that allowed Aboriginal peoples and settlers to live together peacefully.[72] This time, however, the middle ground was established amidst betrayal and a desire for revenge. Revenge and survival increasingly became the motivation for war on the part of Aboriginal peoples. Key British agents well understood this motivation and took drastic measures to address the anger and sense of betrayal felt by the western nations.

Beginning in 1761, Johnson made a series of visits to the region to prevent war. He attempted to extend or renew (it is not entirely clear which it was) the Covenant Chain into the west by kindling a council fire at Detroit. This move was not welcomed by the Six Nations, who resisted it, unsuccessfully, because it ran contrary to their institutional arrangement with the British and their identity as the nucleus of the Indian-British relationship up to that point. The outbreak of Pontiac's War in 1763 was clearly precipitated by settler and military encroachments on western lands. In 1764, Johnson again visited the region and centred his attention on Niagara. At the same time, growing unrest in the colonies, owing to anger at the Royal Proclamation and attempts by central British authorities to govern colonial life, made it increasingly difficult to control the westward expansion of settlers. Assurances and promises by the Crown's representatives not only grew thin, they were also increasingly viewed as duplicitous. The Crown not only had to demonstrate that it had military might but also that it could honour its promises.

At the Treaty of Niagara – held on 9-14 July 1764, just after General Thomas Gage, commander-in-chief of the British forces in North America, ordered Colonels Bradstreet and Bouquet to launch offences against hostile groups in the west – Johnson attempted to broker a peace with all nations in the Great Lakes region.[73] Most who attended claimed not to be at war with the British and had dissociated themselves from Pontiac. Pontiac himself was not present. Johnson could not, therefore, legitimately claim to be conducting a universal peace conference. Nevertheless, the conference can be viewed as somewhat successful, even though historian Jon Parmenter considers it a major failure for Johnson.[74] A large covenant belt of twenty-three rows was issued, apparently the same belt that would be brought forward after the War of 1812 to remind the British of their failed obligations. Although the belt may not have signified a universal peace, it did confirm a relationship of brotherhood and peace, at least with those nations present. The Treaty of Niagara did not end the war, but it was an important step toward peace. It, together with the Detroit Treaty (1761), treaties with Croghan (at Fort Pitt, 22 March 1765) and Johnson (at Johnson Hall, 4-14 July 1765), and the Oswego Treaty (23-31 July 1766), contributed to a growing regional peace.[75]

The greater majority of Algonquian and Huron nations had, in fact, by this time come under the Covenant Chain through the efforts of Johnson and his subordinates. Johnson was able to limit Pontiac's influence to the Ohio Valley because many, if not most, of the nations that attended the council at Detroit in 1761 did not join the raids on forts in 1763. Johnson and his subordinates' efforts to keep the nations at peace with the British divided the western nations; many disavowed any association with Pontiac and claimed to have ignored his calls to war. Indeed, with timely fortune and clever work, Croghan managed to bring even the Shawnee and Delaware into the Fort Pitt and Johnson Hall treaties. In time, these successes moved Pontiac to treat with Johnson at Oswego in 1766. The enormous effort that the Crown invested in treaty making suggests that the British were well aware of the central role that Aboriginal peoples' sense of betrayal had come to play in Indian affairs, both at the personal and political levels. Here, we also gain some insight into the role that reputation played in the moral economy. William Johnson's reputation, as will be made clearer (Chapter 3), was key to the resolution of conflict because he was trusted by both Iroquoian and Algonquian peoples.

In the post-Johnson era, major shifts in the economic and military relationship between the Crown and Aboriginal peoples took place. By the mid-1770s, Aboriginal people once again had to take sides in what must have seemed a never-ending dilemma. A decade after the Seven Years' War had ended, the War of Independence began. The Six Nations were divided. They could not agree at council about which side to support. The majority of Oneida and Tuscarora sided with the colonies; the majority of the other four nations remained allied with the British. The council fire at Onondaga was covered (the confederacy was terminated). By the end of the war, in 1783, the Six Nations were a broken confederacy represented by a broken confederacy wampum belt. Those who had sided with the British were expelled to Ontario, where, led by Joseph Brant, they settled in the Grand River watershed on land purchased by Frederick Haldimand, governor of Quebec, from the Mississauga in recognition of the Six Nations' loyalty to the British Crown. The majority of the Oneida moved to a reservation in Wisconsin, and other allies remained on small reservations in what is now upper New York State.

Most nations residing in the Ohio Valley remained British allies and expected the British to honour the treaty, which designated the Ohio Valley as an Indian homeland to be protected against further incursions. The new US Congress did not see itself as bound by this treaty, however, and settlers continued to pour into the area, precipitating the final war east of the Mississippi in which Aboriginal people figure as a significant nation-based military force. During the War of 1812, some of the Six Nations continued to fight alongside the British on the Niagara front while Tecumseh and Algonquian nations (with the Huron-Wyandot) fought on the Detroit front. The war broke these nations economically, politically, and socially, and they rapidly became destitute. The focus of the fur trade shifted to western Canada as the massive influx of settlers turned former Indian territory into farmland. Remnants of Britain's allies (e.g., the Delaware) either moved to reserves in southern Ontario or were absorbed by other nations. The Potawatomi, among others, were removed from the US to the Canadian side of the border to be included among the Chippewa and Ottawa. Surrender became the dominant form of treaty making, ending the era of peace and friendship treaties. Although surrender treaties had been around before this time, they certainly were not the model for the Covenant Chain.

Treaty records lose their character as a distinctive genre in the aftermath of the War of 1812. For instance, when Colonel McKay, on behalf of John Johnson (son and heir of William Johnson), went to Detroit in 1817, Ottawa, Chippewa, and Winnebago (Winibigo) allies brought out the Covenant Chain belts presented to them at the Treaty of Niagara by William Johnson and a belt from 1786. Ocaila, an Ottawa chief, presented the 1764 belt and, after recounting what the treaty agreement meant to the Ottawa, explained what William Johnson had said:

> Children – you must all touch the belt of Peace – I touch it myself that we may be all brethren and hope our friendship will never cease. I will call you my Children, will send Iamuth [sp?] (presents) to your country and families. My Nation is brilliant as it is and its words cannot be violated Your words were true, all you promised came to pass. On giving us this belt of peace

This replica of the 1764 Belt of Niagara represents the treaty between the British and Far Indians, including the Anishnaabe and western Wyandot (Huron), negotiated by Sir William Johnson. Courtesy of the Ojibwe Cultural Foundation.

you said if you should ever require my assistance Show this Belt and my hand will be immediately stretched for to help.

Ocaila reminded John Johnson, through the colonel, of British obligations that were, to him, clearly recorded in the belts. He then rebuked Johnson for violating the Chain, that is, for failing to fight the "Big Knives" (Americans) until defeated. The peace agreement between the British and the United States, he claimed, was a breach of the Covenant Chain and the primary cause of Aboriginal people's destitution. The superintendent and clerk identified these belts not as William Johnson and his agents would have done, in an engaged manner, but with an almost anthropological curiosity and detachment. In his response, McKay admitted that the sachem was right and promised to send a message quickly to Johnson, but he also instructed his interlocutors to go through their "father," Daniel Clause (son-in-law of William Johnson), for gifts.[76]

The records make no mention of the British following the Covenant Chain protocol or using the language of earlier years. Gone are the origin stories and the renewal, condolence, and purification ceremonies (described in Chapter 2). These records convey a sense of despair and desperation, as Aboriginal orators use the language of the Covenant Chain and present belts without reciprocation. The distress of the sachems as they present their wampum belts is palpable in the record. McKay had met earlier with the Saukie chief Machetemiskikaque (Black Hawk). The secretary describes how Machetemiskikaque held up the war belt as he spoke. But, as with the Ottawa, McKay did not respond in kind.[77] Machetemiskikaque's symbolic act, which would have been reciprocated during William Johnson's time and earlier, had become one of empty desperation.

After the War of 1812, the Covenant Chain relationship rapidly disintegrated, leaving few if any remnants. Gone were negotiations over trade and military alliances and arguments over justice to be replaced by a much more simplified relationship predicated on the assertion of the British and Canadian Crown's sovereignty, and Aboriginal peoples' backwardness. Treaty making became a matter of surrender, a giving over of land in exchange for some hunting and fishing rights and promises of presents. As a result, the shared lifeworld that had once persisted between the two parties also became simplified, if it was shared at all. It became, in fact, an imposed lifeworld in which the concepts of the noble and ignoble savage came into play.

The dominant historical narrative is partly correct. If the relationship between the Crown and Aboriginal people is viewed from the perspective of post-1812 records, the Covenant Chain and similar treaty arrangements were established only because European powers needed economic and military allies. So, the change that occurred between the early colonial and post-1812 period marks a significant shift in British attitudes and recognition of the moral economy. The change also marks a shift in personalities. As I show in Chapter 3, those individuals who were central to the development and maintenance of the Covenant Chain relationship were mostly hard-nosed military officers and businessmen who were not only capable of entering into a shared lifeworld and recognizing the need to exercise a moral economy in their relationship with Aboriginal peoples but also able to establish intercultural institutional arrangements based on these lifeworlds and moral economies. That the British ignored this capacity after the War of 1812 does not mean that they did not exercise it before the war. They not only valued and were committed to developing a shared lifeworld, they also used it to criticize some of their own behaviour and personnel.

Dependency

The Crown's dependency on Aboriginal people, in a way, forced the British to come to terms with certain moral expectations that shaped the Covenant Chain relationship for over one hundred years. According to revisionist narratives, the Crown acknowledged its military dependence on Aboriginal people in its war against the French and even for survival on the continent. The Board of Trade explicitly recognized the importance of the Iroquois as military allies in the 1750s.[78] This dependence was evident in the British response to threats of abandonment. For instance, during the latter part of the Chain's tenure, the Ohio Company of Virginia began to establish forts and settlements in the Ohio Valley to the consternation of the Delaware and Shawnee, who had already been displaced once.[79] Among other events, this encroachment motivated the Delaware and Shawnee to consider alliances with the French against Pennsylvania, Virginia, and the Six Nations. The French had also built forts at Niagara and St. Frédérick (on Lake Champlain) to establish a strategic advantage in trade relations. They sent a major military force into the Ohio Valley to regain control of the region. Different groups within the Six Nations had started to abandon the Covenant Chain – some Seneca and Cayuga had moved to the Ohio to become the Mingos – and many Mohawk had been lured to Kahnawake, from which they began to raid New England. The French and their allies began to surround the English. The Board of Trade recognized that without Aboriginal allies there would be little hope of holding out against the French.

In 1753, Hendrick (sachem of the Mohawk) declared the Covenant Chain broken because his people had been cheated of land so often by Albany merchants. In particular, he complained about what was known as the Kayaderossera patent, which had been used to swindle the Mohawk of eight hundred thousand acres of territory. The Board of Trade well understood the consequences of the declaration. In response, it moved to convene a conference at Albany in 1754, where they would treat with the Six Nations directly in the name of the British Crown rather than through the provinces. A "proper person" would do what was necessary to placate the Six Nations.[80]

The board had plenty of institutional memory to draw on as it considered this move. Francis Jennings argues that Aboriginal allies were decisive factors in many battles.[81] Until 1758, the British won only two major battles against the French during the Seven Years' War, and those battles were led by John Bradstreet from Nova Scotia and William Johnson at Lake George, whose force was made up of provincial soldiers and Aboriginal warriors.[82] Indeed, despite how disgusted the French regulars were with Aboriginal warfare, they too realized that they could not be victorious without having "command" over the warriors, even though "command," according to French commander Louis Antoine de Bougainville, captain of the French dragoons during the Seven Years' War, was an "an irksome job."[83] Commanding Aboriginal warriors involved gift giving and promises, not to mention letting warriors fight in their own way. Since the early days after the English won New York from the Dutch, moreover, the British were ever vigilant of Haudenosaunee (then Five Nations) negotiations with the French. Governor Dongan, in 1683, arranged a council with the Five Nations to stabilize relations and prevent them from treating with Canada and to make peace with the Far Indians. His concern was expressed as follows: "They are now fast to us and we must keep them soe, for if they were otherwise, they are able to ruin al ye Kings Collonys in those parts of America."[84]

Although both the French and British Crowns recognized their dependency on Aboriginal allies, they had to deal with English settlers who felt differently. On numerous occasions, the Crown intervened to protect their allies against settlers, who, from the initial colonization effort in 1585 (known as the Roanoke Venture), seemed intent on eradicating Aboriginal people. Various colonies targeted different nations for elimination in the interest of colonial expansion.[85] The early seventeenth century was replete with skirmishes and wars between Virginia and the Algonquian alliance led by Powhatan. These events led to the eventual elimination of the Pequot in New England by an alliance of New England colonies and various Aboriginal tribes, including the Narragansett. Later, owing to advancing settlement and Aboriginal reprisals, the noted "Indian killer" Nathaniel Bacon began a rebellion against Virginia that was intended, in part, to destroy Aboriginal groups in the Virginia-Maryland area. Governor William Berkeley sided with Aboriginal people and attempted to prevent settlement and settler attacks.[86] He tried to arrest Bacon, despite Bacon's hero status among the settlers. In part, Bacon's Rebellion was fuelled by Berkeley's efforts to protect the allies.[87] Although these events ultimately led to King Philip's War and the destruction of Algonquian power in New England, they also revealed that the Crown would side with its Aboriginal allies, even against its own subjects.

Although they had shared amicable relations with William Penn, the Pennsylvania, Delaware, and Shawnee found themselves at war with Pennsylvania when settlers and businessmen used fraudulent means to dispossess them of their lands. This and many other acts of aggression against Aboriginal people helped precipitate the last French and Indian War, which further dispossessed the Delaware and Shawnee of their territories. During the conflict, the Crown attempted to smooth relations between settlers and Aboriginal people through agents such as Conrad Weiser, but when these measures failed, they resorted to forcibly removing settlers from Aboriginal territory. General Thomas Gage and William Johnson also made futile attempts to remove settlers in the name of the Crown. In all cases, the Crown was well aware of the need to placate Aboriginal people, either because they needed them militarily and economically or because they feared that they would ally with the French. For this reason, they convened many a council to fortify alliances or to convince Aboriginal people (especially the Six Nations) to remain neutral.

In light of the Crown's institutional memory of its dependence on Aboriginal allies, its reasons for attempting to placate the Six Nations' anger over the Kayaderossera patent are obvious. It had to do whatever was necessary to bring a sense of justice to the relationship. Thus, from the beginning, even if the Crown had entered into the treaty relationship because of the French threat, it understood that it had to demonstrate a respect for principles of justice to maintain the relationship. If the English had not been so dependent on its allies, it is questionable whether the Crown would have acknowledged or even been aware of the centrality of such normative forces at work in Aboriginal cultures. Most agents, it seems, did in fact ignore Aboriginal people's claims of unjust treatment, if they could, just as Crown agents did after the War of 1812. But prior to the war, they were compelled to treat their Aboriginal allies as people who belonged to norm-governed cultures, as people with whom an intersubjective normative world would have to be constructed.

Justice-based negotiations and threats of abandonment were not restricted to the war context. Hendrick's declaration that the Chain was broken because of illegal land appropriations by Europeans and Aboriginal people's complaints against unscrupulous traders reveal that justice as legitimation and fairness also operated in the relationship. It does not take a concerted examination of the record to learn that council fires were dominated by complaints and demands for justice over land fraud, unprovoked attacks, and unfair trade practices.

Instances of Haudenosaunee dependence on the British reveal the existence of forces that moved both parties to construct an intersubjective world. Although many accounts tell the story of how Iroquois raids on Algonquian trading parties took an enormous toll, they also tell of French and Algonquian counter-raids into Haudenosaunee country that resulted in the burning of villages and crops (e.g., Tracy's 1666 march through Mohawk territory).[88] These raids, together with the movement of the Algonquian-speaking Ottawa and Mississauga, eventually drove the Haudenosaunee from Ontario to the south of Lake Ontario. In response, the Five Nations, especially after 1700, developed a more entrepreneurial strategy to attract French-Indian trade to Albany (through themselves, of course) and eventually to Oswego and Irondequot. Disease, the French–Far Indian threat, and other factors made it impossible to depend on military force to maintain dominance. The western nations, moreover, outnumbered the Haudenosaunee considerably and were making inroads to Albany, where they could trade directly with the British. Montreal merchants were also trading with Albany for better and cheaper goods than they could get from France in a bid to trade with the Algonquians. At the same time, the British were making gestures to the western Algonquians to join the Covenant Chain. It would have been foolish for the Haudenosaunee to make no effort to renew and guarantee ties with the British. Without these strategic diplomatic moves to cement economic and military ties, it is unlikely that the Haudenosaunee could have risen again to become the political core of the Covenant Chain relationship.[89]

Financial ledgers indicate that, in return for furs, Aboriginal people received, in rough order of importance, guns, ammunition, gunpowder, other weapons, cooking pots and pans, shrouds (wool blankets), alcohol, salt pork, and various other items. Trade with the Dutch for guns had likely been a deciding factor in the 1649 defeat of the Huron at the hands of the Five Nations. As many historians have noted and as Indian affairs records often note, trade was the *sine qua non* of the relationship between the French and British Crowns and Aboriginal allies. During a meeting between the Five Nations and Colonel Schuyler at Albany on 19 July 1712, for instance, the Aboriginal partners said, "Thus (say they) our first entering into a Coven't with you was Chiefly grounded upon Trade."[90] Time after time, the records indicate that various sachems and intelligence agents for the British Crown announced the need for cheap goods and fair trade. When prices for goods increased or when goods no longer became available (especially gunpowder and lead), complaints were brought before the commission, sometimes with barely veiled threats of abandoning the alliance.

This dependence on trade was a double-edged sword. When the Five Nations discovered that they could not depend on the English for cheap goods because of price inflation or for quality goods – when rum was watered down and the gunpowder ineffective – they threatened to abandon the British and form an alliance with the French.[91] In general, the British were able to offer goods more cheaply than the French and even draw "northern" and "Far Indians" away from French trading centres. They were industrialized and had a more open market system than the French, allowing traders to operate independently of government price controls. According to some records, the British could pay between two and four times more for furs than the French, a factor that offset their comparatively poorer political relations with Aboriginal groups.[92]

Britain's dependence on its Aboriginal allies was balanced by Aboriginal people's reliance on the Crown. As the English came to realize how important trade was to the relationship, they began to invite the traditional enemies of the Haudenosaunee, especially the Ottawa, to trade. They even cleared a path for the Ottawa to trade directly at Albany. The Haudenosaunee, however, viewed this arrangement as a violation of the Covenant Chain agreement. It also weakened the Haudenosaunee's economic position. Adapting to the situation, the Haudenosaunee argued that the Far Indians would have to accept a peace treaty with them before they travelled to Albany, since all routes cut through their territory. During certain periods, however, the Haudenosaunee were in no position to protect their territorial rights because the Algonquians, if united, could have defeated them.[93] Richard White shows, however, that the Algonquians were constantly at war or in conflict with one another during this period.[94] The Ojibway-Iroquois war of 1697 had eliminated a large portion of the Iroquois' population, and the "Dowaganhaes" (Waganhaas) continued to attack Iroquois in the west (in Seneca territory). These attacks were a key reason that the Haudenosaunee sought England's protection. Thus, when the English acknowledged their dependency on Aboriginal allies, they were well aware of their allies' economic, military, and political dependence on them. The Six Nations over time became economic and diplomatic mediators rather than a primarily military ally. The English recognized the full potential of a partnership with the Six Nations and did not simply ride roughshod over them, however much later history indicates that they eventually did. Over time, the relationship took on new dimensions of recognition; members were recognized as part of the same body (see Chapter 2), and it became possible to speak for each other (see Chapter 3).

When Oswego was established as a trade centre supplied by Albany, complaints followed, since goods remained cheaper in Albany. In their own defence, traders argued that the cost of transporting goods to Oswego had to be factored into what they charged their Six Nation allies. This and the sometimes exorbitant levies charged for crossing territories or for carrying cargo created a need for a more complex dispute resolution mechanism. Councils gradually acquired the character of political-cum-legal forums, particularly when bad trade relations combined with alcohol abuse resulted in theft, murder, arson, or other injuries. The Covenant Chain increasingly evolved into an internecine forum resolving conflicts over exchange practices.

As a consequence, greater pressure was placed on the relationship to function as an institution for maintaining social order. For example, Six Nations sachems periodically requested bans on the sale of liquor because of the destructive force it unleashed in the communities.[95]

Perhaps because of mutual dependency, the abuse of alcohol aided the development of an intercultural dispute resolution, social-ordering forum. In the Dutch era, traders met Aboriginal trappers in the woods before they reached Fort Orange (Albany). They plied the trappers with liquor to make them amenable to lower prices or to entice them to drink the value of their furs in liquor.[96] Although the colonial Dutch government banned traders from engaging in such practices, traders continued with virtual impunity. Many a trapper returned to his community with nothing to show for his work. Alcohol, at one time, was banned outright. During a series of controversial hearings, representatives of the Onondaga argued that alcohol had stripped people of their ability to act responsibly; when drunk, individuals could not be considered persons or even in their right mind. According to Taiaiake Alfred, contemporary author and activist, the Aboriginal personality is a balance of opposites.[97] Alcohol destroys that balance, allowing the powers of chaos and evil to control behaviour. Richard Atleo (Umeek) likewise describes the Nuu-chah-nulth personality as a struggle between the tensions that existence brings to life.[98] It is the person's responsibility to balance or creatively maintain the tension. The ability to do so is undermined by alcohol. That governors and commissioners accepted the sachem's reasoning and agreed to ban alcohol suggests that they understood something of these psychological effects of alcohol on Aboriginal people and were willing to accept his frame of reference as part of the shared lifeworld.

Later, it will be shown how the British resisted accepting Aboriginal understandings of alcohol, not because they could not understand it, but because they were unacceptable grounds for excusing violations of law. However, when sachems complained that alcohol undermined their ability to govern warriors, Crown authorities listened. These acts of understanding reflect an incipient awareness of the need to broaden the shared lifeworld to include expectations of empathy in the interest of establishing an intercultural system of governance. If for no other reason than their own dependence, then, the English came to share an understanding of expectations with Aboriginal allies based on efforts to achieve mutual understanding of each other's lifeworlds.

Disputes over land put further pressure on the alliance to establish an even more comprehensive set of shared values, ideas, and principles of governance. In 1701, during the negotiation of the Canagariachio Treaty, the British exercised their legal imaginations to pressure the Six Nations to cede territory and, in 1737, they used the Six Nations' system of props and dependency relations to deprive the Delaware of land in Pennsylvania. In other words, they exploited (and distorted) established legal principles and systems to legitimize land grabs. Once settlement began in earnest, particularly by the Dutch and British in the New York area, disputes over land title and the legitimacy of deeds began to replace the use of outright violence to establish territorial rights. Allen Trelease describes how the Dutch – under various early governors, especially Peter Stuyvesant – were in constant conflict with the Mahicans, the Esopus, and other Aboriginal groups along the Hudson River, Long Island, Martha's Vineyards, and so on.[99] Most of these conflicts were settled by force of arms. After the British conquered the Dutch, they found that many local Aboriginal groups had been defeated, but they still had to deal with the unconquered Five Nations, particularly the Mohawk.

One of the first measures the British instituted to deal peaceably with the Haudenosaunee was to establish a dedicated Commission for Indian Affairs at Albany, whose mandate it was to ensure that all land transactions were conducted through proper channels. Peter Stuyvesant had attempted to play such a role on behalf of the Dutch, but without adequate executive power in the form of a standing army, he was virtually powerless to enforce Dutch authority against traders and settlers.[100] The same can be said of the commission at Albany. Aboriginal people came often to complain about traders, merchants, and sometimes even commissioners who had plied their people with liquor to get land deeds signed. Europeans often employed this tactic or had unauthorized people from Aboriginal groups sign deeds. Consistency in following proper procedure was in short order, and the proper representatives were rarely the ones to carry out transactions. Even the Lords of Trade intimated that the commissioners were not entirely reputable. Although the commission was a failed attempt to bring order to land transactions, the fact that it was established implies that the English recognized the need for formal proceedings to adjudicate complaints. The English recognized the need for legitimate land transactions, not only for themselves but also for their allies. Structures and mechanisms were aimed at establishing mutual understanding and framing resolutions to conflicts as acts of justice. Hence, responses to demands for justice were not merely nominal (as in codifications of treaty agreements) but structural in the sense that the system governing Indian affairs included an official body of Crown agents mandated to apply principles of justice to Aboriginal-white relations. No such structures and mechanisms would have been needed if, in fact, the British were dealing with a truly savage people. A large degree of mutual understanding had already been achieved, as evidenced in the fact that both sides complained about the actions of the other through the structure of the Chain and its mechanisms.

As Richard White argues, the French and Algonquian likewise established a common understanding.[101] They developed various understandings to settle disputes and gain mutual advantage, and they used similar protocols (for instance, the pipe and wampum) in their mutual effort to fight the British and Haudenosaunee. Although White calls this common understanding a middle ground, the social arrangements he describes and those described in relation to the Jesuits and Joncaire suggest that the term is too weak. The arrangement enabled the two sides to live together and allowed the French to act as mediators between competing Algonquian nations. This kind of arrangement could not have been the result of a straightforward compromise of power, the exchange of goods, or the manipulation of either side's cultural premises (as if these premises could be treated purely instrumentally). It must have involved the development of a common identity as determined by their shared normative lifeworld. Both sides were cognizant of the conditions that produced feelings of insult, offence, and the desire for restitution or resolution. Although distinctive, the development of the Covenant Chain, especially in attempts to resolve land disputes, placed similar pressure on its members to develop a shared normative lifeworld that, when expressed structurally, gave it the character of a legal institution.

The structural expression of the shared lifeworld was grounded and developed systematically (as opposed to being developed by fiat), and it was systemic (as opposed to *ad hoc*). In order for the relationship to have evolved as it did, the English in particular must have been cognizant of and willing to accept, to a certain degree, Haudenosaunee conceptions of justice. Successful economic, military, and diplomatic relations depended on more than a superficial understanding and acceptance of their ally's conceptions of justice. The transformation of an exclusively *quid pro quo* arrangement into a military-political-legal arrangement precipitated the development of a formally recognized shared understanding of values and normative constraints. Insofar as these values and norms were evolving, the English engaged in a process of coming to recognize what mattered to their allies, why it mattered, and what constituted a violation of these values and norms. Insofar as what mattered in the relationship was socially constructed, the English must have figured out which values and norms could shape the economic, military, and legal relationship and incorporated them into their ways of recognizing and communicating with their allies. The transformation from an accidental, ad hoc trade relationship to a systematically structured institutional arrangement, therefore, required the Chain's members to appeal to their shared lifeworld in a way that had logical force.

Habermas draws a distinction between institutional and free-floating cultural values.[102] Free-floating cultural values have no normative force until they are transformed into legitimate motives for action. Once members of an institution begin to negotiate intercultural modes of governance, they also begin to see how their interlocutor's values, which were once treated as mere curiosities, can become levers to legitimate certain claims. The interlocutor's values therefore acquire normative force for both sides. Learning about and appealing to these values equips members with both the cognitive and motivational means to adapt to the other members' lifeworlds.[103] The Covenant Chain relationship, by becoming more than an ad hoc intercultural arrangement to satisfy the whimsical demands of parties, became a formally systematic institution.

The Duality of British Attitudes

The play of contrary British attitudes toward and conceptions of Aboriginal people reveals important tensions that played out in the moral economy. Religion is one lens through which we gain a glimpse of the duality of underlying attitudes and their diverse effects. Religion had the power both to cement the Chain and rend it apart. Francis Jennings, for instance, blames the abusive and exploitive behaviour of the Puritans on their religious beliefs and suggests that the Quakers' fairer treatment of Aboriginal people and success as negotiators might have had something to do with their religiously motivated moral attitudes. He implicitly connects religion to the moral economy. Cornelius Jaenen begins "The French Relationship with the Amerindians" by stressing France's desire to bring Christianity and civilization to the Indian.[104] Barbara Arneil suggests that Locke's assumption that the Aboriginal people were the ten lost tribes of Israel helped justify the colonization of North America.[105] Some Europeans viewed Aboriginal people as proto-Europeans who needed guidance to exercise the latent powers of rationality required to evolve into civilized Christians. What makes this assumption particularly significant is that it was not extended to Africans. Indeed, the English Crown attempted to prohibit the slavery of Aboriginal people even as it supported and invested in African slavery.[106]

Even though religious matters might have been treated as a means to foster trade, cement alliances, and assert European superiority over Aboriginal people, the fact that the English were disinclined to exploit Aboriginal people as they did African people suggests that religious factors can be studied to gain access to British beliefs about Aboriginal people, enabling us to access more of their shared lifeworld. Sharing a lifeworld meant that the British became attuned to their Aboriginal allies' religious sensibilities in a way that they were not prepared to do for others. Aboriginal people, from the perspective of some central British agents, were more spiritually oriented, rational, and human than other peoples. For others, this was not the case.

This duality of British attitudes was also reflected in the legal relationship. The English Crown in the 1600s had to defend its actions vis-à-vis criticisms from the Dutch, Spanish, and French. During the conflict with the Dutch, England argued that Holland had no right to trade with Aboriginal people in the Hudson River–Manhattan region. Appealing to the idea of *vacuum domicilium* (land unoccupied by civilized inhabitants), the English initially denied Aboriginal people the right to be considered fully human. Unchristian, pagan, and primitive, they could not own property. Therefore, Dutch trade with the Mahicans, Mohawks, and others could not be considered a bona fide trade relationship. In 1672, England seized a Dutch ship for trading in Indian Territory, which it claimed as its domain. The Dutch replied that the English had no right to prosecute since Aboriginal people were the rightful owners of the domain. The English Crown, in response, flatly denied that Aboriginal people could own land. Twelve years later, however, after becoming solidly established on the North American continent, England accepted Aboriginal title to the same land to counter Dutch claims of ownership.[107]

English moral and legal assumptions about Aboriginal people also began to shift in response to changing political conditions.[108] The Crown's early justificatory framework was challenged by Roger Williams, a minister at Salem, Massachusetts. Williams argued in 1633 that "the king had no right to grant lands on which the colony was founded since they belonged to the Indian tribes."[109] Although Williams was banished from Massachusetts Bay as a consequence of his argument, his trial forced the Crown to defend its actions and brought its justificatory assumptions into question. The Crown's position was articulated by John Winthrop, the governor of Massachusetts, who appealed to the doctrine of vacuum domicilium. Once British control was established in New York, however, use of the doctrine became politically problematic as New Yorkers became dependent on the Haudenosaunee and other nations through trade and military alliances. By the time of the Covenant Chain's official inception, the Crown had entered into negotiations, developed diplomatic relations with Aboriginal groups, and formed agreements that had the character of legal documents.

It is worth noting that Dutch land grabbers had not appealed to vacuum domicilium or the concept of *terra nullius* (an empty land) to justify their appropriations of land. Rather, they manipulated "signed" documents to give their deals the appearance of legal legitimacy. Later on, as James Merrell shows, Aboriginal people carried around tattered copies of treaties to show encroaching settlers or English authorities that the land belonged to them.[110] Indeed, Merrell cites instances where these papers were treated as counterparts to wampum belts, as records of treaty agreements. Although often futile, these legitimating claims were a part of everyday interactions between Europeans and Aboriginal people. Over time, it became nonsensical for the English to appeal to vacuum domicilium or refuse to acknowledge Aboriginal people as persons. Neither belief is expressed in the Covenant Chain documents. Rather, the documents describe devious uses of written documents, signing authorities, and councils, references that imply that the British could not and did not conceive of or treat Aboriginal people as soulless and irrational,

or lacking in intellectual capacity. However insincere their acts of acknowledging Aboriginal personhood might have been, the English had to act as
if they recognized Aboriginal personhood, because Aboriginal people would
not have tolerated a failure to be so recognized. Furthermore, owing to the
spiritual-religious dimension of their relationship with Aboriginal people,
these acts of recognition were connected to shared subjective worlds. Such
acts of recognition, then, could not have been mere facades.

As European nations vied for dominance in the New World, demands to
justify land appropriations increased. As the Spanish amassed territory to
the south and the French expanded their system of forts into the west, the
European debate over land rights became more pronounced. The English
employed occupation as a criterion to determine rightful ownership, particularly where its plantations (e.g., in the Carolinas) were concerned. This
criterion was particularly useful for justifying the movement of English
settlers into territory claimed by Spain, since the land was so vast that the
Spanish could not possibly occupy all of it. Other criteria, such as labour
and enclosure, also came into use over time.[111]

During the seventeenth century, few in England had been in favour of
colonization or settlement on plantations, for a range of reasons. Some feared
a drain on England's resources, while others feared the colonies would become competitors with England. Trade, rather than settlement, was the main
focus. But proponents of settlement and the development of plantations for
growing commodities such as tobacco (e.g., Lord Shaftesbury and John Locke)
began arguing that much greater profits could be gained. Their arguments
resonated as competition and conflicts with France, Holland, and Spain over
trading rights escalated. It seemed that justificatory frameworks were constructed to serve foreign policy. Moreover, these justifications followed a line
that would not only satisfy British interests but also be recognizable to other
Europeans.[112] Yet the historical record reveals that these frameworks were
also affected by England's relationship with Aboriginal people. English agents
rarely used conquest, de facto occupation, or labour as a justification for
occupying Aboriginal lands; rather, they based their claims on written documents (deeds) and argued that they were contracts that had been legitimately
negotiated with Aboriginal people. The English treated Aboriginal people as
agents who understood legal process. Conflicts had to be solved through
argumentation. However much the English might have tried to manipulate
or cajole their Aboriginal allies into compliance, they could not avoid responding to Aboriginal people's demands for legal justification.

Admittedly, John Winthrop did claim that appropriating Indian land was
justified on the grounds that there was enough for everyone.[113] Locke likewise
argued the same in *Two Treatises of Government*.[114] While designed principally
to demonstrate English moral superiority over the Spanish, these arguments
were also expressive of a need to defend England's moral reputation, however

inconsistent the arguments might have been with England's general position. John Locke and his main influences, Hugo Grotius and Samuel Pufendorf, articulated various theories of property based on such principles as the right of discovery, rights by virtue of conquest and rights by virtue of mixing one's labour and enclosure. Such theories could be used to argue that Indians did have a basic right to life and liberty, but not to property. On a less skeptical note, Locke did shape his position by distinguishing between African slaves and Aboriginal people, the lost ten tribes of Israel.[115] Since Aboriginal people were conceived of as being proto-rational and educable, they were recognized as rights bearers. From the perspective of those living on the European continent, Locke could get away with this assumption, because Aboriginal lifestyles – as reported by travellers, Jesuits and others – seemed proof enough that they did not understand the value of labour and, therefore, could not understand the full meaning of property.

Indeed, by the late eighteenth century and early nineteenth century, these arguments were being used in North America. Thomas Jefferson asserted that Indians were in an original state and in need of civilization and that they had to abandon their traditional hunting economy, adopt the way of the farmer, and become citizens of the United States.[116] He stated in a message to the Cherokee on 9 January 1809, "I sincerely wish you may succeed in your laudable endeavours to save the remains of your nation by adopting industrious occupation and a government of regular law."[117] He was imposing the Lockean doctrine that although Aboriginal people had a right to land because they had mixed their labour with it, they had no laws to regulate property as determined by a positive constitution.[118] According to Locke, says James Tully, Europe's system of private property and commercial agriculture was superior to Aboriginal hunting and gathering because it used the land more productively, produced more commodities, and expanded jobs and the division of labour.[119]

During the period of the Covenant Chain, however, no such arguments or principles were employed at council meetings. It was only after Aboriginal nations' military and economic strength became insignificant that the British and Americans employed them. I have already suggested that the Crown, at some of the highest levels of its administration, was well aware of having to adopt a different framework of justification from that being developed by intellectuals. It was well aware that Aboriginal people understood fraud, what it meant to acquire land legitimately (e.g., in exchange for protection, as a gift of appreciation, and so on), and the right to control territory. One reason for dwelling on Locke's arguments in relation to the period in which he formulated them is to highlight the omissions. As secretary to Lord Shaftesbury, Locke would have been quite aware of the so-called Indian problem and of the Covenant Chain agreement (the treatises were published in 1688). His membership on the Board of Trade and his well-stocked library shelves, which were full of traveller accounts of North America,[120] would have made him well aware of the complexity of Aboriginal societies and England's political arrangements with the Haudenosaunee and other First Nations. He knew that Crown agents on the ground had to negotiate, bargain, argue, and defend themselves against accusations that the Crown had failed to uphold its agreements or punish violations by settlers and traders. He understood that these agents had to scramble to set things right to prevent their allies from abandoning the alliance or even attacking the colonies. Locke, almost certainly self-consciously, selected and manipulated the data to construct his formal arguments. As Barbara Arneil shows, he used his library's resources to argue that Sir Robert Filmer's theory of government was ahistorical.[121] Thus, Locke's own ahistorical account of Aboriginal people had to have been constructed on a selective use of resources; he chose evidence only as it supported his theoretical and political commitments.[122]

In light of England's dual justificatory framework and the eventual imposition of the theory of property rights, it is fair to conclude that it was only when the British and their political successors enjoyed military and economic superiority over Aboriginal people that Locke's arguments, together with his "official" assumptions about Aboriginal people's lack of rational capacity, became operative in North America. Similarly, as some commentators have argued, appeals to doctrines such as vacuum domicilium were recognizably forced and self-serving.[123] These formal arguments and their underlying assumptions bore little relation to the arguments that took place in council meetings. Crown agents paid little or no attention to the self-serving arguments of their intellectual guides in Europe. Origin stories alone – declarations of the two peoples being of one body, one mind, and one heart – countered suggestions that Aboriginal people could be treated differentially, as far as attributions of rationality and intellectual capacities were concerned. The dual character of British (and, indeed, European) justificatory frameworks has helped to buttress the dominant narrative, by advancing the Europe-based intellectual framework and suppressing the North America–based legal/political framework.

The contradictory character of European attitudes toward Aboriginal people helps to explain discrepancies between the dominant view of Aboriginal-European relations and the terms of reference for conducting affairs between the two sides detailed in historical records. Religion was one of these terms of reference. Not only did Europeans have to deal with shrewd trade negotiators and wary military allies, they had to deal with a people whose thought and actions were directed by belief systems not fundamentally different from those of their own. That Aboriginal people could be converted to Christianity or demand instruction in Christian doctrine and that Crown officials scrambled to meet these demands suggests that the shared lifeworld was based on a mutual understanding of life's meaning and an ultimate source of authority. This is not to say that Christianity was that source, but it is to say that both sides understood that they shared a capacity for thinking through to the ultimate groundings of life and truth.

Both the French and the British found that they needed to engage in justificatory discourse with their allies and use moral suasion to gain favour. Both tried to convince their would-be allies that their competitor was unjust, dishonourable, deceitful, insincere, and exploitive. Use of all of these descriptors assumes moral agency, both in the sense that one assumes one's interlocutor understands the meaning of agency and that the intersubjective world contains conceptions of agency. French and British also cited evidence to support their declarations. Indeed, even in the early period of the Chain, the English often used such language and evidence in council meetings. For instance, Governor Dongan in 1688 appealed to the Six Nations to stand united with the English because they could not trust the heart of the governor of Canada.[124] As mentioned, the French enjoyed considerable success in keeping the Haudenosaunee off balance (wavering between remaining allies with the English, going over to the French side, or staying neutral) by arguing that the English, contrary to their denials, wanted Haudenosaunee land. Both nations asserted that they were the more principled and virtuous European power.

Identifying the moral economy as a significant factor in the Crown-Aboriginal relationship, then, depends on more than simply singling out certain moral feelings or attitudes as constitutive of that economy. The Chain's moral economy was explicitly principled and, as such, contributed to the governance of proceedings between the two sides in ways that allowed for mutual critical evaluation. As the era of the Covenant Chain came to a close in the early 1800s and as Indian affairs eventually came under the auspices of civil departments rather than military departments, the argumentative and justificatory discourse began to fade from the record. When assimilation policies were developed in the 1820s, expressed eventually in instruments such as Canada's Indian Act, recognition of the need to justify plans, actions, and policies to Aboriginal people disappeared from the record, even as Lockean arguments began to take effect. As treaties became exclusively matters of land surrender and the extinguishment of rights, the records of Indian affairs lost their distinctiveness as a genre in which the intercultural play of justificatory frameworks mattered. Manifest Destiny was adopted by the United States as a justification for policy under the leadership of James Munroe. In this context, doctrines such as vacuum domicilium could be exploited freely. Any remnants of the idea that Aboriginal people were rational and shrewd negotiators who could dispute the Crown's actions were removed from the historical narrative. In removing these elements, British and American historians also removed memories of the strong trade and military alliances and intersubjective normative lifeworld that once prevailed.

Conclusion

While policy shifted from trade toward settlement and as intellectual perspectives began to shift, the Scientific and Industrial Revolutions were also taking place. The colonial period was a time of political revolution and a shift toward parliamentary democracy. Feudalism was coming to a close, and capitalism was taking form. Ptolemy's geocentric cosmology was giving way to a Copernican heliocentric universe, and colonizing efforts were exposing Europeans to a plethora of other cultures. Given the lack of such developments in areas of colonization, European colonizers enjoyed an increasing social licence that allowed the ideas of Hobbes, Locke, and Rousseau (and, later, Darwin) the freedom to grow and gain influence. Together, these developments helped produce the historiographic bias that Aboriginal people were not fully developed and, therefore, could be not be considered a civilized people with a clear conception of law. Any remnants of Aboriginal systems of law could be devalued and denigrated with impunity because Aboriginal military and economic power had dissolved. These developments also helped support the view that whatever Aboriginal systems had been in place could do nothing but fall victim to the irresistible revolutionary forces sweeping Europe and the rest of the world.

To lose sight of the Aboriginal-Crown relationship as it once was and view the writings of Hobbes, Locke, and Rousseau as canonical is to perpetuate a gross misrepresentation of Aboriginal people – their cultures, institutions, and relationship with the Crown. As contemporary historians (not to mention nonhistorians) study the record, however, the canon's force is disintegrating and becoming exposed as the product of intentional acts of distortion.[125] If James Tully is correct, Locke's influence on North American historiography is difficult to overestimate.[126] The combination of the demands of empire, colonization, and the differences between European and Aboriginal people would have made adopting the Lockean framework difficult to resist. His ideas on property and acquisition might have been so useful that countering them would have placed detractors at risk, as Roger Williams experienced when he criticized Governor Winthrop's use of the concept of vacuum domicilium. To set the record straight, so to speak, it is important not only to challenge the intellectual and motivational framework that supports the dominant narrative but also to understand and challenge its underlying values.

2
Structure and Function of the Covenant Chain Treaty Relationship

The Covenant Chain relationship, even at its early stages, included more than utilitarian trade and military features: it also included a complex underlying moral economy. Since the Covenant Chain relationship transformed over time into a treaty arrangement that involved various forms of recognition, it should not be defined too strictly or narrowly. For instance, defining the Covenant Chain exclusively as the result of a treaty negotiation, an event with legal properties that have a datable inception, can obscure its other relational and evolutionary properties rooted in a shared lifeworld.

War precipitated treaty-making processes and, as Daniel Richter points out, treaties were brokered principally by military-trained governors and agents,[1] highly suspicious people with whom negotiating was a hard-nosed affair. The idea of a shared lifeworld, then, does not imply that intentions during treaty making were "soft" and motivated by anything like loving kindness. Treaties also typically involved disputes over land. That Aboriginal people carried around pieces of paper as counterparts to wampum belts to authorize their claims shows that treaties had the character of documented, legal title. Core to the idea of the "peace and friendship treaty" was the idea of process – reaching mutual understanding, developing shared lifeworlds, and coming to agreement – by which members avoided war and chaos. This chapter examines the role of ceremonies, protocols, peculiar linguistic forms, and especially the presentation of wampum as the means for engaging this process.

Wampum

Treaties were recorded utilizing both written documentation and wampum belts. The original articles of the 1677 agreement were articulated in both types of record. James Merrell observes, "So vital was wampum as a medium of communication that no frontier negotiator could hope to succeed unless he knew the language of beads."[2] During Pontiac's War, for instance, George

Croghan was sent to the Illinois country by General Gage to do what he could to convince Pontiac and others to come to treaty negotiations with William Johnson. Having been advanced £2,000 for presents and other necessities, he explained to Johnson (to whom he was financially account-able) that he had purchased exceptionally large quantities of wampum and justified the expenditure by arguing that he would "have to furnish Wampum for all the Deputies of the sevl Tribes."[3] Johnson readily accepted Croghan's claims because he had negotiated many a treaty himself and knew that run-ning short of wampum to weave belts could prove disastrous.

Wampum, however, was not strictly an Aboriginal counterpart to written documents; it was used to focus attention on the idea of treaty as relation-ship. Richter describes this concept of treaty as follows: "[T]he *process* of treaty making was always far more important to Indians than the results enshrined in a treaty document."[4] It was more important to establish and maintain the conditions of peaceful relations than it was to itemize and enforce agreements. According to William Fenton, the condolence ceremony, in which "down-minded" (grieving) parties were presented condolences by the "clear-minded," formed the foundation of relations.[5] In this sense, treat-ies under the Covenant Chain were used to restore balanced and healthy relations between members. The term *process* rather than *event* is, then, more appropriate for describing the treaty relationship. Treaties were only second-arily about "agreement" and "law" during much of the Covenant Chain period (although by 1768 the tensions caused by different conceptions of treaty gave way to a more one-sided conception at the Fort Stanwix Treaty).[6]

Wampum was the chief means by which the earlier understanding of treaty was reinforced. It had multiple functions and forms that were not always fully understood by Aboriginal peoples' European interlocutors. When the British and French first arrived in the New World, they found a culture of Algonquian, and later Iroquoian, people who used wampum. The Wampanoag people of the Cape Cod area were producers of wampum beads, which were used as decoration and in jewellery. Beads were carved from the shells of the quahog clam in mostly cylindrical shapes of approximately a quarter inch and drilled lengthwise so that the fibres of elm bark or other materials could be threaded through them.[7] The Dutch called these beads "sewant," the French, "porcelain." Some wampum were pie-shaped and drilled on their flat surface. Both types were placed on strings. Cylindrical beads, however, were the only ones used for belts, which were of various sizes (some up to six or more feet in length). Wampum also served as money for a short period and had an exchange value of five guilders for a fathom (approximately 360 beads of wampum). In the mid-seventeenth century, the Dutch Reform Church established an almshouse in Albany where the poor were employed making wampum beads.[8] In William Penn's records

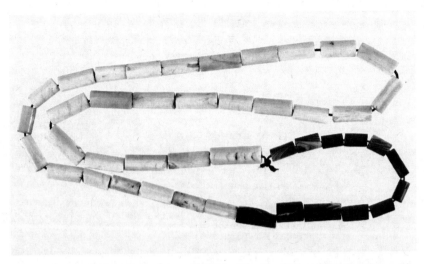

One presentation of wampum was a string of beads. Shown here is a string of white and purple beads, probably from the Iroquois. McCord Museum M13321.

there is a reference to wampum in which it is defined as currency (white was the equivalent of six to eight English pennies while black equalled about fourteen pennies).[9]

Popular history has exaggerated the importance of wampum as currency. The records of Indian affairs for all colonies within the Covenant Chain and those maintained by Robert Livingston and Peter Wraxall refer often to wampum belts and strings of wampum, but the references have little to do with their monetary value. Descriptions of typical council meetings indicate that wampum had several other functions. When a council was called, runners were sent with wampum belts or strings to the invited parties. If the parties refused the wampum, they were declaring that they would not attend; if they accepted, they were declaring their commitment to attend, as if under oath. To begin a meeting, a representative leader of a party whose proposition was being considered would greet the other parties as "brother," "child," or "father," depending on the nature of their relationship. The parties would then ceremonially renew the Covenant Chain, express condolences for key people who had died or been killed in battle, recall what the Covenant Chain signified, and present or throw down a belt or string of wampum. The parties not only promised to take care of each another during council meetings, they also recounted how often they had done so. When one side alleged that the other had broken part of the agreement, it reprimanded the other for lacking honour and integrity. These actions were also accompanied by presentations of wampum belts, strings or, in the early days,

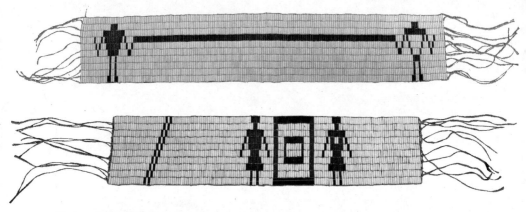

Pictured here are replicas of two Six Nations belts. The figures in the Denny Invitation Belt *(top)* represent the British and Aboriginal people linked by a chain. This representation is consistent with representations on other belts. The second belt *(bottom),* which also represents two figures, is known as the Penn Belt. Courtesy of the Woodland Cultural Centre.

"hands" of wampum. Speakers would hold and handle wampum belts and strings in a specified manner, although most records simply indicate that a belt or string was given or presented. Sometimes they indicate the presentation of a wampum belt or string simply with "a belt" or "a string."

One case in particular helps illustrate the importance of wampum to diplomacy. It involved Teedyuscung, a Delaware sachem who (in concert with Israel Pemberton, a Quaker, and others of the Pennsylvania Assembly) attempted to bring the French and Indian War to a close at a conference held in July 1756 in Easton, Pennsylvania. The meeting was punctuated by the presentation of several unusual belts, including a large all-white wampum that represented proof of sincerity. The Delaware regretted giving so little wampum in return and explained that they could not reciprocate because they were too poor. During these meetings and others, Teedyuscung attempted to situate himself as the head sachem for the Delaware, stating that his nation had made peace with the Six Nations and had come under the Covenant Chain. The problem, in his view, was that there were too many kings (people acting as sachems); if the number could be reduced, he argued, the war could be better managed and peace brought about. Teedyuscung then claimed to speak for ten of the nations (apparently including the western Delaware, who lived in the Ohio Valley and who never acknowledged the authority of the Six Nations' Covenant Chain. In his attempt to place himself in a position of authority, Teedyuscung made the claim that "who ever will not comply with the terms of peace the ten nations will join against him and strike him." He claimed that he had the power to unite the nations and have all join the Pennsylvanian Covenant Chain in an effort to protect their land. However, those present well knew that Teedyuscung had no such authority, particularly over the western Delaware, who not only ignored Teedyuscung's "orders" but also those of the Six Nations.[10]

This record makes it clear that the Pennsylvanians knew Teedyuscung's claim to be tenuous, at best. However, they acknowledged that if his words were to have any chance of affecting any of the ten nations, he would need "a belt of wampum six feet long and twelve rows broad and twelve strings to send to the chiefs to confirm his words." They understood that "without wampum nothing is to be done amongst the indians."[11] Owing to Teedyuscung's poverty, the government would have to furnish him with a great deal of wampum, just as the French had for their allies. The record is peculiar because it draws attention to the fact that members of the Pennsylvania Assembly understood that, however much they might posture and manipulate the situation, all would be for nought unless they produced wampum in appropriate amounts and forms.

Wampum belts and strings carried authority and indicated seriousness or genuine commitment. When Lawrence Claasse (various spellings), Indian agent and translator for the colony of New York, was sent on 1 June 1738 to ask the Iroquois to cease fighting the Catawbas, they "made answer that he was certainly jesting with them for if Corlaer [the Mohawk name for New York's governor] wanted them not to go he ought according to custom to have sent a Belt of Wampum, but as Laur. Claasse spoke without one they should not lay aside their Expedition."[12]

On other occasions, sachems corrected the Commission for Indian Affairs on the proper use of wampum. For instance, on 9 August 1708, the commissioners sent "hanks" of wampum along with a request that the Five Nations not go to war against the Cherokees and Flat Heads. The sachems replied, "[B]ut when such a message is sent you ought to have sent Belts not hanks of wampum, and you ought not to have sent it by a common Messenger but by one of your body – Such proceedings look as if you are not very eager to have your requests complied with."[13] Once the English came to understand the function of wampum, they turned the tables on their Aboriginal allies, sometimes accusing them of not being serious, as did William Keith, governor of Pennsylvania, in his relations with a Cayuga sachem in 1722.[14] Indeed, as James Merrell describes, Pennsylvanians began to send messages to Aboriginal people, for example, about the Stamp Act, through wampum belts and even began to weave their own designs on belts.[15] William Johnson expressed the situation well, "[I]t is obvious to all who are the least acquainted with Indian Affairs, that they regard no Message or Invitation be it of what consequence or nature it will, unless attended or confirmed by a String or Belt of Wampum, which they look upon, as we our Letters, or rather Bonds."[16] Ensuring that plenty of wampum was available when embarking on a mission to Indian Country was of paramount importance. To be without wampum was to be without a voice.[17] Sometimes the amount of wampum needed to conduct proceedings required large bags or even caskets; some belts were six feet in length and a foot wide and included ten thousand beads each.

The authority associated with wampum and the seriousness with which it was employed suggests that wampum carried or represented a legitimating power, a normative force. The Delaware, during the French and Indian War in 1757, even said that they would have come over to the British if a peace belt had been sent.[18] Given what is known about how angry the Delaware were about British encroachment and how much they subsequently devastated Pennsylvania's frontier settlers, this statement is particularly noteworthy. When the Pennsylvania Assembly's deliberations over sending belts to the western Delaware (despite being aware of Teedyuscung's impotence) is factored in, it is clear that the authority associated with wampum was peculiar in that it had the power to compel above and beyond the authority of people or official bodies.

This is not to say that Europeans attributed the same power to wampum as did Aboriginal people, but they acted as if they did. Many a British and French negotiator, including certain principal agents, found the use of wampum protocol tedious and boring. Montcalm, for instance, complained that wampum-based ceremonies were as tiresome as they were necessary.[19] Some, in fact, found convenient excuses to avoid councils and all they entailed, as did Governor Morris of Pennsylvania on occasion.[20] Since there was no option for European treaty negotiators but to participate in wampum protocol and learn about the power vested in wampum, they had to become competent in its use and demonstrate some awareness of the aspects of their interlocutors' lifeworld that wampum use represented or expressed. Aboriginal peoples' insistence that formal talks be in their own tongue would also have compelled agents to widen and deepen their understanding of wampum use to avoid making errors.[21]

Accounts of council meetings and ceremonies provide a glimpse into this process. British agents quickly realized the authority vested in wampum, for they or their clerks began recording wampum presentations and eventually began describing the belts and strings in detail, as if they intended to use these descriptions to explain the meaning of wampum use. For instance, at the Easton conference mentioned above, a belt sent to Teedyuscung by the Six Nations was described as "a square in the middle representing the land of the indians and at one end, a man representing the english, and at the other a figure representing the French."[22] While other facets of this and most council meetings were either described summarily with phrases such as "the usual ceremonies were conducted" or simply ignored by clerks, matters pertaining to wampum presentation were given special attention. Wampum mediated modes of interaction among members of the Covenant Chain.

One of William Johnson's officers who had met two deputies of the Six Nations reported that they had spoken to him "with the belt of Wampum, on which they spoke, a thing necessary for me to produce at a genl meeting with them, as well as hereafter, as a proof of the discovery of their proceedings & malicious intentn toward us for which reason it was forwarded after me by the first opportunity."[23] It is clear that the officer understood the importance of the belt and the importance of sending it to his superior. He treated it with the same sense of urgency as he would have an official letter from his own government. In all councils and virtually all proceedings carried out by Johnson and his officers with the Algonquians and Hurons of the western region, British agents were careful to follow wampum protocol.

To be sure, despite learning how to use wampum, the British never became completely comfortable with wampum protocol, partly because they never felt themselves to be completely competent practitioners. If Conrad Weiser and William Johnson, two of Britain's most successful and respected agents among the Aboriginal allies, felt that they were operating on the margins of competence, others would certainly have been operating even further out on the margins. James Merrell describes how both men admitted that, at the end of the day, they never fully understood Indian ways, even though they had been accepted into clans and knew the language. They had lived in or married into Aboriginal communities, where they danced war dances, fought alongside warriors, bartered, and, in the case of Johnson, had been declared a sachem.[24] Understanding and appreciating the authority vested in wampum was not a simple or straightforward matter; it mirrored the process of complexification in the Crown-Aboriginal relationship and the deepening of the shared lifeworld.

Understanding the lifeworld or mindset of one's allies could only be accomplished to a certain degree, partly because of psychological limitations in the human capacity to make foreign cultures intelligible without knowing the other's language. Both parties would have lacked the ability, usually developed at an early age within one's own culture, to detect and automatically interpret nuances in the behaviour and speech of others. This ability depends on having internalized the web of meanings a culture uses to assign significance to things and gestures. Thus, the ability to enter into an intercultural lifeworld would not have been viewed as an all-or-nothing capacity. Recognizing this limitation, interlocutors would have judged each other on the degree of their commitment to and skill at entering into a shared lifeworld. But once they entered to a degree sufficient to enable effective communication, they operated in an intercultural lifeworld whose mode of mutual understanding differed in kind from that experienced by those confined to a single culture. They might have begun the relationship as strange aliens rather than as children to be nurtured and raised in the culture of the community, and they might have learned about each other by struggling and experimenting with ways to communicate, apologizing for misunderstandings, and inventing communicative devices to overcome barriers, but their shared lifeworld would not be radically different from those who grew up sharing a lifeworld. That commitments had to be made to create a shared lifeworld implies that the two sides took each other seriously and respected each other enough to invest time and energy into attaining sufficient mutual understanding to develop effective modes of communication, which cultural insiders take for granted. The result was something different than the sum, or even the intersection, of the two lifeworlds. Outsiders could not understand or participate in the intersubjective lifeworld that developed. Since the substance of the intercultural lifeworld is established through a process of invention and innovation, people who remain confined to their own culturally defined lifeworlds cannot participate in the intercultural lifeworld. They remain strange aliens. In contrast, those who are willing and able to invent and adapt to create an intercultural lifeworld form a new insider community, one with assurances, expectations, obligations, and especially intentions that contribute to the structuring and functioning of the moral economy.

One way to advance understanding of this intersubjective lifeworld is to examine how wampum functioned as an authority. George Croghan, William Johnson's agent in the Ohio Valley and a key negotiator for Pennsylvania, exemplifies how the authority was exercised by insiders. Johnson sent him into formerly hostile territory just after the last French and Indian War to prepare the way for peace negotiations. On the one hand, Croghan was responsible for presenting the Crown's case and propositions in a way that would enable the Crown to use the proceedings and agreements as legal, or at least quasi-legal, documents. On the other hand, he had to demonstrate competence in and respect for wampum. Croghan used wampum in the same way as his Aboriginal counterparts: he presented belts and strings of wampum to wipe tears away from their eyes, purify their hearts, and clear their throats. Croghan understood that these ceremonies were not mere preliminaries, that he was being watched for signs of understanding, respect, or disrespect. The more time Croghan spent with Aboriginal people and acted according to their expectations (the condition of becoming an effective negotiator), the more he likely felt the need to identify with them and their ways of understanding. Merrell reports that Croghan, indeed, declared himself an Indian at one point.[25]

The record also suggests that British agents and clerks in general went through what Croghan did. As the recording of wampum use became more detailed, as the relationship became more complex and robust, clerks and agents underwent a transformation in the way they understood their responsibilities as recorders of interactions and agreements. In a way, their transformation was predictable. When interlocutors attempt to reach agreements and avoid conflict by trying not to commit blunders, they learn what matters to the other party and how to avoid insulting them or violating their norms and sensibilities. They come to think like them, even if, in the beginning, they do so only for reasons of prudence and utility. At another level, however, once a person starts to think like another, a transformative process begins to occur. This transformation involves a type of learning that makes returning to the former way of thinking impossible. People reflectively compare their own cultural and personal expectations against those of the people they are trying to understand. Comparing one against the other presents an opportunity to judge one's own culture as either inferior or superior, as a whole or on specific matters. People who engage in this learning process tend to understand themselves in a new light through self-critique. As a consequence, acting in accordance with their own culture's expectations will never be the same as it had been prior to entering the shared lifeworld.

The performative aspects of wampum augmented the learning process by embodying the ideas and sensibilities of the shared lifeworld. Wampum protocol involved handling belts and strings in specific ways to convey what was meant, how it was meant, and a sense of reverence. The learning process, then, incorporated embodied modes of communication, and these protocols were not merely skills to appropriate: they were expressions of recognizing and acknowledging a source of normative authority. Constant repetition and tests of sincerity made it difficult not to internalize the sense of authority wampum carried. This internalization process, along with reflective acts of self-criticism, was carried by a shared set of values and other sensibilities. Given that British and Aboriginal agents were hard-nosed military men, the shared values and sensibilities that came to constitute the shared lifeworld were likely hard-won and difficult to dislodge, based as they were on personal commitments and a great deal of invested energy. Likewise, the acceptance of wampum protocol and all it carried would have been hard-won. The English could not have simply capitulated to Aboriginal people's demands.

Habermas's explanation of socialization sheds light on what likely happened to these agents. For Habermas, communicative speech acts result when three worlds – the objective, the subjective, and the intersubjective – interact. The development of a shared lifeworld is social and occurs when

we attempt to communicate with others for purposes of reaching understanding. As we develop words and descriptions, explanations, and modes
of communication that enable us to understand one another, we create a
social field of experience. We cannot focus on or articulate the entire field
of experience, yet we rely on it to provide a backdrop of common meanings
and memories that enable us to make sense of any word or description.[26] In
other words, wherever there is a communicative practice, there is a "cultural
stock of knowledge that is 'always already' familiar," a shared lifeworld that
has already been interpreted as having objective, subjective, and intersubjective aspects.[27] This cultural stock is taken for granted; it is something that
one cannot observe from the outside in.[28] It is not possible to completely
identify the factors that contributed to the lifeworld and intersubjective
lifeworld; thus, the cultural stock must be internalized in such a way that it
can serve as a backdrop automatically, or without explicit recognition.

George Croghan's situation was one in which the lifeworld he shared with
his Aboriginal interlocutors, much of which could not be made explicit, was
embedded in his learning experience. Considering the special character of
wampum protocol, the authority Croghan associated with wampum was at
least somewhat embedded in both Croghan's intersubjective and subjective
lifeworlds. The performative and normative aspects of wampum use reinforced
and deepened this embeddedness as mutual understanding developed.
Moreover, in situations like that of the Covenant Chain, the use of strategic
speech acts was viewed with suspicion, if not as outright signs of disrespect.[29]
In this context, it was extremely difficult to speak and act strategically because
the skills needed to appear sincere were readily detectable in both speech
and bodily behaviour. Successfully entering the world of wampum depended
on developing a shared sense of confidence, on being able to draw on each
side's sense of mutual obligation, normative commitments, and sense of
guilt, shame, and the like. Given the hard-nosed character of the key agents,
the acceptance of wampum and its authority had to have been a matter of
choice based, to some degree at least, on recognizing shared values.

William Fenton's description of the Condolence Council helps explain
the use of wampum as a communicative action aimed at understanding and
developing a shared lifeworld.[30] Condolence ceremonies were integral to the
Covenant Chain relationship. They were structured to enable grieving parties to be condoled by others. Among the Haudenosaunee, different parties
formed a moiety system – a social system that organized relations in terms
of complementary opposites, for instance, father and child or clear-minded
and down-minded. Partners were part of a system of reciprocal relations.[31]
Wampum belts and strings were used in condolence ceremonies to "wipe
away the tears" so that the grieving party could be restored to his or her
proper role in the balance of opposites. The power of wampum, in this

context, was a healing power. Gift giving accompanied wampum, and special councils were sometimes dedicated to condolence. Fenton describes one such council. After the death of Kakhswenthioni (Hanging Wampum Belt, or, as the English called him, "Red Head"), William Johnson, as one of the clear-minded moiety (the other being the Oneida, Tuscarora, Cayuga, and Nanticokes), travelled to Onondaga to condole his down-minded brethren. During the ceremonies, wampum was presented in the form of strings to address the mourners. The Three Bare Words – wiping away the tears, clearing the throat, and purifying the heart – were spoken. One wampum belt was used to cover the grave, another to mourn relatives, a third to admonish relatives to adhere to the Covenant Chain, a fourth to remove the clouds and restore the sun to allow the council to continue, and a fifth to clear the night clouds to enable the stars and moon to shine on the night council.[32] Wampum use promoted and to some extent presupposed an understanding of the suffering of others. The shared lifeworld, as expressed in wampum, then, was constituted not only by economic, military, political, and legal sensibilities but also by the emotions. The expression of appropriate emotions was, then, central to the structuring of the Covenant Chain and critical to its functioning as a communicative forum.

The Covenant Chain was certainly about the rule of law and negotiating agreements, but it was also about maintaining or restoring health, balance and trust, and expressing compassion. Communicative actions were just as much about addressing injury, dysfunction, betrayal, and maliciousness as they were about satisfying contractual obligations. In other words, wampum-based communicative actions were attempts to go directly to the subjective and intersubjective worlds of moral feelings and responsibility. The intersubjective world into which interlocutors entered led to expectations of good will. Involving oneself heavily in wampum protocol required interlocutors to enter into another's emotive subjective world and to create an intersubjective emotive world in which acknowledgments of suffering and affirmations of the other's value were integral. This aspect of the relationship may explain why many Europeans claimed to have become Indians or why others perceived them as such. Ironically, it also helps explain why Conrad Weiser, after having lived with the Mohawks and been a negotiator for Pennsylvania for decades, sought to resign in 1754. He asked to be relieved of his duties as principal interpreter because he was "no longer Master of that Fluency he formerly had, and finding himself at a Loss for proper Terms to express himself is frequently obliged to make Use of Circumlocution."[33] It was onerous work being a competent member of the wampum world. It demanded that agents remain constantly attuned to one another. But once attuned, they could make use of the bonds and obligations made possible by shared values and norms.

The main point is that the peculiar kind of socialization that wampum use effected operated explicitly in three worlds: the subjective, the inter-subjective, and the objective normative. To practise wampum protocol meant freely committing to agreements based on acknowledgments of shared values and norms. In this respect, wampum represented or called upon the moral forces that governed self-avowed members of an alliance. Put another way, the structure and function of the Covenant Chain alliance were not intended to make people feel compelled to obey the normative expectations of the agreement. The devices used to produce mutual understanding and agree-ments operated by, first, creating awareness and, second, presenting a choice. They were designed to clear the mind rather than force it into compliance. Wampum protocol, then, was not some external force that compelled people to conform to norms but rather represented forces that became in-ternal to the relationship as it evolved through the use of communicative actions.

Protocol, Paradigms, and Lifeworld

Treaty councils, for the most part, followed a strict protocol. Even British agents not so close to their allies recognized the importance of protocol, as is indicated in a letter from Lieutenant Colonel Thomas Gilbert to Thomas Hardy, governor of New York. In it, Gilbert proposed to send warriors on scalping and settlement-destroying expeditions into Canada in an attempt to counter French incursions into New York. He cautioned, however, that it "is a work wch will require previous Ceremonies & a more formal Application than can be made here."[34] Getting warriors to go to war was not an im-promptu affair. Given that warriors could not be ordered into battle and that proper protocol had to be followed before any request to join in battle could be made, requests for alliances required wampum. Suing for peace also required that wampum protocol be followed. One of the best accounts of this protocol is by Father Barthelemy Vimont in the *Jesuit Relations*.[35] Both Francis Jennings and Robert Williams Jr. (among others) cite the passage to make it clear that Aboriginal people were far from being passive victims of colonial forces.[36] The passage tells of Kiotsaeton, a Mohawk spokesman, coming from Mohawk territory to Three Rivers in 1645 to treat with the French, Huron, and Algonquin, with whom the Mohawk had been at war. At the initial encounter, Kiotsaeton stands in his canoe while covered in wampum and signals for silence so he can begin his speech. After being al-lowed to land, he sets up poles and ties a cord between them. His party then carries seventeen belts of wampum; some are strung across their bodies while others are carried in a pouch. With each statement uttered, Kiotsaeton places a belt of wampum over the cord. When he returns a prisoner, Guillaume Costure, as a gesture of good will, he ties wampum around Costure's arm. He uses some of the belts to describe why he came. One belt indicates that he is returning a prisoner, one is given to help people forget the pain of previous warfare, one reminds the Huron of their good will, and one clears the skies of clouds so the people can see clearly. By the end of the speeches, of which there are many, each wampum belt has an appointed place.

To confirm the peace negotiated at Three Rivers, the parties then agree to meet at an appointed place with parties from all nations. They meet in the fall of that year. At the meeting, the Iroquois ("Hiroquois") take a Frenchman and an Algonquin by the arms to dance and sing a song of peace. The Haudenosaunee term to describe the linking of arms is *teHonanē:shō* (they have joined arms).[37] Although the passage illustrates the multiple functions of wampum, the case also emphasizes wampum's power to unite or bring people under a common bond.

In a second passage, in what appears to be a wood's edge ceremony, George Croghan delivers an opening address for the council meetings of 6-12 April 1760, which were attended by William Johnson and hundreds of representatives from the Six Nations, Delaware, Shawnee, Twightwees, and Mohicans. On 6 April, Croghan welcomes the Aboriginal representatives with wampum:

> [W]ith this String I wipe the Sweat & dust off Your Bodies Pick the bryars out of Your feet, & clear Your eyes that You may see Your brethrens faces & look Chearful – Gave a String. Brethren, With this String I clear Your hearts and Minds that You may speak perfectly free and open to us – Gave String – Brethren, With this String I wipe the blood from off the Council Seats, that Your Cloaths may not be Stained nor Your Minds disturbed.[38]

No business is mentioned or transacted. The Aboriginal participants reciprocate and then light a pipe, which they all smoke. They then drink a glass of wine and depart from the ceremonial grounds.

A third paradigmatic case, which shows how healing is linked to unity, occurred on 3-13 August 1682 and opened a series of councils between the Five Nations, Maryland, and Virginia. New York played a mediating role. The issue discussed was the Five Nations' raiding, murdering, killing livestock, and taking prisoners from New England through to Virginia. In the record, the parties meet at Albany, where Colonel Henry Coursey serves as mediator. Maryland and Virginia (represented by Governor Effingham) present their accusations and give an ultimatum: if they are not given satisfaction, they will war against the Five Nations and reduce them to the same position to which other Indians have been reduced. The Five Nations acknowledge their guilt and begin the process of rectification. Arnout Viele, a Dutch trader, and Akus Cornelius, whom the clerk describes as a "former Indian," translate. In the exchange, the Five Nations speakers present "peaks" (wampum belts). Four peaks in total are presented, two of which have sixteen rows. On 4 August 1682, the clerk notes that the belts have been left on the floor and that the Haudenosaunee have left. When they return the next day, the Haudenosaunee see that the belts remain on the floor. They express consternation, and in response, Cornelius is ordered by the commissioners to tell them that they are in a peace talk and that they have nothing to fear, after which they make a loud noise and seat themselves. The agents, as they are referred to by the clerk, ask what the Five Nations delegates meant by delivering up the belts. The agents offer an interpretation: "forasmuch as wee hue understood from you this morning that the Belts of Peak whch you laid down yesterday, were only for a beginning, and to get a right understanding in order to our further Treaty." The Five Nations representatives confirm the interpretation.[39]

This record is one of the first in which interpretation and details of the protocol are the clerk's focus. It is informative because of the clumsiness of the interaction and the obscurity of Aboriginal protocol in English eyes. In these early meetings, the use of wampum protocol was an occasion for misunderstanding, as might be expected. However, agents and clerks learned not only that it was important to distinguish between belts and strings but also that it was important to understand the symbols on them and the manner in which they were presented. The record demonstrates that the English quite consciously and intentionally sought to understand wampum protocol and to recognize its unifying and healing functions. They could have simply followed up on their threats to eliminate their interlocutors; instead, they invited the development of a shared lifeworld.

A good illustration of wampum's multiple functions is contained in the records of the peace council – held on 23-31 July 1766 at Oswego – that followed Pontiac's War in the aftermath of the last French and Indian War in the Ohio region.[40] The Western Confederacies and the Six Nations attended the council to confirm a peace agreement with William Johnson and to establish the Chain of Friendship between three great links: the English, the Six Nations, and the Western Nations. The council had been preceded by councils at Detroit and Niagara in 1761 and by the Treaty at Niagara in 1764. The war sachem Pontiac had, however, been wreaking havoc on British forts and absent from these treaty councils. Johnson worked to bring Pontiac to treat from the 1764 Niagara council on, instructing his right-hand man, George Croghan, to take whatever opportunity he could to encourage Pontiac to come to the council. Reports were sent to Johnson and Thomas Gage that detailed Pontiac's whereabouts, movements, and influence among the various tribes in the Ohio and Detroit areas.

Upon convening the Oswego council, Johnson begins using wampum and pipe protocols to express sympathy for deaths in the communities and to purify hearts and minds. He opens the council with three strings of wampum, performing, as Guy Johnson, William's secretary and nephew, tends to describe them, "the usual ceremonies." Next, Johnson offers condolences for the death of Aughstaghregi, chief of all the Huron, in the usual form. He "gave three Black Strouds &ca and covered his grave with a Black Belt of Wampum." He then "causes" Pontiac's pipe to be lit, and after it is handed around for all to smoke, he begins his speech. He accompanies each aspect of his speech with wampum of various forms. He concludes with, "I hope the Great Spirit will enable, and allow us to meet and see each other often in this Country," and then presents a belt.[41]

Once the Huron begin to speak, Guy Johnson provides more detailed descriptions. Opening remarks by Tiata, chief of the Huron, who prays for the Great Spirit's assistance, are accompanied by a belt of nine rows. His proposition to quit all evils and remain steadfast to the Chain of Friendship is accompanied by a belt of ten rows. A request to have a smith sent to the community to repair guns and other implements is accompanied by a string of wampum. When Pontiac speaks about taking Croghan by the hand the previous year, a belt of seven rows is presented. An admission that some of his people's minds have been poisoned against the English is accompanied by a belt of nine rows. A promise to set things straight is accompanied by two belts of five rows and one belt of six rows. One belt is used to cover and strengthen Johnson's Chain of Friendship. It has ten rows. A farewell good wish is made with a bunch of wampum. Communications between Six Nations chiefs and Pontiac are accompanied by strings, some of which are single, some of which have four branches, and some of which are made of multiple and separate strings.

These four cases illustrate how integral wampum belts and strings were to council proceedings and how members attributed various powers to them such as healing, purifying hearts, clearing minds, making throats clear, legitimating propositions, and speaking for others (as in the 1682 case). In light of wampum's many functions, it is worth drawing a distinction between its power and its authority to explain its significance to the shared lifeworld. Wampum's power was connected with action (e.g., healing or condoling) while its authority derived from its ability to assign status to propositions (e.g., agreements or requests). Its healing power was recognized first during council fires, followed by its authority, indicating that the relationship was more important than its substance.

Each use of wampum was associated with a communicative function, and its appearance was associated with specific meanings. Colours, shapes, symbols, and the like had to be interpreted to understand what a belt or string meant, a complex process that required considerable learning and mentoring. That the record rarely provides explanations for belts, even though they are often described, indicates that learning how to use wampum meant learning a high-context language. The authority and power of wampum might never have been spelled out or explained.

Yet there is much to be learned about wampum from the record. What is immediately apparent is that forms of wampum were categorized into types. The belts Kiotsaeton presented in 1645 were peace belts (predominantly white) while others were war belts (predominantly black or purple). There were Covenant Chain intercultural belts and Five Nations intracultural belts. There were condolence belts and belts to renew treaty arrangements, as well as belts and strings to establish equanimity. Eventually, clerks also began to record colour, size, shape, and patterns because they came to understand that everything on belts conveyed meaning that could be "read." Even if much of the meaning of belts and strings has been lost, the records at least make clear that they were, as an intercultural medium, readable and that being able to read them was a matter of critical importance to the Covenant Chain relationship, in every respect. It might even be fair to say that wampum use constituted a distinct paradigm of communicative action.

Although not obvious in the records, wampum use gave voice to its holder or presenter. Giving voice was one of its powers. In 1699, when the French were once again threatening to attack the Five Nations unless they came to Canada to treat, Dekanisore, a key sachem for the Onondaga and spokesman for the confederacy, described his dilemma to Governor Bellomont of New York.[42] Bellomont, in turn, reported the event to the Lords of Trade. In his report, he relates that upon learning that the Five Nations (the Mohawks had withheld approval) were to hold a council at Onondaga to appoint sachems to meet with the governor of Canada, he had sent Johannes Schuyler and Johannes Bleeker to the council to convey the Crown's objection. On the way, the two men stopped at the uppermost Mohawk "castle," where they conferred with sachems. Schuyler and Bleeker reported that the sachems had sent seven hands of wampum "with us for to have their Voice in the General assembly and also that they would stand by the propositions made to the Governor."[43] This is the only record that uses the locution "to have their voice," but it is clearly a function of wampum to empower speakers to participate in communal and intercommunal negotiation and decision-making forums. The presence of wampum obliged others to listen, and this obligation was reinforced by procedure. Responses to propositions and condolences typically involved repeating what was said so as to ensure proper understanding. To have voice, then, was to make the others who also had a voice in council commit to understanding what was said.

The Authority and Power of Wampum
To legitimate, authorize, heal, or give voice is to exercise a capacity to bring about or produce consequences. That the British were aware of this capacity of wampum and that it had more than a merely formal function is evident in intelligence reports concerning movements of the enemy. When British agents reported that the French or the Far Indians were going among the

allied nations (especially the Mohawk and other Five Nations) to win them over or to convince them to remain neutral, their superiors expressed special concern when invitation or peace belts accompanied them. Considerable effort was made to find these belts and to compel the allies to send them back. The British warned of French intrigue and dishonesty in an attempt to counter the effect of the French belts. A record dated 29 March 1746 indicates that the Mohawk received a belt from the governor of Canada, who claimed that it should be considered as good as having the governor himself present. The belt was sent to "inform" the Indians of the mischief that the British would soon bring. The governor promised to break a path for the Indians and mark it clearly with bent twigs. When the time came, he would be ready to help them as he expected, and they would be ready to help him in return.[44] The commissioners of Indian affairs viewed the French belts as sufficiently threatening to warrant sending a letter to the British government warning it of the dire consequences that would follow if no action were taken. Many other instances, including George Washington's attempt to convince the Delaware and Shawnee to return French belts on behalf of Governor Dinwiddie, could also be cited.[45]

Events at the council at Easton in July 1756 indicate the capacity associated with wampum.[46] During the council, the Delaware presented a belt with a square in the middle, which represented the land of the Indians. Each end of the belt contained a figure of a man that represented the English and the French, respectively. The belt signified that the Delaware were caught in the middle. They resented the Pennsylvanians for encroaching on their land and mistrusted the French for sending troops into the Ohio Valley. The Delaware were also under pressure to take sides. At the meeting, the Delaware were reinstated as "men" (their skirts were removed to signify that they would no longer be treated as dependants of the Six Nations) so that they could be called to join in the war effort against the French without having the Six Nations mediate the proceedings. As indicated, about three decades prior to this meeting, the Delaware had been denied the right to treat for themselves by the Six Nations, who had made them "women," a problematic assertion.

The Easton meeting was convened in part so that Teedyuscung could report that the belt he held was a sign that the Delaware had been made men and that it gave him the authority to speak. Teedyuscung's claims must have been at least partially bluster, but the Pennsylvanians were becoming desperate. When the English called him the Delaware king, they were using the occasion to encourage the warring nations to treat. On 31 July, the day after Teedyuscung gave the belt to the governor, Conrad Weiser expressed some doubt about it but advised the governor to reciprocate all the same. He advised that a belt should be constructed and given to the "king," especially since the French had been giving large quantities of wampum to their allies.

This was done, and the secretary was then ordered to give to Teedyuscung all of the wampum in the council's possession: fifteen strings, seven belts, a parcel of new black wampum (seven thousand beads), and a newly commissioned belt woven by a woman (five thousand beads). The commissioned belt had a figure of the governor in the middle and five men on each side (the ten nations). Thus, despite Teedyuscung's dubious claims and status, the Pennsylvanians responded to his presentation of wampum because they knew that not doing so would leave them no other recourse but to continue at war with the other nations.

A letter from William Johnson to his commander-in-chief, Jeffrey Amherst, shows that the significance of wampum was recognized even in high-ranking circles. The letter was sent at a time when the Crown suspected an uprising by the Six Nations, the Seneca in particular. The issue occupied the two-month-long conference at Niagara and Detroit, where Johnson had established the new council fire and invited the Western Nations into the Covenant Chain. Owing to advancing European settlement, military duplicity, and the increasing poverty of Aboriginal communities, some Aboriginal groups (the Seneca, it seems) sent a war belt to various nations in Canada requesting that they join in an effort to eliminate the English. On his travels to Niagara and Detroit, Johnson met with various nations and used the opportunity to query them about the belt. Everyone denied knowing anything about it until Johnson arrived at Detroit. There, the Huron and Ottawa described how two Seneca, Kanághorait (actually a white Mingo) and Kayashota, had presented the belt to the Huron, who had rejected it. Guy Johnson recorded the proceedings, taking pains to note when belts and strings were being presented. Likewise, when Johnson reported to Amherst on the possibility of an uprising, he copied Captain Campbell's record of the proceedings (previously cited) in which the captain reports the presentation of a belt of Wampum, "a thing necessary for me to produce at a genl meeting with them." Johnson then reported that he had sent a "Belt of Wampum from Oswego to assemble some of the Chiefs."[47]

Two points can be raised: first, wampum use put forces (in this case, antagonistic forces) in motion that required appropriate responses; second, wampum protocol had become embedded in the discourse not only between the British and Aboriginal groups but also among British agents in their communications regarding Aboriginal people. The first point is implied in the previous explanations of wampum, but it is worth making it explicit. The second point is new. Why would Johnson and others not simply abbreviate descriptions of proceedings or events by simply reporting that a certain proposition had been made or that a message had been sent? Why mention the accompanying belts and strings so systematically rather than simply stating what business had been conducted and agreements reached. As was the case with other formalities, why did they not simply say that "the usual messages were sent"? In another noteworthy communication from Daniel Claus to the Pennsylvania secretary dated 10 July 1755, Claus describes speeches made at Fort Johnson in which references were made to raising the Tree of Shelter and Friendship for all the United Nations, of lighting council fires with wood that would never burn out. He follows this description with a detailed account of the belts used to make a number of propositions.[48]

The more familiar one becomes with the record, the easier it is to explain why the British used the language of wampum, even in correspondence among themselves. Wampum was entrenched in communications involving and concerning Aboriginal people so agents could ascertain the significance and meaning of events. Gradually, those meanings did not need to be spelled out because they had become part of the high-context language used to talk about and with Aboriginal people. Moreover, the British never, as far as I can tell, referred to belts in a disparaging way, as they did other practices and characteristics of Aboriginal life. They felt quite free to cast disparaging remarks about Aboriginal people's religion or warfare practices, for instance, but for those engaged in diplomacy, no such words were spoken about wampum. This phenomenon was, in part, the result of being socialized to recognize the authority and power of wampum, as far as an intersubjective shared lifeworld was concerned.

As the reporting of belts and strings became more detailed, the language of wampum (as in the use of the Three Bare Words) also became increasingly integrated into the discourse. To illustrate, the Livingston records from 1666 to approximately 1672 read more like the reports of a novice reporter. They describe events in a style that resembles point form. The presentation of wampum, for instance, is noted as "Give thereupon 1 fathom wampum." By 1674, however, the descriptions had become somewhat more complex: for example, 14 February 1674-75, "Give thereupon 7 strings of wampum: 1 of 13, 2 of 11, 1 of 9, 2 of 5, and 1 of 6 high." By 1677, the beginning of the Silver Covenant Chain, the language had become one of oneness: "one hart and one head, for the Covenant that is betwixt ye Govr: Genll and us is inviolable yea so strong yt if ye very Thunder should break upon ye Covenant Chayn it wold not break it in Sunder."[49] Finally, as seen, in Johnson's era, 1750 through the 1760s, the use of Aboriginal metaphors, wampum belts, and strings is recorded in detail.

Wampum even played a part in the religious aspects of the Covenant Chain relationship. William Smith, secretary of the Correspondent Commissioners of the Society in Scotland for Propagating Christian Knowledge, wrote to Johnson in October 1764 from New Jersey about a belt the Oneida had sent to Samson Occum, an Aboriginal preacher, in November 1763. Samson had sent the belt to the Reverend David Bostwick, president of the commission, who was ill and probably unable to attend to it before he died. It had since been in the hands of William Smith, who did not know what it was about or who had sent it. Once Smith became aware of what the belt meant (it was a request to send missionaries to the Oneida community), he sent word to Johnson that missionaries had been sent. His reason for writing, however, was to ask that Johnson convey his sincerest regrets to the Oneida for the unintentional delay. He wanted Johnson to ensure that the accident had not been seen as a slight.[50]

The entrenchment of wampum into communications between Crown agents had other dimensions, especially where William Johnson was concerned. In correspondence with General Braddock, for instance, Johnson wrote to describe the actions he had taken to keep the Six Nations on side and to prevent them from going over to the French: "Immediately upon my coming home I dispatched a String of Wampum thro the Six Nations to apprize them that a Reinforcement was marching to Oswego." He went on to report that

> some of the Mohock Sachems advised me to send a Belt of Wampum with a special Messenger to prevent their being alarmed at so unusual a Number of Soldiers marching through their Country, besides as I doubt not the French will endeavour to blow up a Jealousy amongst them upon this Occasion & therefore to prevent any ill consequences I have with my Belt of Invitation sent another upon this Occasion with proper Instructions to the Interpreters thereupon.[51]

Johnson could have simply reported that he had been advised to send a message and that he had sent an invitation. But he specifically mentioned that he had been told to send a belt of wampum and specified that he had sent an invitation belt.

At times, Johnson even went further. During a meeting with Lieutenant Governor DeLancey on 8 February 1755, for instance, he presented strings of wampum from the Mohawk and Canajoharie castles in the same manner that those belts would have been presented by Aboriginal people at a council meeting. In this case, however, no Aboriginal people were present at the meeting.[52] He could have said that the Indians were becoming disenchanted with the British. He instead reported that the Mohawk see "once clear skies turning to dark clouds" and are thinking of "removing those clouds." He then presented four strings of black wampum to DeLancey. DeLancey was Johnson's superior, so it is unlikely that Johnson was simply being playful.

The DeLancey example is somewhat unusual, but Johnson's correspondence with Braddock is typical. Both cases suggest that both the language of wampum and wampum protocol had, to some degree, been integrated into the internal procedures and communications of Indian affairs. This characteristic of the record adds to its peculiarity as a genre and may be one of the homegrown metaphors of which Benjamin Franklin spoke. If the incorporation of wampum into the discourse of Indian affairs was one of those metaphors, its use was normalized through the colonial government. In light of the British propensity for formal and legal (that is, technical) language, it is difficult to understand why Johnson and others reported in this language, unless communications would be adversely affected by their absence. Aboriginal protocol and language had then acquired a kind of official and technical significance for the British. Weaving references to wampum into reports and even face-to-face communications between British agents seems to have been intended to guarantee that the meanings were not missed or distorted.

Records that describe the facility with which agents such as Croghan, Johnson, and Weiser engaged in the condolence ritual demonstrate that they had no difficulty acknowledging the power associated with wampum. At a series of council meetings held on 7-11 September 1733, where condolence was the focus, New York's Governor Cosby opened by offering his condolences on the deaths brought about by the smallpox epidemic in various communities.[53] He wiped away tears and opened the grieving people's understanding so that "we may behold one another with joy." He gave three strings of wampum and a belt. After apologizing for not coming sooner, he told the Six Nations that the king had ordered him to tell them that he loved them as a father does his children and that his affection had been occasioned by the fact that they had demonstrated bravery and honesty, two qualities he valued most in nations and persons. Cosby had been commanded to renew the Old Covenant Chain and to make it bright, if not shinier than ever. He gave a belt. In response, a few days later, the Six Nations expressed gratitude for the condolences so that they could open their sorrowful hearts and see each other with joyful eyes. They recognized deaths on the British side and wiped away tears so that they could see each other in gladness. They too gave a string of wampum and said:

> You spoake to us a few days ago and said that you was sorry we lost so many of our People by a Disease; You have also wiped off the tears from our Eyes that we might see one another with joyfull Eyes and open'd our sorrowful Hearts, & what Blood might yet be remaining you have wiped up, wherefore we return his Excellency thanks. We do in like manner condole the death of all y'r People who died since our last Conference – Gave a String of Wampum.[54]

They then gave a bundle of skins as a token of remembrance and to express sympathy for the death of Governor Montgomerie. This act was followed by statements of renewal: "[T]hat this is the Place where Our ancestors have mett together on this Place we lay a match which will never be extinguished when there be Occasion for it that a consultation may be held by the fire, and it may be Concluded between your Excellency and us what may be for our mutual benefit and Advantage." Afterward, they reminded the governor that he had renewed the Covenant Chain and strengthened it; if there had been any rust, he had made it clean and bright again. Thus, everyone – from the soldier to the most powerful Crown representatives on the continent, even the Lords of Trade – became familiar with and worked within the wampum framework of power and authority.

The point here is not to show that all Indian affairs agents became Indian or attributed power to wampum but that there was a systemic preparedness to enter into a shared normative lifeworld through the power and authority of wampum. By practising wampum protocol, the agents did more than merely tolerate the attribution of power and authority to wampum; they contributed to it by extending this power and authority beyond the inter-cultural lifeworld. Some of the beliefs, values, and ways of viewing the world connected to wampum use had to have been internalized to account for these officials' behaviour and modes of communication. Insofar as the practice was systemic, these beliefs and values were institutionalized.

To gain further understanding of the function of wampum, it helps to distinguish between legitimacy and authority. Legitimacy has to do with acknowledging rightness or appropriateness. It refers to a more passive at-titude toward power. We seek legitimacy to attain permission or acceptance for what we propose or do. Authority is a more active power. When we ex-ercise authority, we assert our legitimacy. Those who wielded wampum as-serted their authority to speak and act. Insofar as belts could speak for themselves, as in the 1682 case, their power was perhaps best understood in terms of authority and secondarily in terms of legitimacy.

The English likely adopted wampum protocol initially as a necessary means to get what they wanted from the relationship. Given that socialization and internalization take place in relationships over time, however, it would not have been unreasonable for their Aboriginal allies to expect the British to view and value wampum as they in fact did, especially if they knew from the beginning that the relationship would last for over one hundred years. Those closest to the allies (council negotiators and go-betweens) were likely the first to adopt the high-context language of wampum and to do so the most deeply. Those at a distance would have adopted it later and more superficially. Those who were closest to the Aboriginal allies were also the agents on whom those at a distance depended both to conduct daily affairs and to help ensure that they themselves did not commit diplomatic blunders. Wampum was, of necessity, a part of the culture of Indian affairs. Even if a particular agent did not believe in the power or authority of wampum, he likely acted as if he did and rationalized his actions in whatever way he could. The situation in which agents found themselves would have been little different than that of university professors today who do not believe in grading students' work. They may reject the legitimacy of the practice but use it and defend it all the same because their livelihood depends on it and because they are forced to admit that it is the best motivator, given the overwhelming lack of genuine interest in most students. The historical record, however, supports the view that many agents internalized the expectations of wampum protocol.

Negotiating a shared lifeworld is not possible if the terms of reference do not make sense or resonate in the subjective worlds of both sides. The British would not have accepted and used wampum protocol unless it somehow resonated with their own personal and cultural sensibilities. Initial strangeness likely gave way to familiarity before they internalized wampum protocol and became competent users. Perhaps wampum use readily resonated with Europeans' cognitive and normative sensibilities because the values it enforced were not foreign to English or other European cultures. At some level, the language of wampum – the language of healing, compassion, justice (fairness), unity (loyalty), and their consequences (for instance, social and political order) – resonated with the English. Since the use of wampum did not demand the acceptance of Aboriginal people's gods, following wampum protocol did not imply religious conversion or anything of the sort. Rather, it focused the mind on establishing conditions of social and political order and well-being. Certainly, in the European tradition, the notion of the Good, from Plato through Christianity, had much in common with the authority and power associated with wampum – the authority to establish social and political order and the power to heal. The Good (God) was also connected to the power to unify diversity. It would not have been a far stretch for the English to connect the conceptual framework and values of wampum protocol to the European idea of the Good. Hence, as much as the shared lifeworld was a product of negotiation and compromise, it was also a product of the mutual discovery of common values and sensibilities.

Wampum belts, as Johnson explained, could also be treated as the Aboriginal counterpart to European legal documents. However, as James Merrell points out, Aboriginal people often mistakenly identified treaty documents as the English equivalent of wampum and carried illegible copies of treaties to prove to white settlers that they had rights to a particular piece of land. Even though they could not read these documents, they nevertheless behaved as if they had the same kind of power and authority as wampum belts, even though, more times than not, their European interlocutors ignored their appeals.[55] On more than one occasion, Aboriginal people expressed mistrust of written documentation, particularly as they came to mistrust those who appealed to it. Teedyuscung, for example, at a conference held

July 1757, even demanded that his own minutes, taken by a trusted Quaker clerk, be accepted alongside those of the government.[56] The request was unprecedented and refused at first by Governor Denny. Eventually, the request was granted, and Charles Thomson, a trusted Quaker from Philadelphia, became the Delaware's clerk. Written documents, then, in some instances, were seen as manipulated records of proceedings and agreements. Consequently, when Teedyuscung requested wampum to construct a belt to take to the other chiefs during negotiation of the treaty at Easton, he, by implication, was saying that documents would be insufficient to empower him to speak. Aboriginal people did not believe that written documentation had the same binding force as wampum.

Treaty agreements were contained "in" the belts so that proper (specially trained and designated) people could read them. Commissioners at times recognized the need to have Aboriginal people confirm the written record by referring to their oral tradition. British agents understood that Aboriginal people's sense of integrity and a variety of social forces were central to wampum-based agreements. By contrast, the force of their written documents was backed by an external enforcement agency. Their use of written documentation reflected a culture in which it was assumed that people would act out of self-interest and ignore agreements. For some British agents, in fact, the wampum tradition was more trustworthy than their own, especially when settlers ignored decrees or when proclamations and laws intended to prevent encroachments onto Aboriginal lands could not be enforced by the military. It is then reasonable to assume that the British adopted wampum protocol not just because it was necessary to do so but because they recognized the kind of internal moral force it evoked. It seems fair to say that the intercultural lifeworld that developed included a shared ethos, an unarticulated set of moral sensibilities that shaped people's normative inclinations. This may explain why some agents could and did deeply internalize Aboriginal practices and why the system of wampum was so readily adopted and not derided.

Other factors would also have contributed to the recognition of a shared ethos. When conflicts emerge between parties who wish to remain at peace, for instance, the parties may initially focus on their differences, but they eventually seek points of commonality and agreement when they see the advantages of maintaining the relationship. In efforts to resolve conflicts, common memories (e.g., of fighting alongside each other or of mutually beneficial trade relations) can reduce tensions by showing how sacrifices and risk taking by one side benefitted the other. The shared memories of debts owed make disputing parties more aware of commonly held values and principles. Cases in which parties blame each other for damaging the relationship or accuse each other of some infraction can have a similar, albeit obverse, effect. Interlocutors try to cast themselves as blameless, trustworthy, and honourable. In attempting to resituate the blame or to justify what might appear to be a blameworthy action, the accused party, in effect, defends its honour and integrity. Both parties refer to honour, integrity, and the like and in so doing acknowledge the force that these values have in their own subjective lifeworlds. When they find sufficient reason to remain in the relationship, both parties will also find ways to ignore infractions, to forgive or rationalize them, thereby committing more of their subjective resources to maintain and protect the intersubjective world. They invest more of their subjective world into the relationship. Thus, even negative circumstances can contribute to building a shared ethos.

The religious dimension of the relationship now takes on new meaning in light of the notion of a shared ethos and the power and authority attributed to wampum. George Snyderman focuses on functions such as condolence, renewal, and healing to identify what he considers the spiritual power of wampum.[57] He argues that hatchets, furs, and money were sometimes substituted for wampum as gifts, but these items could never heal or polish the Covenant Chain relationship like wampum could.[58] The existence of this healing power suggests that wampum must have been connected to another dimension of life, a spiritual dimension. At times, the historical record itself comes close to identifying something like this spiritual element. For instance, Aboriginal allies sometimes referred to wampum as medicine, which is itself a complex notion but clearly something different from commodity, contract, or agreement.[59] Insofar as medicine can be related to healing and the offering of condolences, such references point to the power carried by wampum. Some commentators believe that early wampum belts were only diplomatic-political belts and that they did not acquire religious or spiritual significance until the 1800s.[60] Even William Fenton, in a key essay on wampum, describes wampum belts more in terms of their political and diplomatic functions than in terms of their spiritual significance.[61]

Scholars of Aboriginal heritage, by contrast, such as Raymond Skye and Tehanetorens, have been quick to connect wampum, ceremonies, and related practices to the Creator.[62] Robert Williams Jr. seamlessly links the metaphors of ceremony and ritual with the idea of sacred text.[63] He does not hesitate to call the language used in treaty negotiations sacred. John Borrows also utilizes the idea of sacredness in his analysis of treaties and Aboriginal rights.[64] If these Aboriginal scholars so readily see a spiritual element in the early treaty record or treaty process, there is good reason to believe that those who fail to see a spiritual element are overlooking something. I use this idea of the spiritual element, not to draw out wampum's religious meaning but to draw out the existence of a largely hidden but recognized power in the Covenant Chain relationship, a power connected to a shared ethos that operated through wampum protocol.

Hybridity and the Common Ground

Although the British did most of the adapting, Aboriginal people did adapt somewhat to English legal sensibilities. Wampum belts were sometimes treated as more reliable than written documents, but written documents were sometimes used to interpret belts. The rough equivalency of wampum and written documentation is illustrated clearly in a record of a council fire with the Six Nations at Johnson Hall on 24 April 1762. At the council, the Onondaga present a Covenant Chain belt that had been given to them at Albany by an unidentified person. Those of their nation who had been present at the original council were now dead, however, so the belt can no longer be read. The Onondaga request that Johnson remind them of what the belt says and present a large Covenant Chain belt. Johnson cannot remember, but promises to inform them once he has had a chance to read an account in the folios at his house.[65]

If a wampum keeper died or became incapacitated, the message of a belt could be lost. On such occasions, Aboriginal people sometimes relied on written records to explain belts. The ability to treat wampum and written records as rough equivalents is indicative of the hybrid character of the Chain's structure and function, what White calls the middle ground:

> The middle ground depended on the inability of both sides to gain their ends through force. The middle ground grew according to the need of people to find a means, other than force, to gain the cooperation or consent of foreigners. To succeed, those who operated on the middle ground had, of necessity, to attempt to understand the world and reasoning of others and to assimilate enough of that reasoning to put it to their own purposes. Particularly in diplomatic councils, the middle ground was a realm of constant invention, which was just as constantly presented as convention ... Perhaps the central defining aspect of the middle ground was the willingness of those who created it to justify their own actions in terms of what they perceived to be their partner's cultural premises. Those operating on the middle ground acted for interests derived from their own culture, but they had to convince people of another culture that some mutual action was fair and legitimate.[66]

White's emphasis on the role of justification is confirmed by the historical record, but his focus on strategic rather than communicative speech acts suggests that the primary goal was to obtain the agreement of the other side with as little compromise as possible. The relationship was of a sort that would quickly dissolve if one party was incapable of appealing to the other's cultural premises in negotiations. Even though White focuses on strategic speech acts, he does recognize that the Algonquians and French entered into a shared lifeworld that included recognizing each side's culturally determined criteria of legitimacy. He assumes that both sides had some ability to grasp the cultural and, therefore, conceptual framework of their interlocutor and to communicate that understanding in arguments. But if my analysis is correct, White truncates his analysis in focusing on the strategic aspects of communication. To apprehend another culture's frame of reference in the way thus far described means that both sides grasped the logic and some of the richness of each other's language, their intersubjective world. It means that they also took shared values and beliefs for granted. The hybridity of French-Algonquian and English-Haudenosaunee relations, then, went beyond the incorporation of particular practices and customs. It incorporated ways of understanding the world or worldviews. The Covenant Chain's particular type of hybridity therefore required the use of more than strategic speech acts when appealing to the other side's cultural premises. It required communicative speech acts.

Admittedly, acts of incorporation – such as struggles over status – were sometimes attempts at assimilating the other. British agents typically asked Aboriginal people to call them "father," to accept the designation "child," and to accept English law as the basis for their relationship. On occasion, the Six Nations tried to designate the British as younger brother and themselves as elder brethren.[67] Canasatego challenged the legitimacy of the governor of Maryland's claim to have possessed lands in Maryland for one hundred years by arguing the following. The English could lay claim to lands beyond the sea, from whence they came, but it was the Six Nations who belonged to the land: "You must allow us to be your elder brethren."[68] This meant that the Six Nations had jurisdiction over the land and that the English had to accept their authority. He then recounted the story of the Covenant Chain to add force to his argument. In a case that had the opposite result, the Shaahkook and Kath Hill Indians (probably those defeated in King Philip's War) corrected the commissioners at Albany for calling them brethren rather than children, presumably because they had been conquered and had become dependent nations.[69] The correction implied that the Shaahkook would accept the authority of the English. These two cases indicate that the use of familial language could imply the manipulation or subordination of one side by the other. But both presuppose a shared conceptual and normative framework.

Clearly, having a shared understanding did not result in complete mutual understanding or agreement over the meaning of terms. The meaning and significance of familial relations was not always obvious, for instance. The French were successful in their attempts to be designated as "father" by their Algonquian allies. Onontio, as the governor of Canada was called, was viewed as father to his Aboriginal children. Both the British and French tried to define *father* in terms of sovereignty or the right to command so that *children* would connote subjecthood and subordination. The same meanings were not always assumed by the Algonquians. Richard White shows that Onontio, in being designated father, was not in a particularly desirable position. *Father* implied more of a responsibility to protect and provide than a right to command.[70] The word was also associated closely with the role of mediator, which western Algonquians seem to have invited the French to adopt after attempts to end conflicts among themselves failed.[71] Moreover, like the Iroquois, the Algonquians did not hesitate to punish the father if they saw that he wished to do them harm.[72] *Father* and other terms could have both similar and different implications for the two peoples. Both sides, however, could understand the different meanings and what was at stake when certain uses and definitions were allowed to stand.

The term *hybridity,* then, does not imply a straightforward mix of cultural ideas, norms, and ethoses. It does not imply a simple compromise. That the other's cultural premises can be sufficiently understood to enable each side to utilize logical constraint to ensure compliance means that the room for misunderstanding and miscommunication that remains could just as easily bring about a deeper mutual understanding as it could prove to be an insurmountable cultural difference. Thus, whatever enabled a shared lifeworld to develop was something more complex than what is identified by Richard White. The ability to translate the meaning of terms, employ cultural beliefs to justify claims, and so on presupposed a set of core shared sensibilities that interlocutors discovered, rather than invented, in the interest of constructing successful negotiation forums. What actually enabled the two sides to enter into a dialogue and negotiate agreements was not a middle ground but rather a common ground, that background set of beliefs, values, ways of knowing, and so on that underpins the ability to communicate.

The outcome of the 1682 council between the Mohawk, who acted as intermediaries for the other members of the Five Nations, and Virginia and Maryland indicates that the two sides had moved beyond trying to establish a middle ground to recognizing a common ground. The council had what William Fenton calls a dualistic system of reciprocity.[73] This reciprocal relationship was founded on the moiety system, which structured social relationships according to familial categories. It functioned, particularly in times of crisis, to restore proper relations. In the case of condolence ceremonies, the down-minded were condoled by the right-minded.[74] Such dualities could obtain at various levels: family, clan, nation, and confederacy. Being divided into dualities yet bound together as a moiety allowed the Five Nations to resolve conflicts by enabling one or more members to act as healers or intermediaries. The moiety system was a system in which opposites were recognized, formulated into roles, and then integrated to form a unity. Fenton elaborates further. It was important not to use too much power when healing or mediating, so they followed a four-part process: (1) separate or approach, (2) alternation and reciprocation of acts, (3) interdigitation of rites, and (4) threaten to withdraw or appeal to stay. Each subsequent stage increased the severity of the consequence of not resolving the issue at hand.[75] The balancing of opposites fostered a procedure by which each side expressed its demands and needs without assuming a zero-sum result. The unity function did not allow the procedure to result in losers and winners; it was aimed at restoring proper balance. To produce winners and losers would defeat the purpose. By taking different sides, individuals or individual communities were not so much negotiating a balance of power; rather, they were producing a balance of responsibilities and privileges. Furthermore, since no individual or clan was defined essentially as the down- or right-minded – that designation depended on circumstances (e.g., a death in the family) – any member could become the down-minded or right-minded. These shifting roles meant that sometimes one member would be expected to interact or even negotiate from a position of strength and, at other times, from a position of weakness. As a consequence, acknowledging weakness was expected to evoke a sense of obligation to restore balance on the part of the strong-minded.

Insofar as Governor Effingham was, in a manner of speaking, forced to comply with the moiety system in 1682 because of the stature and influence Edmund Andros, New York's governor, held among the Five Nations and the Crown, we can imagine what he must have experienced. Rather than receiving justice according to English legal terms of reference – a form of severe punishment – the Five Nations were to be viewed as down-minded and in need of being brought into a balanced relationship with Maryland and Virginia. Effingham was expected to demonstrate an understanding of the Five Nations' situation and why they might have breached the Covenant Chain agreement. He was to accept that, by admitting guilt, being publicly shamed, and obliged to offer presents, the four guilty nations would be brought back into right balance with the colonies. Like most committed to the English system of justice, this form of righting wrongs would hardly seem appropriate to Effingham. Moreover, the expectation that he should demonstrate an understanding of the Five Nations' situation would likely have exacerbated his outrage, rather than making him right-minded. Despite this likelihood, he would have engaged in a complex process of moving the discourse away from accusation and defence toward understanding and reconciliation.

The resistance of people such as Effingham to adopting the moiety system militates against the idea that a common ground was established. Yet being a member of the Chain required that he and all Indian affairs agents speak and act despite their resistance. At some point in the proceedings, owing to the presence of Andros and the interests of the Crown, he would have felt pressure to act in conformity with the expectations of the moiety system. However insincere he might have been, the use of communicative speech acts to reach understanding with the down-minded would have obliged him to show an awareness of the other side's subjective world, to speak from the point of view of the established intersubjective world and to appeal to the normative shared lifeworld. He could, as did the Mohawk, use phrases such as "You foolish people" in speech acts intended to berate the guilty parties. Using this locution presupposed an acceptance of the legitimacy of the need to correct an incompetence, to heal rather than punish. It presupposed an acceptance, to some degree at least, of the need to bring those who had slipped from adulthood to childhood back to adulthood. Such language placed some pressure on the speaker to identify with the accused, making it difficult to maintain a single-minded adversarial attitude toward him. Like parents who berate their children for being bad, Effingham had to frame his speech acts so as to demand that the guilty parties correct their bad behaviour and become reconciled with the family of right-minded members. The logic of the moiety system required speech and action to conform to the end of mutual consideration and unification, or the re-establishment of mutual consideration and grounds for reconciliation.

How did condolence ceremonies move the members of the Covenant Chain toward a common rather than a middle ground? The function of condolence ceremonies was to show that members understood and sympathized with each other's suffering, even the suffering that they themselves had caused. The protocols of the Chain demanded reflective awareness of the other party's suffering in a way that assigned the highest value to communicative speech acts and devalued the use of strategic ones. The moiety system, together with the condolence function of the Chain, encouraged sympathetic understanding aimed at producing empathy.

Decades after the Effingham case, the Commission for Indian Affairs and Governor Montgomerie faced a similar demand to move from a strategic mode of discourse to a communicative one. In 1733, when dealing with the murder of a Six Nations sachem, the commissioners invoked a version of Article 2 in the original 1677 agreement: "[I]t has been concluded by the antient covenant between Our ancestors that if any such accidents happen'd that it should be reconciled and forgiven & that it may be thrown in a great Pitt which is the Earth whereto is a Great Strong door whereon is a large Rock which can't be mov'd, wherein all such things are burry'd in Oblivion therefore we desire that the Soldier may be Releas'd."[76] Although articulated using Aboriginal language and metaphor, the English attempted to interpret Article 2 in accordance with English legal terms of reference. An English legal authority, typically the Commission for Indian Affairs or the governor himself, conducted the proceedings and made the decision. They were hardly free, however, to exact whatever punishment they desired.

The Montgomerie case of 1730 illustrates why this was the case. On 4 July 1730, after a number of murders had been committed by both sides, the sachems of the Mohawk and Onondaga came to Albany to express their condolences over the loss of a trader, Joseph Brower, who had been murdered by two Onondaga men in a drunken rage. The sachems recounted the murders and a number of misdemeanors that had been committed against them by English folk. They emphasized that they had not taken immediate action in the past to revenge the murders of their own people, including a Seneca sachem, but had delivered the perpetrators up to Albany for justice, according to the agreement. After being tried and found guilty, the perpetrator had been sent back to the Seneca, who, in the end, pardoned him, not wanting to risk a breach in the Covenant Chain. From the sachems' point of view, the Covenant Chain had never been broken, despite these acts of murder, because they had maintained the agreement by following proper procedure. Although, in the end, the soldier had not received due punishment (i.e., capital punishment), everyone had received "all due satisfaction" in the eyes of the Onondaga. The implication was that the demands of law had been satisfied and that the commissioners should treat Brower's killers in the same way. The commissioners, however, demanded their own form of justice – capital punishment.[77]

The subsequent argument between the Onondaga and British over the proper definition of *due satisfaction* reveals that the dialogical expectations of the Chain moved the two sides first toward separation (abandonment) and then toward a common ground. In response to the commissioners, the Onondaga's argument was that they could not accept the commissioners' argument. The sachems said, "[I]f we Tooke Life for Life, it would make us appear like men out of Natural reason; and more Like drunken men, and occasion a breach in our Covenant, the Issue of which might prove war between us, so we surrendered the Criminal wholely up to the Christians who pardoned him."[78] They followed this statement with a question, "but shall we have reconciled there [sic] murders Without in the heart Looking for revenge or desiring blood for blood?" While the precise meaning of the passage may be unclear, it is clear that the sachems argued that the commission's conception of justice was irrational (as if a consequence of drunkenness). They had mentioned that one of the perpetrators of Brower's murder had escaped and that they saw this as "satisfaction for that murder." This statement likely meant that the perpetrator had exiled himself and was no longer recognized as a member of the community. This negative consequence of an illegal act was, in their eyes, far more reasonable to expect than capital punishment.

The commissioners, in turn, understood the Onondaga's argument and sense of justice but rejected them, as one would reject a theory of law. They acknowledged that crimes had been committed by their people and that much of what the Onondaga had recounted was correct. They then itemized murders and crimes that the Onondaga had failed to mention and accused the Six Nations of using alcohol as an excuse. In response to the Onondaga's act of renewing the Covenant Chain and requesting that they live in the light by having the governor of New York regulate the behaviour of his people, the commission replied that, in order to walk in the light of the Covenant Chain, the Six Nations would have to regulate their people by governing themselves according to English law. As infused with Aboriginal protocol and metaphor as these proceedings were, they constituted a legal process that provoked both sides to adopt seemingly entrenched positions and accuse the other of making no sense, when in fact they understood one another perfectly well.

In the midst of these accusations and counteraccusations, the Onondaga recited the origin story, which initiated a shift toward the reconciliation or healing process. They said that after they had learned to understand one another better, they had formed the Covenant Chain as brothers.

> When you first Came here and anchored the first Ship here, wee Took Each other as broth'rs and soon after we made a Covenant w'th you (That is to Say) a Strong Silver Covenant Chain w'ch was Inviolable, and w'ch Chain we no w'th the Mohawks Nation Joyntly renew & Strengthen it was Likewise Assured us that in Case there Should any Flaw or breach Come in that Chain, w'ch was then above ground that then there was another underground w'ch could not be damaged by rust or any other Penetrating matter.[79]

In this passage, the legal function of the Covenant Chain is intertwined with its evolution and sense of tradition, which, in turn, are foundational to the relationship, including its sense of law. In the passage, the Onondaga distinguish between levels of governance: the "above ground chain" and the "underground chain." The first level comprises explicitly formulated, legal agreements (articles) while the second includes the "below-ground" foundations of the relationship. The claim that nothing could cause the underground chain to rust or be penetrated means that not even a severing of the legal relationship could undermine the relationship altogether. The Chain was constituted by something more fundamental than any explicit law or agreement could capture. The Onondaga were claiming that something deeply constitutive of the relationship bound and united the two sides, however much they might have reason to separate from each other.

Records of this sort are rare, but not idiosyncratic, since they follow the same pattern as the Effingham case. Claiming that an underground chain bound both sides would not have come as a complete surprise, even if the use of the idea of an underground chain was a surprise and unprecedented. The idea of an underground chain belonged to a set of ideas propagated by origin stories, which spoke of unifying forces and the connections between the two sides, none of which were ever identified as the codified laws that they or their ancestors had agreed to. This idea was expressed in terms of the geopolitical aspects of the relationship and in terms of brotherhood, peace and friendship, and becoming one body, one mind, and one heart. The functional idea of law, accordingly, was embedded in a framework that placed unity at the centre of the Chain's value system. The function of law was to protect that unity; when it did not, it was open to questioning. For this reason, the Onondaga did not carry out the letter of the law when they had the right to execute a soldier who had killed one of their sachems. They expected the English to reciprocate.

The British, however, were not about to abandon their legal practices and resisted the move to question their legal sensibilities. After the commissioners and the Six Nations made their arguments, they still failed to reach a decision. The commissioners delayed, and a stalemate ensued. The case had to await adjudication by Governor Montgomerie, who could not come to Albany until after the spring thaw. When he arrived several months later, Montgomerie claimed that God's law and the law of all nations demanded execution of the murderer, repeating what the commissioners had argued earlier.[80] Yet another stalemate and threat of abandonment followed. After conferring with the commissioners, who unanimously agreed that a reprieve should be given because they thought it unwise to endanger relations with the Six Nations, Montgomerie reasoned that, since the murder had not been premeditated, the perpetrator could be reprieved. Montgomerie accepted the Onondaga's argument, namely, that the accused had not been in his right mind when he killed Brower and that liquor had caused the man to act out of character. Montgomerie did not entirely abandon British conceptions of justice to accommodate the Six Nations – he did not admit that he had given in or that Haudenosaunee law superseded British law – but he did attenuate his and the commissioners' English legal sensibilities.

Was this nothing more than a calculated compromise? At a meeting with the River Indians during the same visit to Albany, Montgomerie acted quite differently. These props of the Six Nations had been accused of violating Colonel Rensselaer's title to Squampamick by continuing to use it as if it were their own. Montgomerie made a summary judgment in the case. After renewing the Covenant Chain with the River Indians, he simply asserted that they were in the wrong and that the deed produced by Rensselaer proved them so. Moreover, he advised them not to act as judges of wrongdoing (not to take the law into their own hands) but to appeal to him or his appointed deputy to decide whatever matter had led them to their actions against Rensselaer.[81] Whatever might have been the River Indians' traditional sense of justice, it was irrelevant to Montgomerie, although he did see the necessity of justifying his decision to them. When they could, the English did impose English law. Thus, Montgomerie's willingness to attenuate English legal sensibilities in the Onondaga case could hardly have been motivated by anything more than prudence.

All the same, Montgomerie's accommodation was more than simply a grudging acceptance of the Haudenosaunee's position. It was preceded by arguments that all parties understood. And when the Onondaga invoked the origin story to remind everyone of the purpose of the law, they were challenging the way the English understood that purpose. When they appealed to the underground chain, the Onondaga shifted attention away from legalistic discourse and toward recognizing the foundations of the relationship, not by force but by reasoned argument. Montgomerie's response was also reasoned and based on premises that were not foreign to European minds.

Comparing the Brower case with another helps expand on this point. Crimes of passion had already been treated as nonpunishable offences. On 13 March 1724, in an exchange with the Kahnawake of Canada, who had been raiding New England in alliance with the French, the commissioners accused them of breaking the Covenant Chain, which they had enjoyed with the British when they lived with their brethren in the Mohawk Valley. The commissioners had stipulated that they would not consider the covenant broken even by acts of heat of blood (crimes of passion), but since the Kahnawake attacks had been deliberate acts of aggression, they were clear violations of the covenant.[82] The commissioners drew a clear distinction between violations that constituted a break in the Covenant Chain and those that did not. The latter were those motivated by forces that overrode or supplanted the autonomy of agents. In other words, Montgomerie could have appealed to this precedent when he made his judgment in 1730. He could have recognized the murder of Brower as a crime of passion. Perhaps the commissioners had forgotten about it, or perhaps Montgomerie had simply not been apprised of it. At any rate, a precedent had been set for differentiating between types of murder. That the commissioners and Montgomerie took so long to use the category "crime of passion" to settle matters in 1730 suggests that they were trying to force the Onondaga to accept English law. Their failure to do so forced them to recognize the deeper foundation of the relationship. Failure, then, revealed the potential of the Covenant Chain's structure to shift discourse toward more fundamental groundings. The conflicts of 1724 and 1730 altered the discourse to allow the disputants to carry on a discussion about the conditions of accountability. Such discussions served as occasions for invoking origin stories to draw attention to the more fundamental grounding of the relationship. In other words, moving the discourse away from punishment and toward reconciliation was not done willy-nilly. The Chain was structured to ensure that unification and healing remained the core function of the relationship.

In their arguments with Montgomerie, the Onondaga appealed to the origin story and used wampum to engage with their interlocutors and plumb more deeply into their shared lifeworld to find a common point of reference. As Fenton explains, they used the threat of abandonment and withdrawal as part of the formal procedure of reconciliation and healing, not as a last, desperate measure. Recontextualizing threats of abandonment in this way reveals that the British either expected or could have expected the Onondaga to use a threat of abandonment as part of the procedure. When the British agreed to accept the argument against capital punishment, they were acting in compliance with formal procedural expectations. Acknowledging deeper roots than codified law and explicit agreements allowed was not, therefore, necessarily an act of abandoning principled discourse or even an act of acquiescence.

If the above analysis is correct, the Covenant Chain's dispute settlement mechanism had to invoke more than a middle ground to resolve differences: it had to be based, in some way, on a sense of holding something deeply in common. Aboriginal groups might not have articulated this common ground in terms demanded by the English legal system (in terms of technically formulated concepts and principles), but the structure and function of their legal arrangement enabled them to utilize this common ground to maintain the alliance. The two sides might have failed to produce uniformity between their respective legal systems, but they could appeal to this implicit set of normative sensibilities as a common ground to resolve their conflicts through dialogue.

The Language of Unity

Sometimes the language of unity – one heart, one body, one mind – appeared empty because of constant violations of the agreement. In light of how origin stories and wampum functioned, however, use of the language of unity was aimed at reinforcing a sense of solidarity and loyalty because it had the effect of moving discourse toward recognizing a common ground. The language of unity represented the institutional structure of the treaty relationship metaphorically, in a way that constantly reminded members to engage in dialogue aimed at mutual understanding and protection. It defined participants as occupying a shared lifeworld (a common set of memories, experiences, and so on) and framed their discourse in terms of communicative speech acts. The overt intent was to create a common identity and common sense of responsibility to protect each other. When members used wampum to clear minds and throats, to purify hearts, to open roads, to remove briars from feet, and to wipe sweat from bodies, they used performative communicative actions in ways that embodied their commitment to sympathetic understanding, which further reinforced unifying processes.

When members used the language of unity to express demands for allegiance in the face of a common enemy, they explicitly articulated the unity expressed in the structure and function of the Chain.

The historical record is replete with examples of agents trying to ignore or resist acknowledging these unifying procedures. Clerks often omitted descriptions of ceremonies or abbreviated descriptions with phrases such as "the usual ceremonies took place" or "in their usual manner." When the records are examined chronologically, however, the importance of the language of unity is more obvious because it is recorded more frequently and in greater detail in later entries. The earliest records from Albany – the four folio volumes that Johnson presented in the June 1755 council, which are summarized in the index – contain few references to the language of unity.[83] The earliest index entries simply state that initial meetings happened. Like the Livingston records, however, the entries become increasingly detailed over the years until a shift in genre occurs, and the language of unity becomes increasingly pronounced. It should be emphasized that this shift partly came about because Aboriginal people did not trust written documents or the clerks who wrote them (as is indicated by Teedyuscung's insistence that a trusted Quaker serve as clerk). Livingston himself served as clerk of Indian affairs and on at least one occasion reported being told by an Aboriginal speaker to "be careful and observe well and write what we say."[84] The problem of trusting clerks never seemed to disappear. Since Aboriginal partners were suspicious of clerks not recording accurately or missing important details, they periodically demanded that written documentation be corroborated by wampum belts and oral tradition. This atmosphere of suspicion placed pressure on clerks to err on the side of caution by recording even details that were opaque and perhaps meaningless to them. Once they better understood the importance of these details, they offered more detailed accounts. Aboriginal people's mistrust, then, seems to have motivated clerks to record wampum protocol, origin stories, and condolence ceremonies in increasing detail. It was not simply the growing interconnectedness of interests and lifeworlds that accounted for increased use of the language of unity; it emerged in response to Aboriginal peoples' demands for trustworthiness and reliability.

When a broader source of documents is considered, for example, the massive collection of Iroquois-related treaty documents compiled by Francis Jennings and colleagues, a similar pattern of transformation can be detected.[85] The collection comprises many sources, including archives in England, France, and Holland. It also includes independently published records such as *Documents Relative to the Colonial History of the State of New-York*.[86] These records contain both descriptions of council meetings and correspondence between agents, between governors and the Lords of Trade, and between military officers and their superiors. The document base can also be widened to include Pennsylvania colonial records housed at the American Philosophical Society in Philadelphia. Even in their differences, these record groups can be described as belonging to the same genre as the New York documents, as do documents from Maryland and Virgina. All colonies to some extent were subject to the same transforming influence of unification. Since these records were official documents that were often read by superiors on the North American continent and in Britain, the fact that clerks came to take careful note of unification stories, metaphors, and devices (wampum) was not an accident or the product of New York's clerical and leadership idiosyncrasies. For this reason, the records relevant to Indian affairs represented a concerted, systemic attempt to record what mattered in the British–North American treaty relationship, writ large. Hence, the language of unity so central to the New York–Six Nations discourse was only one instance of a more comprehensive understanding of a Covenant Chain treaty relationship.

Re-examining the place of origin stories in light of their function to direct attention back to the relationship's unifying forces would reveal how they were modified, sometimes only slightly but at other times quite significantly, to draw attention to different aspects of the unity function that mattered. The use of "one heart, one mind, one body" also varied. The reasons for these variations were never given in the record, but they seem to have been reason enough for clerks to take note of the variations as much as they took note of the commonalities, suggesting that these stories and protocols were not in general considered mere gestures or niceties but something that required close attention. Paying close attention was vital for council proceedings. For instance, after the business of council meetings got underway and one side had made its propositions, the other side was expected to retire for a time to consider the proposition. These deliberations sometimes took days, but they typically took a part of a day or a whole day and night. The response began with an often verbatim recounting of what had been said by the first party. Clerks rarely wrote, "They repeated what was said the day before." They instead recorded the verbatim recitations. For each belt presented during the stating of propositions, the responding party reciprocated by giving a belt in return or by returning the belt. Clerks recorded each event separately. That these details were recorded while others were merely mentioned suggests that subtle differences in the way speeches and presentations of wampum were performed had specific meanings. Maintaining unity, then, depended heavily on each side understanding the other and on demonstrating that understanding in particular instances as much as in general situations.

Consider how corroboration of British documents was conducted. In 1723, the commission at Albany requested that representatives of the Five Nations tell them what had taken place at a treaty meeting in Boston, even though a New York agent, John Schuyler, had been there and had reported it in writing. The Five Nations asked that the document be read so that they could tell the commission whether it accurately represented what had been said. The commissioners responded by stating that they were "sensible you have good memories to retain and repeat what you have [heard and acted] at Boston and as you are great men who Represent your Respective Nations so we will not give Credit to any thing but what you yourselves so inform us, neither is it honest to take things upon trust."[87] In 1737, "French Indians" likewise stated before the commission, "You tell us you Committ your Affairs to writing w'ch we do not and so when you look to your books you know what past in Former times but [empty brackets in original] keep our Treaties in our Heads & therefore shall begin w'th what passed long ago."[88] On both occasions, and many others, "Indian memory" was both respected as an accurate record of what happened and recognized as being central to the interpretation of agreements. It was not respected merely as a reliable repository of information, like a computer's hard drive. The British respected Aboriginal memory as a means of explaining what treaties meant to their Aboriginal allies and, by implication, how they themselves should understand each treaty. Keeping careful notes on the use of wampum and the language of unity was a response to demands to establish a proper understanding of their partner's interpretive frameworks, that is, an understanding that took account of Aboriginal perspectives to ensure mutual understanding of particular treaty agreements. Peculiarities in the way they represented Aboriginal perspectives, using Aboriginal metaphors and descriptions of wampum, indicate that they tried to frame their understanding to reflect the way they would have to interact with Aboriginal people in different contexts.

In the William Johnson–Conrad Weiser era (the mid-eighteenth century), descriptions of council proceedings reached their greatest complexity. Clerks were more aware of belt details (although they paid relatively little attention to strings). They described the numbers of rows, colours, lengths, widths, and even how they were handled. Unlike the Jesuits, however, British clerks typically omitted details about other gestures, such as "taking them by the arm and dancing the dance of peace." Perhaps recording these kinds of actions had turned out not to be politically or legally important. Pipe ceremonies were described in quite abbreviated ways, as were parting ceremonies. The special attention paid to origin stories and wampum, then, supports the view that the Chain's unity function and recognition of a common ground were central to the treaty relationship and drew its members to become attuned to the shared lifeworld.

Conclusion

This chapter describes the structure and function of the Covenant Chain with an eye to identifying its moral economy or normative forces. Placed within its historical context, the Chain emerges as an institution that evolved to order trade, military, and legal relations in accordance with principles of justice, fairness, loyalty, sincerity, trustworthiness, integrity, honour, and compassion. Recognizing and acting on these principles were not mere displays of diplomacy: they were material to the process of cementing alliances and trade relations. Granted, the analysis thus far has revealed that members of the Chain felt compelled for various extrinsic reasons to express compassion, appear honest, and so on. To maintain trade and military alliances, people had to appear as if they were driven morally to act in solidarity with their brethren. Yet, given that the partners shared a normative lifeworld and had established a degree of mutual understanding, they must have internalized the values expressed in the language of unity to some degree. It would have been extremely difficult to engage in the moral economy of the Covenant Chain in a purely strategic manner without internalizing at least part of the moral economy of the shared lifeworld. The ground on which the shared normative lifeworld was established went beyond (or was deeper than) mere utilitarian calculations.

3
Reputation and the Role of Key Agents

That the Covenant Chain's moral economy operated at a level beyond that of diplomatic discourse and explicit norms – at the level of law and moral principles – is no more evident than in the role played by key agents and how their reputations enabled them to work with Aboriginal people. Examining roles played by key agents also discloses the place of moral agency in the moral economy, and consequently, the nature of this agency. In turn, the way in which moral agency operated in the economy indicates why Aboriginal people cannot be described as passive victims of colonial forces in any sense: they worked with Europeans to generate a moral economy and insisted that their allies conform to the expectations of that economy, even as they were expected to reciprocate. Both sides viewed a reputation built on moral qualities as a vital element of the Covenant Chain relationship. Examining what agents demanded of one another, deliberated about, felt they had to achieve, and how they came to decisions offers further insight into the nature of the common ground.

Focusing on reputation satisfies another purpose. It initiates a transition from a description of the moral economy to a discussion of the universalizability of the Chain's moral framework by describing how certain values, moral commitments, and arguments of key agents drew interlocutors away from their culturally bound ways of thinking and communicating. William Johnson's reputation will serve as the central focus here, even though he was not the only agent whose reputation was vital to establishing and maintaining the Covenant Chain. Johnson might have been special, but he was not unique. Nor was he exceptionally moral. The Johnson Records in particular describe the play of moral forces in the context of economic, military, and political intrigue in an especially rich manner. When contrasted with those of Conrad Weiser, Johnson's life and experiences offer a nuanced picture of how reputation reflected the operation of the moral economy.

Because I limit my investigation to British sources, the analysis includes key Aboriginal figures only tangentially. The voices of Kondarionk, Hendrick,

Canasatego, Sassoonan, Shikallemy, Scarouady, Pontiac, Tecumseh, and even Teedyuscung are mostly silent in the record, and to the extent that they are represented, it is through translation. Nevertheless, owing to the constraints placed on British clerks and others, many of their voices do come through indirectly because British agents found they had to record what was said and done in ways that could be corroborated by Aboriginal allies.

Moral Agency and Reputation

Hugh Shewell describes the development of Indian policy in Canada as being directed by liberal democratic terms of reference, especially individual freedom and equality of citizenship: "These are the concepts that provided – and still provide – liberal democracy with its moral purpose, and with its self-acquired image as the fountainhead of progress, civilization and individual rights."[1] Various Indian affairs agents (e.g., Duncan Campbell Scott) held and promoted these values, which, in turn, enabled them to conceptualize Aboriginal people as backward. If the colonial record is read from their perspective, it is difficult to see how reputation, as shaped by Aboriginal people's expectations, operated in the moral economy at all. Aboriginal culture and even the intercultural Covenant Chain were not liberal in the sense described above. Nor were the conceptions of moral agency – a philosophically thorny issue in itself – liberal. The preceding chapters have been necessary, in part, to avoid inadvertently imposing liberal, individualistic conceptions of moral agency and the moral economy. They present, rather, a complex picture of the context in which moral values mattered and how they were related to conceptions of rights, equality (as reciprocity), and community (as a member of one body and mind). By assuming this context, I attempt to describe moral agency in ways that avoid certain assumptions (e.g., about free will or more modern conceptions of agent causality). The goal is to allow a description of agency to emerge in accordance with the assumptions one must make in order to make sense of the record.

Just as the peculiar language of the early historical records disappears and is replaced by a more distant third-person perspective after the War of 1812, so too does the role of key agents become less pronounced, until it becomes almost irrelevant. Aboriginal people are represented as objects to be investigated and managed rather than allies with whom agreements or mutually acceptable arrangements must be negotiated. With this shift, the concept of the passive Aboriginal victim of colonization begins to appear in the record and dominates the historical narrative. As the power of the bureaucracy increased, agents who dared to challenge the dominant system were either sanctioned or fired, and all remnants of the former discourse between allies disappeared.[2] Recovering this discourse in which reputation and moral agency figure centrally and noting the distinction between the colonial and contemporary understandings, particularly with respect to how agents interacted with Aboriginal people, brings the dynamics of the relationship and how those dynamics enabled the interlocutors to draw on a common ground into high relief.

My account is recognizably minimalist. A richer and more complete account would have been possible had the activities of other "go-betweens" been recorded. James Merrell does manage to piece together records to show that agents (e.g., Andrew Montour, Elizabeth Cornish, Barefoot Brunsden, James Narrow, and Conoy Sam) besides those mentioned here were indispensable communicators, even though they were often seen as undesirable, unfortunate necessities, as rogues whose loyalties were uncertain.[3] It is important to acknowledge their role, because scribes of the day often focused only on signed documentation and paid little attention to the people who had prepared the way for formal proceedings. The go-betweens, long before any formal treaty procedures took place, travelled with Aboriginal negotiators, shared meals, strung wampum, and settled squabbles.[4] Yet, because both Conrad Weiser and William Johnson can be categorized as go-betweens (despite their relatively lofty status), I have not entirely neglected their role.

Merrell also notes that descriptions of go-betweens make it difficult, at times, to differentiate between those who worked for the English and those who worked for Aboriginal people. For example, the roles of Tanaghrisson, Shikallemy, Scarouady, Tunda (Moses) Tatamy, Conrad Weiser, and even William Johnson are obscure, because it is not always clear whom they represented. Sometimes messages, accompanied by wampum, were sent to Onondaga or Shamokin through Aboriginal agents, as if they were intermediaries for the Crown. Some of these men, for instance, Shikallemy and Scarouady, were Six Nations representatives sent by the council at Onondaga to oversee their client nations (props) in Pennsylvania or the Ohio Valley. The relationship between Pennsylvania (as well as New York) and the Six Nations – the latter were recognized and often treated as holding sovereignty over the Susquehanna, Wyoming Valley, and other "conquered" territories – was such that Crown agents, including the Lords of Trade, were aware of the need to negotiate through the Six Nations. This meant that they had to work through Six Nations representatives such as Shikallemy. But Shikallemy was sometimes sent by the Pennsylvania government with Weiser to negotiate treaty arrangements at Onondaga. Weiser often sought Shikallemy's advice, which appears to have been freely given. Indeed, these two men were pillars of the Crown-Aboriginal relationship, as far as Pennsylvania was concerned. The relationship between the Mohawk sachem Hendrick and William Johnson was also ambiguous. The records name yet other men – such as Arnout Viele and Lawrence Claesse, as well as traders and the subordinate commanders of forts – as translators, commissaries (commissioned Indian agents at various forts), and messengers to various Aboriginal nations. These individuals were often deeply engaged with Britain's Aboriginal allies, as were their French counterparts, men such as Joncaire who had their Algonquian allies, and certain Seneca. The Vieles and Claesses would have required a fairly intimate understanding of Aboriginal ways to be entrusted with as many missions as they were. While these men's roles remain ambiguous, they highlight the degree to which a shared lifeworld must have existed and the multiple levels at which it operated. The reputations of the agents described here must, therefore, be understood as part of a more comprehensive network of reputations and relations. We cannot, as a result, simply describe how one side recognized the other, or how one side's agent represented the values and commitments of that side, as we might were we to adopt a comparative cultural analysis approach. The moral economy in which key agents operated, then, was likely more complex and robust than the sources indicate.

Early Key Figures

Arendt van Curler shows up only sporadically in the records of the 1600s, but he was, nevertheless, clearly an important figure in early Dutch-Mohawk relations, as evidenced by the fact that the Haudenosaunee appropriated van Curler's name (modified as *corlaer*) as the title for the governor of New York. As a young man of eighteen, van Curler was sent to perform the role of assistant commissary on the frontier, where he became central to Dutch trading relations with the Mohawk. Allen Trelease remarks, "Whether it was due to honesty in these dealings – sufficiently rare among traders – or some other quality which no longer stands out, he won their confidence and retained it for the rest of his life."[5] Milton Hamilton is less uncertain. Placing van Curler among the "few wise men" who won the confidence of Aboriginal people by treating them as equals, adopting their manner of negotiation and learning to speak their language, Hamilton contrasts van Curler with other interpreters: "[T]oo often they were unscrupulous self-seekers whom the Indians did not trust ... An exception, during the Dutch period, was Arendt Van Curler, known as the founder of Schenectady ... Because of his honesty and sincerity, he won the Indians' respect, and they chose to deal with him instead of others in the Dutch department."[6]

It was van Curler upon whom the Dutch at Rensselaerwyck depended to manage Indian affairs. Apparently, it was he who established the peace and friendship treaty of 1643, since records of a subsequent treaty renewal council in 1659 report him saying that "sixteen years have now passed, since we made the first treaty of friendship and brotherhood between you and all the Dutch, whom we then joined together with an iron chain."[7] Upon his death in 1667, the Mohawk spoke of him as "long resided ... and ruled in this region."[8] It was considered an honour for later governors of New York to be given the title corlaer.

Trelease also notes that no other person except Peter Schuyler and William Johnson would have such influence with the Mohawk. In contrast to the many unscrupulous traders and Dutch officials, van Curler stands out as a successful negotiator. Trelease cites his reputation for fairness to explain his success among the Mohawk and other Aboriginal nations. Whereas other traders made use of alcohol to manipulate Aboriginal hunters, van Curler used an approach designed to produce peace and friendship by constantly renewing the relationship, thus enabling the initial relationship to evolve from a rope into an iron chain.

Edmund Andros, unlike van Curler, was a military man with a dominating personality. Andros enters the historical record at the time of King Philip's War, when he was given the responsibilities of governor general in the domain of the Duke of York. He was instrumental in developing an alliance with the Mohawk, in suppressing Metacom (a.k.a. Philip, the Wampanoag war sachem) during King Philip's War, and in converting the once mighty Mahican and Susquehannock nations into props of the Six Nations. He was an imperialist, loyal to the English king and to the Duke of York. As a successful military commander, Andros viewed the world through a military lens and governed accordingly. Unlike many of his contemporaries, however, he learned that it was better to develop alliances with warlike Aboriginal people than it was to attempt to subdue them with military power.[9] In 1676, when England won New York back from the Dutch for the final time, Andros was assigned as "lieutenant and governor-general of all his royal highnesses territories in America."[10] His role was to administer and enforce the Duke of York's claim to the territory of New England.[11] Despite the relative sparseness of Europeans in New York, that province soon overshadowed New England, largely because of Andros's relationship with the Haudenosaunee. Stephen Webb suggests that this period "demonstrates the importance of determined individuals and geographic place."[12] With an Iroquois and Mohegan alliance controlling raids on New England settlements, Andros was able to make New England dependent on New York.

As governor general, Andros brought social and economic order to New York by rebuilding the city after the destructive departure of the Dutch (they burned much of the city following their defeat). He brought order to New York and Long Island, sometimes through creative interpretation of the terms of surrender with the Dutch – for example, by forcing the burghers to declare an oath of allegiance to the British Crown and, when they refused, imprisoning them and confiscating their property. Andros must have been somewhat concerned that he would end up like his predecessor, Colonel Francis Lovelace, who was dying in the Tower of London after failing as a soldier.[13] But unlike Lovelace, Andros had established a reputation as an effective and loyal soldier during his experience in Barbados and, consequently, approached his duties with apparent confidence.

Andros had also learned diplomacy skills in his dealings with the indigenous peoples of Barbados. The nature of these skills was illustrated at a council with the Delaware on 13 May 1675 to address a series of killings of white travellers. Andros invited key sachems (*sachemakas*, in the record). When they arrived, he thanked them for coming and declared his friendship with them. He made it clear that he was not asking for their help in dealing with the perpetrators. He assured them he could deal well enough with them on his own. Rather, he stated that, if the sachems were willing to be kind and peaceable, even to the settlers' livestock and gardens, he would maintain the peace and enforce justice. Sachem Renowewan rose and accepted these terms by presenting a large wampum belt (it had fifteen rows and was as long as the sachem's body). The clerk recorded that the sachem walked around, took note of certain people, and then threw the belt at Andros's feet. A second sachem performed a similar ritual. Andros reciprocated with presents. The sachems expressed their pleasure with "[K]enon, kenon."[14]

Throughout the record, Andros is described as cementing relationships with acts of good will and the exchange of goods. He recognizes those whom he should honour in the eyes of the Delaware and makes it clear that his military capacity will be effectively exercised, if necessary. By all accounts, Andros, like his superiors, made his imperialist commitment transparent to his would-be allies, a commitment backed by his reputation. He had, after all, conquered the Dutch and ruled in Barbados. Yet his imperialism was predicated on a sense of fairness and justice. However we might question this sense of fairness, Andros exercised his idea of it and expected his subordinates to act in the same manner. In a letter to Edmund Cantwell dated 14 August 1675, he instructs his captain to be "kinde to Renowickhan in particular manner, who shall not lose for his constancy."[15] As if to demonstrate his commitments publicly, Andros tried James Sandylands, whom the sheriff suspected of murdering a Delaware. Although the jury acquitted Sandylands, Andros proceeded to strip him of his militia captaincy. This act apparently helped reinforce his reputation with the Delaware, which aided New York when King Philip's War erupted.[16]

Webb recounts how, at the onset of King Philip's War, the Connecticut Puritans refused to accept Andros's offer of military aid. Rhode Islanders, in reaction and in an attempt to prevent an all-out war with the "Indian rebels," accused the Puritans of rogue behaviour and championed Andros for having an unblemished reputation for fair dealing.[17] The Islanders' attempt to bring New England under the command of Andros failed and, as a result, much New England blood was shed. New York, however, remained relatively unscathed. New York's insulation from the blood-spilling of King Philip's War was due not only to good relations with the Delaware, who seemed to have significant influence over the tribes of the region, but also, and more importantly, to developing relations with the Haudenosaunee. Few Aboriginal

nations (except the Far Indians) during this period dared attack the Haudenosaunee or those considered under their protection. Webb suggests that
these good relations began during meetings in August 1675 at Tinontougen,
only three months after the council with the Delaware.[18] It was there that
the silver links to the Covenant Chain began to be forged. Years later, on 18-
21 September 1688, at another council, sachems for the Six Nations referred
to this earlier meeting as the one that had initiated the long-standing relationship with Andros.[19]

It was at this Tinontougen (sometimes *Tionondoge*) council meeting that
Andros was given and accepted the title of corlaer, "the name of a Man that
was of good disposition & esteemed deare amongst us (to witt) The Old
Corlaer."[20] With this part of the council completed, the parties renewed
their commitment to the covenant. Any violations by one another would
be thrown into a bottomless pit. They performed the ritual of the Tree of
Welfare, a tree that "reaches to the clouds so that the sun shines on it forever."[21] Not much more information about this council is available, but it
is clear it had significant implications. At the 1688 meeting, Andros used
both his reputation and the earlier 1675 council agreement to establish the
Crown as the father of the Five Nations. Curiously, the Five Nations accepted
these designations following a private caucus, even though they at first
insisted that they were all brothers. During the remainder of the multiday
meeting, the other Five Nations addressed Andros as "Father Corlaer." This
outcome is exceptional, since, for the most part, governors after Andros were
addressed as "brother." Children were supposed to address the king, not his
governors, as father. Later records indicate that the Five Nations did make
this distinction. It seems, then, even though Andros gave himself the priv-
ilege of the king's title, he somehow got away with it.

Explanations lie in the fact that throughout this period the French and
their Algonquian allies raided the Five Nations. Castles (villages) and crops
were burned to the ground and people displaced. From 1669 on, many
Mohawk, among others, moved to Kahnawake, where they became Christians and allies of the French Crown, and turned their war energies against
New England. On the one hand, then, even though the English enjoyed the
Five Nations' protection against the Algonquians to the east and south, the
Five Nations' military power had begun to dwindle. In this context, a strong
alliance with the English would have been not only a vital defensive strategy
but also an offensive one. The Five Nations likely called Andros father and
accepted being designated children because of the protective responsibilities
fathers had to assume.

The Five Nations likely respected and trusted Andros's hard-edged military
sense of fairness and reputation for carrying out his duties. As a military
man perceived as being unafraid to use force when he deemed it necessary

and who had gained his reputation through military accomplishments, Andros could and did expect to be paid a high degree of respect. Given this context and personality profile, it is not surprising that Andros would demand recognition as father and that his Aboriginal allies would be open to recognizing him as such. Moreover, unlike almost every other colony, Rhode Island and New York under Andros's command did not think first to do battle with Aboriginal people. Andros instead tried to negotiate peace and friendship treaties.[22] He demonstrated that he was not a warmonger; rather, he was a man who resorted to battle only after carefully considering the situation, a quality consistent with Iroquois practices (i.e., holding war councils to debate the proposition of going to war). It is not too far a stretch, then, to suggest that Andros's reputation as a protector was instrumental, perhaps central, in enabling him to be called father.

The resistance Andros received from New Englanders – he was eventually overthrown by rebellious Bostonians – stemmed from his reputation of being more concerned to protect Aboriginal people than colonists. The colonists either believed or trumped up rumours that Andros had been equipping certain Aboriginal people with weapons, which were then turned against settlers. In the absence of substantiating evidence, affidavits were signed and broadsheets published to that effect. Andros responded to this smear campaign in several ways, including appealing to the Privy Council to have the accusation declared empty.[23] New Englanders hated Andros for the very reasons his Aboriginal allies respected him. He treated Aboriginal people justly, even when it meant meting out punishment to whites for crimes against Aboriginal people. He fought what both Webb and Jennings describe as a predominant New England racial prejudice and bore the hatred expressed toward him by his countrymen.

Andros, however, was quite prepared to exercise his sense of justice, even against the Haudenosaunee. To illustrate, in 1677, Five Nations warriors attacked the River Indians, who had come under the Covenant Chain at the same time, and continued their attacks all the way down to Narragansett Bay. This attack contravened the Covenant Chain agreement. Andros did not hesitate to demonstrate his anger because the Five Nations sachems rushed to Albany to apologize and make reparations on 12 July. At one point, Andros sent his officers to summon the sachems to "put them in Mind how I protected them in the time of warr, & gave their old men, wives & children, admittance within our Towne & Fortifications, & that I doe expect that whosoever doth shall come in & submitt themselves & live quietly with our Indyans shall be protected from any outrage or force & I shall ... looke upon any violence ... as done to myself."[24] In the same record, Andros acknowledges that the attacks were expressions of a war culture. In an attempt to assuage the warriors' impulses, he then requested that they turn their aggression against another traditional enemy, the Abenaki. In this way, he matched his sense of justice with an understanding of his allies' cultural expectations, setting the tone for how affairs would be conducted by generations of governors and agents. Montgomerie, for instance, used a similar approach when he admitted that alcohol could be accepted as a mitigating factor in the trial of an Onondaga man for murder.

When Andros castigated Haudenosaunee sachems for violating the treaty and for failing to return his protection in kind, he knew full well that they did not directly control the warriors. He drew, instead, on the internal social mechanism of shame and honour. By understanding how the warrior society operated and demanding that the warriors redirect their aggression against the Abenaki, Andros offered the entire community recourse to redemptive actions. If they agreed to his suggestion, they could recover their honour, and Andros would have his eastern front protected. Just what effect this offer had is not clear, because there is little evidence that the Six Nations actually attacked the Abenaki. Rather, they sent messages warning the Abenaki that they would face disciplinary measures if their raids did not cease. The messages were ignored. But raids on the River Indians and other allies of the English did cease. Andros's actions and responses to them, then, illustrate how a reputation for fairness, justice, integrity, trustworthiness, and good understanding influenced both Crown-Aboriginal relations and inter-colonial relations.

While Edmund Andros drew out the hard edges of the moral economy into relief, his younger contemporary Peter (Pieter) Schuyler, born in Beverwijck and first mayor of Albany, drew out other aspects. His was a role that has remained somewhat hidden in the major works on the history of this period, perhaps because his geopolitical significance was contained more or less to Albany. The Indian Affairs records of New York suggest, however, that Schuyler played a central role in the emerging Covenant Chain relationship and an even more central one in the Five Nations–Crown relationship. He, like Andros, earned a reputation as a warrior who understood his allies' cultural values. He was one of the few commissioners of Indian affairs at Albany whom Aboriginal people trusted. He was also known for escorting four Iroquois "kings" to England to visit Queen Anne in an effort to emphasize the importance of England's alliance with the Five Nations. Upon Schuyler's death in 1724, even some Algonquian sachems who had been allied with the French came to give their condolences: "Some Farr Indians came to condole the Death of Colonel Schuyler, saying that it is their custom to bury the sachems of neighbouring nations and that they do likewise for Col. Schuyler."[25] On 15 July, the commissioners thanked the Far Indians for burying Schuyler according to their customs.[26] On 7 August 1724, others performed a condolence ceremony and gave gifts of twelve hands of wampum "to mark off the tears of relations" in memory of Schuyler.[27] Three years later, on 10 June 1727, representatives from Detroit (speaker Ochsachronde or Ajastoenies) and a representative from a nation called "poatamis" by the French (likely Potawatomi, speaker Wynamac) came before the board "with Calumet pipe pointed & blew." They made a speech to the effect that they had been sent by the sachems of Tughsackrondie to give condolences for Peter Schuyler and to bring a beaver blanket to cover his grave so that the rain would not fall on it: "They fill'd the Calumet with tobacco lighted it, with one of them went about & lett all the Comm's take some whiffs Out of It as a Ceremony among them of peace & friendship which they use in their treaties with the neighbouring Nations."[28]

Schuyler (named *Quider*) was often addressed, along with Corlaer, by Aboriginal speakers during council meetings. For example, on 25 July 1707, a report was given to the Mohawk sachems, to which Kunnsore, one of the sachems, responded, "Brother Corlaer and Quider."[29] Even the Far Indians acknowledged Quider in the same breath as they addressed Corlaer, as they did during a council on 20 July 1708. Far Indians from Tughsackrondie opened with the salutation, "Brother Corlaer and Quider."[30] Schuyler was often sent either to renew the Covenant Chain with the Five Nations or to accuse them of breaching the agreements (on 6 August 1707, for example).[31] He even took the place of Corlaer on occasion, as he did on 30 September 1708.[32] Allen Trelease describes Schuyler as a man who won the respect and devotion of the Iroquois. As a result, he was indispensable to various governors, who made him their chief lieutenant in military and diplomatic affairs in the Albany area.[33] Although Schuyler was viewed as a man of integrity and courage, these characteristics did not hamper him from acquiring a minor fortune from the fur trade.

A series of events cemented Schuyler's reputation. In the wake of the chaos caused by what was known as Leisler's Rebellion and renewed French-Algonquian attacks on Mohawk castles, which all but destroyed them and their winter food stores, Schuyler led a small army of militia and River Indians to meet the enemy. Although he was prepared to attack when he discovered the French and Algonquian at the Mohawk castles, the commander at Albany, Major Richard Ingoldsby, refused to give the go-ahead until reinforcements could be gathered. Since his Aboriginal allies were infuriated by the lack of support and action shown by his brethren, Schuyler disobeyed orders and pursued the Canadian force. Owing to a sudden thaw that prevented a hasty retreat, Schuyler was able to intercept the Canadian army and fight it, more or less, to a standstill. His party managed to negotiate the release of Mohawk prisoners once the Canadian invaders began to starve.[34]

After hearing of Schuyler's situation, Governor Fletcher quickly mobilized an army and reached Schenectady in three days, arriving "as fast as an arrow." Upon his arrival, however, Schuyler was already on his return march. Fletcher dismissed his troops and proceeded to consolidate the settlers' homes, apparently in an attempt to satisfy the Five Nations' complaints about settler encroachment. During a subsequent meeting, the Five Nations bestowed upon him the title *cayenquiragoe* (lord of the great swift arrow). Trelease argues that the Five Nations bestowed a great honour upon him, even though Fletcher's political foe Peter de la Noy considered the title an ironic gesture.[35] Schuyler, indeed, seems to fade from the record of these events, while Fletcher receives all the glory. It should be kept in mind, however, that Fletcher had done nothing. Later records side with de la Noy. At a council the following year, the Five Nations criticized the English for not sending sufficient support in the war effort against the Canadians.[36] Then, when Bellomont, who had succeeded Fletcher, argued that the Five Nations had suffered losses because of their own neglect, the Five Nations criticized Fletcher – and by implication Bellomont – for the many times he had failed to keep his promises. They also made a point of praising Quider (Schuyler) for being the only person who had come to their aid in their time of need.[37] The Five Nations knew that Schuyler had continually lobbied his superiors in New York to send money, arms, and supplies.[38] Giving Fletcher the title cayenquiragoe, then, was at least partially an act of mockery for taking the credit someone else deserved. In these sorts of instances, clerks should have, for our sake, recorded glances and other sorts of gestures to convey the full meaning of events.

During the late 1690s and the early eighteenth century, the Five Nations of the upper New York area were in a state of near panic because French-Algonquian forces were advancing into their territory and their population was being ravished by disease. The Livingston report of 1700 corroborates others that describe an exodus of Mohawk and other Five Nations warriors and their families to Kahnawake to receive religious instruction from the Jesuits. Schuyler's report of August 1700 to Bellomont confirms that the English were afraid that the Five Nations were going to go over to the French. The Five Nations had in fact accepted an invitation by the Canadian governor to a grand council in 1701, the Great Peace of Montreal, as it is now known in Canada. It was there that Kondarionk made his pivotal speech to help broker a peace among all the Great Lakes nations, including the Haudenosaunee Confederacy. After the English governors failed to keep their promise to send ministers to the communities (they had known full well that they could not supply them), and after the Five Nations had reminded the governors of their failure to provide military support, there was little to keep the alliance intact. During these times, Schuyler was sent often to the communities to renew the ties of the Covenant Chain. As late as 1754 (well after Schuyler's death), at the Albany Conference, where the Lords of Trade sought to unite the colonies so that they could treat with the Six Nations jointly, Hendrick recalled the days when the Six Nations had been strong and how

Colonel Schuyler had frequently come among them to keep the relationship strong.[39]

Schuyler's reputation, though in some ways similar to that of Andros and van Curler, was distinct, partly because of the role he played. His role, as one who constantly strove to supply and protect his allies, especially in light of the failures of his superiors and the intrigue of others from Albany, was to fight and lobby alongside his Aboriginal allies. As one of the few who tried to keep English promises and who risked reprisal for insubordination, Schuyler was held in high regard by Aboriginal people for his commitment and loyalty. Given the accolades bestowed upon him at his funeral, and for years afterward, it is safe to say that he was one of the few who held the Covenant Chain together in the early years, heavily tarnished and threatened though it was in the late 1690s and early 1700s.

William Penn, first governor of the proprietary colony of Pennsylvania, was a contemporary of both Edmund Andros and Peter Schuyler. When Pennsylvania was established in 1681, New York was not a welcoming neighbour, having had some of its territory carved away for Penn. The treaties Penn formed with the Delaware and the Haudenosaunee were seen as threats to New York's growing dominance among the colonies. When Pennsylvania began treaty relations with the Onondaga, who allowed the colony to acquire land around the Susquehanna and Delaware rivers, Albany hurriedly renewed its alliance with the Five Nations.[40] There seems to have been no love lost between New Yorkers and Pennsylvanian colonists, whose influence with Aboriginal peoples (even the Haudenosaunee) gradually came to rival that of New York. A significant, if not pivotal, factor in Pennsylvania's growth was William Penn himself.

Francis Jennings spends a section in *The Ambiguous Iroquois Empire* describing Penn, whose practicality, piety, and decency made him a special person, not only to new settlers but also to Aboriginal people.[41] He established Pennsylvania as a colony of peace and tolerance without military force and did not attempt to divide the tribes into factions, as did the other colonies. He did not establish Christian missions but rather employed persuasion and respect for Aboriginal people to demonstrate the virtues of Christianity.

His inaugural speech to the Delaware in 1681 discloses something of how he was perceived by Aboriginal peoples:

> My friends – there is one great God and power that hath made the world and all things therein, to whom you and I, and all people owe their being and well-being ... this great God hath written his law in our hearts, by which we are taught and commanded to love and help, and do good to one another, and not to do harm and mischief one to another. Now this great God hath been pleased to make me concerned in your parts of the world, and the king

of the country where I live hath given unto me a great province, but I desire to enjoy it with your love and consent, and that we may always live together as neighbours and friends, else what would be the great God to us, who hath made us not to devour and destroy one another, but live soberly and kindly together in the world? Now I would have you well observe that I am very sensible of the unkindness and injustice that hath been too much exercised towards you by the people of these parts of the world, who sought themselves, and to make great advantages by you, rather than be examples of justice and goodness unto you, which I hear hath been matter of trouble to you, and caused great grudgings and animosities, sometimes to the shedding of blood, which hath made the great God angry; but I am not such a man, as is well known in my own country; I have great love and regard towards you, and I desire to win and gain your love and friendship, by a kind, just and peaceable life, and the people I send are of the same mind, and shall in all things behave themselves accordingly; and if in any thing any shall offend you or your people, you shall have a full and speedy satisfaction for the same, by an equal number of just men on both sides, that by no means you may have just occasion of being offended against them. I shall shortly come to you myself, at what time we may more largely and freely confer and discourse of these matters. In the mean time, I have sent my commissioners to treat with you about land, and a firm league of peace.[42]

Penn was believed because his actions confirmed his sincerity in the eyes of the Delaware and Haudenosaunee. He did not exploit the concept of vacuum domicilium, as did others of his time (e.g., John Winthrop and Samuel Purchas). Jennings describes his actions as concerted attempts to act on each commitment he made in this speech. Although dates and proceedings are uncertain, it is clear that Penn treated with the Delaware to establish a chain of friendship that had no political connection to the Iroquois Covenant Chain.[43] Conceptually, it was almost identical: it was a hybrid agreement that combined Aboriginal protocol, language, and ceremony with British articles of agreement (e.g., if an Aboriginal person injured a white, he would be brought to an English court for justice). Perhaps the only element that was missing in the Delaware Covenant Chain was the image of the Great Tree of Peace, whose roots spread far and whose branches protected all those who agreed to the terms and conditions of the Covenant Chain.

The effect of Penn's moral reputation was most obvious in the devastating events that followed. Owing to the tendency of the Delaware to believe that the honour and trustworthiness of the father was passed on to the sons, Penn's reputation was exploited by his offspring to bring about the infamous Walking Purchase.[44] On September 1737, Thomas Penn, William's son, finalized a land surrender begun in 1734. In his treaty talks with Manawkyhickon, he reminded the Delaware sachem of William Penn's great love and justice for the Indian. In reciprocal fashion, Manawkyhickon acknowledged the relationship of love and acknowledged the legitimacy of the agreement, made by his forefathers, to give land to William Penn. But when land-hungry Pennsylvanians wanted to legalize and finalize the deed fifty years later, they twisted the terms of the agreement to suit their purposes. The Pennsylvanians demanded far more land than had been promised. In a defensive move, the Delaware stipulated that the deed guaranteed as much land as a man could walk in a day and a half without puffing or straining.[45] But, after Henry Hamilton drafted a misleading copy of the deed and Manawkyhickon signed it, the Pennsylvanians began surveying and clearing a straight path for runners to mark out the boundaries. Although the Delaware complained that the men were running rather than walking, the Pennsylvanians marked out sixty-four miles in a day and a half, and with the aid of some creative geometry, they managed to claim all of the land the Delaware occupied.[46]

The effects of Thomas Penn's manipulation did not end with the removal of the Delaware from their land. Paul Wallace and Francis Jennings argue that the anger generated by the Walking Purchase had far-reaching consequences. It is not difficult to imagine that the stories of the Walking Purchase, told in intertribal councils, were replete with the language of betrayal. The Delaware and their grandsons, the Shawnee, built consensus among their people based on resentment toward the Pennsylvanians. It is difficult to deny that raids on Pennsylvanian settlers during the Seven Years' War were a direct consequence of moral outrage, resulting from the Walking Purchase and other land grabs. The degree of violence Delaware and Shawnee warriors inflicted on settlers was matched neither by the Six Nations nor by the nations of the Ohio Valley during Pontiac's War. Those who were instrumental in the Walking Purchase were hunted and, when found, killed. The runners, for example, were targeted for retaliation. One of the runners, Edward Marshall, escaped, but his wife and children did not. This war, then, was as much a war of revenge as it was a war of defence.

William Penn was perhaps unique in his extreme commitment to scruples and fairness. His character sketch does not quite fit the pattern established by other key agents. He was not a military man and apparently conducted affairs without a show of force. Although he was intent on expanding Pennsylvania, he did so by purchasing lands from the Delaware and Shawnee at prices that exceeded those set by the Crown. He was also intent on converting Aboriginal people to Christianity, but only through example and just action. Including Penn's reputation as a critical part of the narrative is paradoxical, because, in the end, it is not a positive example of the moral economy at work. The trust and respect Penn developed was manipulated by his sons with devastating consequences for the Delaware people and the Crown's relationship with them. All the same, these negative consequences demonstrate how factors such as a reputation for fairness, integrity, trust, and sympathy were deeply significant, precisely because they made the Delaware and Shawnee more vulnerable than they would have been had they never come to trust the Penn lineage. This darker side of the moral economy reveals how historical outcomes were profoundly affected by the intersubjective normative lifeworld.

Conrad Weiser (Tarachiawagon or Zihguras)

According to Paul Wallace, Conrad Weiser was a jack of all trades, farmer, father of fourteen, justice of the peace, colonel in the first Pennsylvania army, prisoner, and monk, to name just a few of his roles.[47] Named Tarachiawagon (He Who Holds the Heavens) by his Aboriginal allies and Zihguras (or Segorus, the Killer) by others, Weiser was an indispensable go-between for the Crown, Pennsylvania in particular.[48] When he took ill in 1748, the provincial secretary for Pennsylvania, Richard Peters, requested funds from Thomas and John Penn to train a new go-between, for without one, he argued, Pennsylvania would find itself in a dreadful situation with the Indians. Weiser's position in Crown-Aboriginal relations was of immense importance. More importantly, his ability to interact with Aboriginal people and his reputation for being able to do so effectively made him a special individual. Wallace makes Weiser out to be a preternatural hero in Pennsylvania's history. James Merrell comes close to doing the same. Like William Penn, Weiser stands out as a central figure in establishing good relations in Pennsylvania and to some extent in Virginia, Maryland, and even New York. Unlike Penn, however, he was a hard-knuckled Lutheran who, legend has it, proved himself in brawls with Mohawk warriors during his sixteen-year stay among them.[49] He is reputed to have won a footrace against a young Mohawk man to decide a wager. He won by first knocking the fleet-of-foot-but-slight competitor into a wall, almost killing him. This, of course, ensured his victory.[50] During his attempts to lead a monk's life, he fathered fourteen children with his wife, Ann Eve.[51]

In other words, some caution needs to be exercised when characterizing Weiser as a hero. Weiser appears in the record in many ways, but more like an inconsistent, ordinary man who struggled with his beliefs and ideals. He was sometimes angry, confused, and uncertain, sometimes obsessed with mysticism. He struggled with government incompetence and malicious intent because his moral-religious commitment drove him to seek fair and considerate treatment of Aboriginal people, both formally, in terms of adherence to treaties, and informally, in terms of respecting the honour, dignity, and suffering of Pennsylvania's original residents.

Weiser overcame a difficult childhood and humble origins as an immigrant from the German Palatine to become an indispensable treaty negotiator, someone on whom governors and their secretaries depended for advice on treaty matters. As was the case at the Lancaster Treaty – negotiated in June 1744 between the Onondagas (for the Six Nations), Pennsylvania, Virginia, and Maryland – Weiser's adeptness at backwoods politics helped propel Pennsylvania to a position of prominence in Crown-Aboriginal relations.[52] His reputation as a go-between was even acknowledged by settlers beyond the Blue Mountains who called him father when they requested protection.[53]

Having spent sixteen years living with the Mohawk and learning their language, Weiser was considered half-Indian and half-white by many. In 1742, during a Six Nations–Pennsylvania council, Canasatego of the Six Nations said, "When we adopted him [Weiser], we divided him into two equal Parts, one we kept for ourselves and one we left with You."[54] His special connection to the Mohawk enabled him to develop a close, if not symbiotic, relationship with Shikallemy, overseer of the Delaware, Shawnee, and other props in Pennsylvania. Shikallemy and Weiser worked in concert to become the single most important channel of communication shaping diplomatic relations between the Six Nations, Pennsylvania, and the Delaware-Shawnee. This connection, in turn, involved Weiser in the Walking Purchase affair, since he was instrumental in beginning the land cession process in 1732, when the Six Nations signed over the lands claimed by the Delaware to the Penns.[55] In so doing, he supported the Six Nations' declaration that they had made the Delaware women. He maintained this position throughout his career, apparently because he believed it was the only way to maintain peace in the region.

This connection with the Six Nations brought him into conflict with both the Delaware and the Quakers, who supported Delaware autonomy and who dominated the Pennsylvania Assembly. As pacifists, Quakers attempted to treat with the Delaware as an independent nation, a move that, in effect, threatened the chain of friendship between Pennsylvania and the Six Nations. The competition between the Quakers and Weiser over control of Indian affairs was largely a conflict based on moral commitment. Both believed they were doing what was morally correct. During King George's War, and especially during the French and Indian (Seven Years') War, Quaker pacifists maintained a principled resistance against establishing a standing army or militia. They, as did the founder of Pennsylvania, resisted trade in guns and ammunition and insisted on fair dealings with the Delaware, Shawnee, and other Aboriginal groups in the area. Neither the Quakers nor Weiser were obsessed with gaining power; both, in their own way, avoided acquiring too much power or using it for personal gain. For the Quakers especially, supporting Teedyuscung could not have been for political gain, because he was an emperor with few clothes. The real military threat was the western Delaware, who had moved to the Ohio with many of the

Shawnee to escape settler encroachments. Indeed, during the French and Indian War, Shingas of the Delaware treated with Pennsylvania independently, ignoring Teedyuscung's declaration that he was king of the Delaware and nine other nations. Given Weiser's constant resistance to the efforts of the governor to assign him more political power and his constant desire to be able to retire to his farm and lead a spiritually oriented life, it is clear that his support of the Six Nations was not for personal gain but rather a genuine desire for peace and order. The conflict between Weiser and the Quakers was, therefore, largely over the moral high ground.

When looked at from the point of view of the Quakers and eastern Delaware, Weiser appears as a party to an oppressive system of governance. From the governor's and Six Nations' point of view, he was an instrument for maintaining law and order and a good understanding between the Six Nations and Pennsylvania. From both perspectives, Weiser was a man of honour. The Quakers understood that they were competing against a man who could not be bribed, a man who was respected and one to whom almost all Aboriginal people listened (including the Delaware) because of his reputation for honesty, fairness, and integrity. They simply thought some of his political commitments were wrong.

Weiser's importance became clear during the events that preceded and included the 1744 Treaty at Lancaster. Weiser travelled to Onondaga several times to broker a peace between the colonies, the southern nations (the Catawbas, especially), and the Delaware and Shawnee. Meanwhile, the French threatened a virtually defenceless Pennsylvania frontier. Disputes over ownership of the Susquehanna and Wyoming valleys threatened to bring Pennsylvania into all-out war with its Aboriginal neighbours. In an attempt to stave off war, three colonies (Maryland taking the lead for Pennsylvania and Virginia) requested a treaty council with the Six Nations, since cementing an alliance with them was critical to maintaining a buffer against the French. Colonel Lee of Virginia seems to have forgotten this, since he believed that the best policy would be to crush the Six Nations, until Governor Thomas of Pennsylvania reminded him that they were necessary to protect the colonies.[56] When news arrived that the Six Nations had finally come to Shamokin (a principally Delaware settlement upstream on the Susquehanna from Philadelphia), it was Weiser who greeted the delegates and accompanied them to Philadelphia. Throughout this prolonged at-the-edge-of-the-woods meeting at Shamokin and during the following two-week council period, Weiser ensured that the Six Nations were properly treated. He was Pennsylvania's instrument to steer certain colonial officials (mostly Virginians) and their aids away from acting in ways that would exacerbate the animosity created by previous blunders.[57] He also convinced Richard Peters, secretary to Pennsylvania, that Governor Thomas should be at council to maintain proper protocol and order. After the treaty council, Canasatego named Weiser "Tarachiawagon," thanked him for all he had done, and expressed hope that Weiser would be preserved to a good old age. Until Tarachiawagon is underground, he commented, "there is no room to complain."[58] The comment was of a piece with Weiser's reputation as guardian of the Indians of the Ohio, as it was expressed at an earlier council at Onondaga in 1743.[59]

To be called Tarachiawagon was a peculiar and special honour. According to Horatio Hale, Tarachiawagon is a national god of the Iroquois.[60] He guided the early fathers in their wanderings, protected them from enemies, and instructed them in the useful arts. Certain records even indicate that William Johnson did not exactly celebrate Weiser's title. In his journal, where he describes the Treaty of Easton of 1758, Richard Peters reports that Johnson instructed or requested the Six Nations not to address Weiser as Tarachiawagon, since it was too prestigious a name. They should, rather, address him by his other title, Segoruras, which would ensure that they did not forget Weiser's devious ways of winning races.[61] Johnson's name (Warraghiyagey, "He Who Does Much Business") would have appeared diminutive beside that of Weiser.

It is apparent now that the category "go-between" fails to capture the significance of Weiser's role or his diplomatic efforts. No other person, including Johnson and respected governors, received so illustrious a name; thus, oral tradition likely contained references to Weiser's special significance. As a protector and provider, Weiser's reputation was even stronger and more widespread than Schuyler's before him. It spread not only among the Six Nations but also among the nations of the Ohio Valley and Pennsylvania. Weiser was often entrusted with the responsibilities of a governor and was addressed as "Onas" in that capacity by Aboriginal people. His recognized importance to Pennsylvania was amply demonstrated during the Lancaster conference. When the Virginians became impatient at a long delay in the proceedings, they blamed Weiser for it and called for his replacement (one of their potential blunders). Governor Thomas of Pennsylvania refused. He argued that a treaty with the Six Nations could not be made without Weiser.[62]

Interestingly, Thomas Lee, one of the impatient Virginians who had sought to crush the Six Nations, eventually became Weiser's friend and came to appreciate his respect for the common humanity that existed between the Six Nations and colonists.[63] Lee came to accept Weiser's advice, reversing his opinion of the alliance with the Six Nations on almost all counts. Like Governor Thomas, he agreed that "a Good will for them [the Six Nations]" brokered through Weiser was necessary. Lee even stated that, because of the trust the Six Nations had in him, Weiser deserved a pension for life.[64] In a correspondence with Weiser, Lee requested an account of the Six Nations' religion. Weiser's careful response cautioned that, if Lee meant a doctrinaire system of beliefs and rules, the Six Nations had none. But if he meant "attraction of the soul to God" or "Union of the Soul with God," then they were truly religious.[65] The more Lee corresponded with Weiser over such matters, the more he came to depend on Weiser's understanding and to respect the Six Nations. At some point during the relationship, Lee shifted from being a hard-nosed military man who would crush the Six Nations to one who appreciated that understanding and moral reputation were more effective for expanding and protecting the colonies than brute military force. He shifted from a strategic attitude to a communicative one.

Weiser's commitment to developing a mutual understanding with Aboriginal people is reflected in his criticism of William Johnson. According to Weiser, Johnson was a man who played loose with Six Nations warriors, demonstrating little regard for the proper channels of treaty making.[66] To be fair, Weiser was complaining about a young and headstrong Johnson and he died before Johnson demonstrated diplomacy and sensitivity to the proper channels of treaty making in the 1760s (described in the next section). Nevertheless, this criticism reflects the constancy of Weiser's character and his commitment to establishing good understanding as a basis for diplomatic relations.

As was the case with William Penn, Weiser's reputation became an exploitable resource. In a devious scheme to gain territory and increase trade with the interior nations, the sons of William Penn, along with Richard Peters, secretary to the Pennsylvania Assembly, schemed to achieve their ends by exploiting Weiser's reputation. Peters wrote to the proprietors:

John Bartram ... sayd ... That in his opinion Mr Weiser must make one [scheme] and must have a Message to deliver to the Indians, and as he was the known Interpreter he & he only coud cover such a design he added that Lewis Evans tho an ingenious man was not agreeable to the Indians nor to Mr Weiser; and that therefore somebody else should be appealed to coud do Evans's part. On these reasonings Wm Parsons was thought of and he & Mr Weiser consulted on the Occasion – and when this was done, it was thought that considering the present posture of affairs at Ohio, a Message to the Indians as well settled there as to the Six Nation Indians might with great propriety and use be drawn up & given to the charge of Mr Weiser with Strings of Wampum and then he might as usual pretend a Visit to his Relations among the Mohocks & so carry the whole affair thro without the least suspicion – And as the cover entirely depended on Mr Weisers publick Character and the Importance of his Errand it was thought unnecessary to clogg the thing with any more Persons – Indians were to be provided in order to carry the Luggage who would still further confirm the Embassy & give an Air of publick business to it.[67]

Once Weiser was apprised of Peter's plan, he communicated his distaste for it to the Penns. The mission was dropped. But clearly, Weiser's reputation was viewed as being of major import to Indian-white relations, and this reputation had little to do with his trading practices or military prowess.

In Weiser's life, we see reputation playing a stronger role than in perhaps any other key figure's story, including that of William Johnson. Without being able to depend on Weiser's reputation, it is likely that the Pennsylvanians, and certainly the Virginians, would have attempted to use force against the Six Nations and that the Six Nations would have retaliated. Above all else, Weiser's reputation for fairness and honesty carried the most currency. He was, indeed, nicknamed "Honest Conrad." In 1750, Thomas Lee of Virginia again acknowledged Weiser's value and reputation: "I greatly rely on you, and your Friendship for the Indians is what I like, for as far as I can Judge, they ought to be used justly and kindly and that as British subjects we ought to be tender of their lives and Safetys Cresap had noe directions from me to act ye part, for as to Indian affairs I shall make use of noe other whilst I can have your honest assistance."[68] Lee recognized Weiser's role in transforming him from one who would "crush" the Six Nations to one who would unite with them in peace.[69]

Both Aboriginal people and the British depended on Weiser's reputation to broker diplomatic relations. His understanding of Aboriginal culture and ability to demonstrate how important such an understanding was to diplomatic relations helped produce a shared lifeworld built on moral values that moved Europeans and Aboriginal people away from violence and toward peaceful relations. Although Weiser was not central to trade and military relations, he was central to diplomatic and political relations because of the way he brought both sides together in the spirit of mutual understanding. By playing the role of standard-bearer, Weiser created an atmosphere in which the members of the Pennsylvania Covenant Chain felt pressure to maintain a moral bearing toward each other. His participation in the moral economy was, accordingly, peculiar. No other person's reputation, apart from its connection to trade and military values, seems to have had such a strong bearing on historical outcomes. No other figure seems to have evoked moral sensibilities as strongly as Weiser. Weiser's case does, consequently, help identify what it was about reputation that affected people's attitudes and behaviour. The force with which his reputation influenced people's attitudes, decisions, and behaviours shifted their subjective worlds and opened them to the possibility of establishing an intersubjective world with Aboriginal people. His reputation affected people's values and belief systems, for example, that which people believed was necessary to get what they wanted. It even affected what they wanted from and in relation to Aboriginal people.

William Johnson (Warraghiyagey)

A number of comments have already been made about William Johnson, some of which have not been entirely flattering. Francis Jennings and Paul Wallace, among others, view him as an opportunist and a somewhat dark character. According to Wallace, "Dark ways and subterfuges did not bother him as they bothered Weiser; his eyes were accustomed to darkness. He did not look far ahead, and we lack in him the bold and penetrating vision of Weiser and James Logan; but he mastered the cross-currents of political intrigue, turned them to his own benefit, and in the end made his own interests serve the interests of the state."[70] Jennings describes Johnson as lording it over the Iroquois, whom Johnson viewed as peasants. Johnson was not altruistic, but seeing that the Iroquois were his means to power, he lied and used divide-and-conquer techniques as needed to serve the Crown.[71]

Different opinions about Johnson's abilities, personality, and moral disposition have been expressed, as should be expected with such a central figure. In a fictionalized account of Johnson's relationship with the Mohawk, Robert Moss identifies him as "Firekeeper" and narrates his life as if only a spiritual point of view could suffice to capture the depth of the man.[72] Milton Hamilton, one of the editors of the *Papers of Sir William Johnson*, makes a number of similar claims about Johnson's moral character:

> Furthermore, William was an honest and openhanded young Irishman who wanted to make friends and who respected the rights of others as he wished them to like and respect him ... His greatness is more remarkable because he gained his power over the Indians through his honesty, fairness, and brotherly love shown in dealing with them. And he used his power for honest aims and for the good of the Indians as well as for the whites ... He was universally trusted. He was content to wield his influence without show of personal ambition or political preferment.[73]

One could view these differences of opinion as split between scholars centred in Pennsylvania and those in New York. It has struck me in the course of studying the colonial period that no other figure evokes such deeply contradictory judgments about his moral character. But at least all commentators view him as having an exploitable reputation among Aboriginal people. The New York records support the opinion of New Yorkers, while the Pennsylvania records tend to support that of Pennsylvanians. In New York, despite his Loyalist commitments, people still refer to William Johnson as "Sir William," whereas in Pennsylvania the attitude is not so respectful. However, almost all scholars who study Johnson seem compelled to make a moral judgment on his character, leaving little doubt that the man evoked a wide range of judgments by those he encountered. For this reason, his character stands out as a valuable resource for understanding how the complexity of the moral economy played out. My own encounter with the records describing him suggests that there is truth and error on both sides.

Johnson's involvement in events on the North American continent, from King George's War in the 1740s onward, and records for the years 1753-55 and 1761-67 offer extensive evidence for the operation of the moral economy. The context in which Johnson lived was one of looming chaos and a constant threat of violence. Prior to his arrival, the Six Nations had complained about settler encroachments and the failure of the English to protect them from French attacks. They complained about the unfair practices of traders and land grabbers, threatening, as a consequence, to go over to the French. On more than one occasion, attempts had been made (sometimes even initiated by the Six Nations) to form a united Aboriginal front to remove the British from North America. In other words, Aboriginal people resented, mistrusted, and were angry with the British. During this same period, the Crown, as represented by various colonial governments, had become increasingly cognizant of its dependence on key agents who could maintain alliances and treaties to keep the Six Nations and others on side against the French.

By 1753, as Peter Wraxall, secretary to William Johnson, notes, the commissioners for Indian affairs at Albany had gained a reputation for being underhanded, conniving, and even traitorous men out to serve their own interests. Not only Aboriginal people but even governors and the Lords of Trade viewed them this way. Both Wraxall and the Six Nations held them in contempt. They were known for using their position to defraud the Six Nations of land and for continuing trade with Montreal, even during periods of war with the French.[74] If the records of the council at which Hendrick, sachem for the Mohawk, came to New York to confront Governor Clinton about these issues are examined from a slightly different point of view, the significance of Johnson's reputation to the Crown-Aboriginal relationship comes into focus. On 12 June 1753, Hendrick described the long history of England's failure to live up to its obligation to protect the Six Nations against French invasions, even after the Six Nations had protected the English during King George's War. He detailed how the English had failed to come to the aid of their Ohio Valley brethren when the French and their allies attacked. He complained of land frauds in which the English had been granted small tracts of land by the Mohawk but had taken far more. He complained of a deed known as the Kayaderossera patent, which was being used to swindle Mohawks of eight hundred thousand acres of territory.[75] At the first conference, Hendrick announced that the Covenant Chain would be broken if the Six Nations were not satisfied. After conferring for a couple of days, Clinton gave his reply on 16 June. He promised to look into matters concerning the raids on the Ohio but essentially dismissed complaints concerning land fraud by deferring the matter to the Commission for Indian Affairs at Albany.

In response, Hendrick declared:

> When we came here to relate our Greivances [sic] about our Lands, we ex-
> pected to have some thing done for us, and we told you that the Covenant
> Chain of our Fathers was like to be broken, and brother you tell us that we
> shall be redressed at Albany, but we know them so well, we will not trust to
> them, for they are no people but Devils, so we rather desire that you'l say,
> Nothing shall be done for us ... By & By you'l expect to see the Nations down
> which you shall not see, for as soon as we come home we will send up a
> Belt of Wampum to our Brothers the 5 Nations to acquaint them the
> Covenant Chain is broken between you and us. So Brother you are not to
> expect to hear of me any more, and Brother we desire to hear no more of
> you. And we shall no longer acquaint you with any News or affairs as we
> used to do.[76]

With this declaration, Hendrick sent the province of New York, along with
the Lords of Trade, into a panic.

Governor Clinton reported back to the Lords of Trade and included the
minutes of the meeting with Hendrick. Now, from at least 1702 onward, the
Lords of Trade had viewed New York and its alliance with the Six Nations
as central to the Crown's interest on the North American continent. The
members recognized the "necessity of preserving the friendship of the Five
Nations of Indians, which are a barrier between his Majesty's plantations
and Canada, by treating them kindly, and showing them a force constantly
maintained in New York, ready to protect them upon all occasions."[77] This
awareness was the result of lobbying by various governors (at least from
Fletcher on) and other key agents (especially Schuyler and Livingston) who
wrote a number of letters apprising the Lords of Trade of England's vulner-
ability to the French-Algonquian alliance and the need for support in the
form of armaments and troops. Given this context, the last thing Clinton
should have done was tell the Six Nations to air their complaints to the
commissioners. He should have at least suppressed the record of his actions
or edited them before sending them to the Lords of Trade.

The Lords of Trade acted quickly. First, they removed Clinton from office
and recalled him to England. Second, Lords Halifax and Dupplin apprised
Lord Holdernesse of the Six Nations' act of severing the Covenant Chain
and expressed just how important it was to address British failures in the
eyes of Indian allies. They recommended that an interview with the Six
Nations be held as soon as possible.[78] On the same day, they wrote to Danvers
Osborne, whom they had sent to replace Clinton, not realizing that he had
died, apparently en route to New York. They conveyed their confidence in
him to do everything necessary "to obviate the fatal Consequences which

might attend this affair." After emphasizing the importance of maintaining a friendship and alliance with the Six Nations, they continued:

> We cannot but be greatly concern'd and surprized that the Province of New York should have been so inattentive to the general interest of His Majesty's subjects in America, as well as to their own particular security as to have given occasion to the Complaints made by the Indians but we are still more surprized at the manner in which these complaints were received the dissatisfactory answers given to the Indians and at their being suffered to depart (th'o the Assembly was then sitting) without any measure taken to bring them to temper, or to redress their Complaints.

The Lords of Trade pressed the point that the Assembly had to be made well aware of the need to re-establish friendship and affection to tie the Six Nations to British interests. They also acknowledged that Albany was obnoxious to the allies, owing to the commissioners' ill reputation, and suggested that Onondaga once again be recognized as the appropriate meeting place. They continued: "We likewise hope that in the choice of the persons who are to attend and assist you in that Interview You will have a regard to such as are best acquainted with the Indians and their Affairs, and not obnoxious to them and as a great deal depends upon the Interpreters, we desire you will be particularly careful to appoint such as are well acquainted with the Indian Language and men of ability and integrity."[79] The Lords of Trade instructed the governor to bury the hatchet and renew the Covenant Chain and to let the Six Nations know about the presents that were being sent. The governor was also to listen closely to complaints about land frauds, redress them, and admit that lands had been "unwarrantably taken" from Aboriginal people. All colonies were to send representatives to make one treaty rather than one for each province.

This attempt to consolidate the power of the Covenant Chain in New York failed, but it indicates where the Crown's interests were focused and that it was aware of the implications of severing the Covenant Chain. This communication also demonstrates that the Crown was well aware of the role that the moral economy played in diplomatic relations with Aboriginal nations. However, since Osborne died before he could assume his duties as governor, none of the instructions were carried out, and a period of chaos ensued.

In a letter to the Lords of Trade date 30 October 1753, Thomas Pownall, secretary to the deceased Governor Osborne, attempted to explain that William Johnson was the proper person to smooth things over with the Six Nations. Pownall wrote that Johnson had travelled to Onondaga in an attempt to keep the Six Nations on side but that there had also been considerable controversy over whether he or the commissioners at Albany should control Indian affairs.[80] James DeLancey, lieutenant governor of New York and Johnson's superior, also claimed to have tried to bury the hatchet. He identified himself as a "proper person with a publick character" who had gone to Onondaga, "which is the place of the General meeting of the five Nations and where they keep (as they express themselves) their Great Fire & the Tree to which one end of the Covenant Chain is fastened."[81] DeLancey used the language of the Covenant Chain to make his claim. He did not simply say "to treat with" or "to negotiate a peace" to make his claim, and he did not use the more legalistic "official council meeting location." Rather, he used "Great Fire and the Tree" to indicate the geopolitical importance of Onondaga. He was, at least, trying to impress upon the Lords of Trade that he was familiar with Aboriginal ways and could converse effectively with Aboriginal people. He was trying to demonstrate that he had a good understanding of the Crown's allies and could be counted among the few proper persons who could be assigned a key role in Indian affairs.

In their communication to Osborne, the Lords of Trade explicitly acknowledged the importance of key agents, or proper persons. By *proper person* they meant "people who were not obnoxious to the Indians and who had gained their respect." DeLancey claimed he was a proper person who could represent the Crown, particularly New York. Pennsylvania had sent Weiser to the Six Nations as just such a person in an attempt to repair the damage done by Clinton and likely to gain an advantage over New York. His journey to Onondaga, however, was never completed. During his travels, he stayed with Johnson, who had "welcomed" him to Onondaga but by his demeanor indicated that he preferred that Weiser not attend.[82] Weiser's official account of this incident omits his more cynical remarks about Johnson not accomplishing anything of importance at Onondaga, suggesting that Johnson was not the proper person to conduct Indian affairs. Weiser intimates that both New York and Johnson did not want him at Onondaga precisely because he was such an effective go-between. Before he was recalled, Clinton had actually sent Johnson "under the Broad Seal of the Government" to negotiate a settlement. This competition between DeLancey, Weiser, and Johnson for recognition as the proper person to engage with the Six Nations discloses an underlying web of intrigue governed by the moral economy.

In this chaos, who could be called a *proper person* – closely associated with *proper understanding* – was played out in discourses and interactions among Crown agents in their attempt to mend diplomatic relations with the Six Nations. The importance of reputation was brought to the foreground as a key factor in any attempt to dissipate the anger of the Six Nations. Johnson's subsequent report to Clinton, just prior to Clinton's removal from office, includes a description of a preliminary meeting with the Mohawk speaker Hendrick held about a month earlier than the Onondaga meeting. After responding to an invitation belt sent by Johnson to request a meeting,

Hendrick arrived at Fort Johnson on 26 July 1753. He emphasized how glad the Mohawk were that Johnson had been raised up again and "impowered to receive and impart the news" while making it clear that the Mohawk would not have responded to a call from the commissioners at Albany. Johnson, seemingly brazenly, responded by chastising the Mohawk for their brash manners and unreasonableness at New York and for creating such an uncomfortable situation for the governor. Since the governor had to be replaced by another for alleged medical reasons, by one who would address the Mohawk's land issues, Johnson asked that they wait for the new governor to settle the matter. He then asked the Mohawk to confer with him about matters to be discussed at Onondaga.[83] Why was Johnson allowed to speak so brazenly, behaving in a manner clearly out of keeping with being a proper person? And why did Hendrick single him out as the only person in political circles at Albany to whom the Mohawk would respond?

Johnson had arrived on the continent in around 1738 to manage his Uncle Peter's (Peter Warren's) property in the Mohawk Valley. He established his own property just across the Mohawk River after negotiating a land cession with the Mohawk. As John Christopher Guzzardo describes it, Johnson quickly acquired land and developed strong trade relations with the Six Nations.[84] He leveraged his success to establish himself as a virtual feudal lord, populating his ever-growing land holdings with immigrant Irish and Palatines from Germany. He was a man who did much business (hence the name Warraghiyagey) and satisfied much of his ambition through close ties with the Six Nations, especially the Mohawk.

During King George's War, in the 1740s, Governor Clinton ordered the commissioners at Albany to treat with the Six Nations, only to have them boycott the meeting. After failing twice to find suitable agents – he tried John Glen and John Lydius in 1745 – to negotiate treaties with the Six Nations, he finally assigned Johnson to the role. Owing to his success as a trader and landowner, which in turn had led to political success in his fiefdom, Johnson was hated within Albany. He had redirected much of the town's "Indian trade" to Fort Johnson and, in so doing, had established a prosperous plantation and good relations with the Mohawk. Therefore, when Clinton arrived for treaty negotiations, no commissioners were present.

Apparently, unbeknownst to Clinton, Johnson was attempting to persuade the Six Nations to come to Albany for treaty negotiations. Clinton, as a result, found himself virtually alone to prepare for war against the French on 28 August 1746.[85] After a couple of anxious days, Johnson entered Albany, dancing a war dance with Six Nations warriors. The commissioners apparently found it imprudent to stay the course and joined the proceedings. To Clinton's relief, Johnson had assembled a warrior force, which some would say was the decisive factor at the subsequent battle at Crown Point. Johnson earned his reputation as a warrior among the Six Nations there. But at this point, his reputation was based on doing fair and mutually advantageous business. His reputation seems to have made him an effective treaty negotiator, so much so that the governor of Canada placed a bounty on his head in 1746.[86] Success bred success. Once military prowess was added to Johnson's reputation, following the battle at Crown Point (he actually fought the French to a draw), the already diminishing power of the commissioners was dealt yet another blow. In 1750, Clinton extinguished the council fire at Albany and rekindled it at Fort Johnson. Five years later, Johnson was commissioned as sole superintendent of Indian affairs in the north.

It may have been brash of the young Johnson to use his influence to bring the Six Nations into the war. As Wallace explains, Weiser was none too pleased with Johnson's dancing. In his exuberance, Johnson endangered the Six Nations, whereas Weiser was committed to their protection by keeping them neutral.[87] Weiser's biographer does, indeed, indicate that Weiser was always far more concerned to effect peace and protect the Great League than he was to use the Six Nations' military might to protect the Crown's interests. Johnson, in contrast, made use of his reputation and exploited Aboriginal peoples' propensities for war to bring them into the conflict with Britain's enemies. This raised his profile well past that of Weiser in the eyes of the Crown. Johnson eventually became a brigadier general, baronet, and sole superintendent of Indian affairs, whereas Weiser died in pain during the bloodiest war the colonies had seen to that date. Although not yet superintendent, by the time he met with Hendrick in 1753, Johnson had fought alongside the Mohawk leader and become central to trade with the Six Nations. His brash behaviour was nothing new to the Mohawk; it was part of his reputation as one who spoke his mind.

As different as Johnson and Weiser were, they shared a reputation for honesty, integrity and, indeed, toughness among Aboriginal people. Both men were deeply immersed in Aboriginal culture – Weiser among the Mohawk and Onondaga, Johnson principally among the Mohawk. Weiser was raised in a Mohawk community, while Johnson became so intimate with the Mohawk that he "married" into the Mohawk castle Canojoharie when Molly Brant, with whom he had four children, became his "housekeeper." Johnson had stayed with the Brants whenever he visited the Mohawk village and came to know Molly in the context of her role as clan mother.[88] Thus, like Weiser, he gained an understanding of and respect for Aboriginal culture through direct contact and engagement with Aboriginal people. Unlike Weiser, however, who was a loyal husband, "playboy Johnson," as Wallace calls him, gained part of his reputation by fathering many a Mohawk child. Rather than doing his reputation harm, however, it seems to have endeared him even more to the Mohawk.

Johnson could "get away" with brazen speech, then, because the Mohawk considered him one of their own. Johnson, like Weiser, was seen by his superiors as having a special relationship with the Mohawk community because his interests were closely tied to those of the Six Nations and because he had what we today would call social capital on which to draw. By 1753, Johnson was more a brother to the Mohawk than a mere agent of the Crown. Thus, he was not only a proper person who had earned the respect and trust of the Mohawk, he also had the right to speak freely as a community member.

Johnson was more than willing to use his community membership as leverage in negotiations. In 1753, for instance, he and the Mohawk travelled together to Onondaga, where they were met by sachems at the wood's edge on 8 September. After the Onondaga sachems healed the travellers with belts of wampum and gave condolences with "strouds" to cover the graves of the dead, Hendrick proceeded to speak for Johnson. We can assume that, at the previous Fort Johnson meeting, the two men had agreed to this arrangement, although no hint as to why it was made is contained in the record. Johnson, after all, was quite accustomed to speaking before the council. All things considered, it is safe to assume that Johnson trusted Hendrick.

Johnson was sent on this mission to resolve conflicts generated by illicit land appropriations, particularly the Kayaderossera patent. But the issue seems not to have been raised at council. Rather, the discussion focused on French incursions into the Ohio region, which the Six Nations blamed on British neglect. This neglect, in turn, was formulated as something that was tarnishing the Covenant Chain. Johnson raised the issue of the Six Nations' treaty negotiations with Canada, among a number of other items, in a counter accusation. Everyone seems to have left the meeting satisfied that the Covenant Chain had been renewed and brightened, without addressing the Kayaderossera patent. It would appear, then, that Hendrick and Johnson, in their preliminary meeting, had agreed not to raise the land issue and to convince the Onondaga to defer discussion until the new governor was in place. Granted, that issue was principally between the Mohawk and the British, not the Onondaga, although the patent did affect the Oneida. Yet all of the Six Nations would have recognized that land frauds were of interest to the entire confederacy, not just the Mohawk and Oneida, because the impact of fraudulent land transactions would eventually become their problem. And since Onondaga was the council fire for the Six Nations, any nation-to-nation resolution to deal with land frauds would have to be made there, as the Lords of Trade recognized. Moreover, Johnson knew that the Lords of Trade wanted to renew the council fire at Onondaga and to deal with the land fraud issue in a way that would satisfy the Six Nations. Hence, for whatever reason all agreed not to raise the issue, it had something to do with the agreement Hendrick and Johnson had made earlier. When Weiser cynically criticized Johnson's actions (or inactions) at this council, he had good reason to suspect something was amiss. He expressed his opinion by saying, "It looks very Strenge to me that when Coll: Came to onontago he dreshed the old Straw over again [offering condolences for the death of Canasatego, three years in his grave], and did nothing else."[89]

Johnson did not address the issue, but he did discuss the matter of the French threat and requested that the Six Nations cease treating with the French and not go to Canada. This, after all, was the underlying concern of the Lords of Trade. Therefore, to be fair to Johnson, he did accomplish something. What is not clear is whether what he accomplished was of genuine benefit to the alliance. Whatever the meeting accomplished, it showed that Johnson's ties to the Six Nations allowed him to act as an insider. Indeed, his reputation and identity as an insider were quite different from Conrad Weiser's, but they were just as effective in allowing him to communicate with the Six Nations. Johnson and Weiser were well aware of the other's effectiveness in Indian affairs, and this awareness generated mutual jealousy, which was evident in their competition for influence and in the (sometimes not-so-polite) criticisms each made of the other. Weiser especially wanted to be recognized as the agent with superior understanding of Aboriginal ways, whereas Johnson wanted to be recognized as the more effective negotiator. Where Johnson emphasized warrior values, Weiser emphasized the sachem (political) values of the confederacy – peace and friendship. In times of war, consequently, Weiser was bound to lose the competition for influence, particularly during the 1750s.

These two men's experiences suggest that the definition of a proper person for the times was one who could succeed in gaining the respect of Aboriginal people (and vice versa) by demonstrating a kind of integrity, as the Lords of Trade understood. Clearly, acceptance into (belonging to) the community was also critical. Their shared past and shared struggles produced a shared identity. Crown agents were well aware of this criterion, insofar as they recognized the need for negotiators who had a capacity for backroom politics or "speaking in the bushes." The British saw this aspect of crosscultural politics as the darker side of personal relationships, as did many Aboriginal people. As the meeting with Hendrick and many references to private conferences in the record suggest, however, matters of importance were, in fact, negotiated in the bushes. Both Johnson and Weiser were masters of bush politics. Colonel Daniel Claus later (in 1777) describes Johnson as being unequalled in the private conference, "which was based on mutual respect, sincerity and trust between the participants."[90] Weiser's bush politics with Shikallemy and others was treated almost as official policy.

Although aspersions were cast on bush politics, the forum depended on proper persons even more so than did official treaty councils. If we do not know exactly what went on during the course of conducting bush politics, we do know that these meetings were crucial for maintaining the relationship between the Crown and Aboriginal allies, as they were among the

French and their allies. The French Jesuits and Joncaires provided ample evidence to the British that bush politics was absolutely necessary, if British interests were to be protected. It is no surprise, then, that the Lords of Trade and various governors recognized their dependency on proper persons, and by implication the moral economy, in the conduct of Indian affairs.

Johnson's reputation also had an effect in official political circles, as is illustrated in his relationship with Governor William Shirley. When General Edward Braddock, commander-in-chief in North America, made Johnson the sole superintendent of Indian affairs in the north on 15 April 1755, Johnson had already been denied the post once.[91] The Lords of Trade recommended to the king that Johnson should be appointed to the post since he had preserved the Crown's friendship with Aboriginal allies by virtue of his having lived among them and his knowledge of their manners and customs.[92] He was also given the rank of major general to complement his baronetcy, much to the chagrin of people such as Shirley.

Shirley had previously recommended Johnson to the Lords of Trade for the post. In other words, he helped catapult Johnson to a position of influence that exceeded his own. In a way, Shirley became a victim of Johnson's reputation, but he also reaped what he had sown. Years before, on 2-5 July 1751, Johnson had quit his post as an Indian agent because it was bankrupting him. Both Hendrick and his brother Abraham lobbied Governor Clinton, "We desire to have an answer to what we have said and that Coll. Johnson may be reinstated, for he has large Ears and heareth a great deal, and what he hears he tells us; he also has large Eyes and sees a great way, and conceals nothing from us."[93] Johnson was eventually reinstated and compensated for his expenditures. Shirley supported Johnson's reinstatement. Later, however, in 1754, Johnson's reputation as a man with good understanding, the willingness to listen, and the ability to communicate was pitted against that of Shirley's right-hand man, Colonel John Lydius. An Oneida sachem refused to treat with Lydius present because he considered him a conniving snake. The sachem warned Johnson to clean the council fire of such filth; otherwise the council would not proceed. This was the same Lydius who would, just after the 1754 Albany Conference, conduct the illicit Susquehanna Valley land transaction for Connecticut by plying several sachems with liquor and getting them to sign title over to him. Johnson removed Lydius, to the chagrin of Governor Shirley (who was also commander-in-chief of North America at the time). Although Shirley commanded Johnson to strike the report of the incident from the record, Johnson kept it in a private record.[94] Somehow, it must have come into the hands of the Lords of Trade, since Shirley was soon after removed as commander-in-chief. Thus, the following year, when Johnson was raised to the position of sole superintendent of Indian affairs, Shirley was not a happy man. The two men's relationship reveals the role that moral reputation played in the conduct of Indian affairs. Moral values played a key part in determining who advanced and who did not, who was successful and who failed.

Employing the values of the moral economy to one's advantage, as has been shown, had a dark side. For instance, some commentators refer to an incident in which Johnson cheated the Mohawk of five hundred acres of prime land. The story goes as follows. One day, Hendrick came to Johnson, saying that he had had a dream in which Johnson gave him a fine red jacket (British military uniform). Since dreaming was connected to authority in the Aboriginal cultures of the region, Johnson gave Hendrick a jacket of the same description. Later, Johnson claimed that he had dreamed that Hendrick had given him five hundred acres of prime Mohawk land. While signing the deed to Johnson's newly acquired land, Hendrick is reputed to have said that he would never again dream with him.[95] Wallace cites a different source for the same story to suggest that Johnson exploited his understanding of Aboriginal culture and personal relations whenever the opportunity arose.[96] However, even Honest Conrad was not above exploiting such opportunities. After Shikallemy dreamed that Weiser had given him a rifle, Weiser claimed that he had dreamed that Shikallemy had given him an island in the Susquehanna River.[97] These events indicate how both Johnson and Weiser exploited communicative actions and transformed their intended purpose into strategic actions.

The competition over reputation mattered, partly because winning the competition gave the winner an economic and political advantage. From this point of view, even Wallace, who heavily criticizes Johnson for being a shortsighted rogue, considers Johnson the greatest Indian agent (as opposed to Indian ambassador), particularly for his ability to find acceptance within Aboriginal communities.[98] Indeed, Johnson's brashness sometimes endangered his allies. When he persuaded Six Nations warriors to do battle against the French in 1747, for instance, he did not go through the proper channels at Onondaga. His actions threatened to undermine the League of Peace, and, of course, the battle resulted in the loss of lives. For this reason, Weiser was contemptuous of Johnson.[99] Johnson, however, did not simply paint himself and dance the war dance with the warriors; he risked his life and his fortune by serving as an Indian agent. He was not a man who spoke merely with his mouth, as Aboriginal people often accused the British of doing. During the battle at Crown Point, Johnson, while fighting on the front lines, took a bullet in the leg, which confined him to his tent for the remainder of the battle. He carried the bullet there for the rest of his life. It was no act of cowardice, moreover, that kept him confined to his tent.

It is not clear that Johnson's good reputation was always deserved. His victory, as it was cast by Crown officials, was proclaimed because Johnson had captured a French officer and had not been defeated. The Crown Point battle came just after General Braddock's army, including Braddock, had been slaughtered at Fort Duquesne. Every French incursion into British territory up to that point had succeeded. Both the English and the Haudenosaunee were under threat of losing territory and control over their domains. A certain embellishment of the Crown Point outcome was therefore helpful in boosting morale, and a little brashness and a few blunders by Johnson could be overlooked or recast as confidence because Johnson was one of only two rays of hope, the other being John Bradstreet, that the British had at the time. Johnson was not the hero he was made out to be, but the fact that British officials exploited and embellished his reputation indicates just how critical reputation was to military affairs and the political economy.

In a way, the less-than-superlative title *Warraghiyagey* was a well-suited moniker for Johnson and remained so for the rest of his life. Johnson got things done and used his reputation to enhance his effectiveness. He was not only a trader, negotiator, and military leader, he was also the magistrate for his fiefdom in the Mohawk Valley, which he turned into a lucrative agricultural plantation with his Irish and German "subjects." As leader of the region's masonic lodge and supporter of the Society for the Propagation of the Gospel, Johnson filled his plate to overflowing. When scholars and Johnson's contemporaries condemn his less-than-sterling moral character, they overlook that he was operating in a complex context of trade, competition, and war. Indeed, his hard-nosed trading practices and desire for personal gain, when measured against the sacrifices he made, could be interpreted as contributing to his profile as a strong, trustworthy person. Even his detractors in Albany could not dispute the claim that Johnson used "fair dealings" with the Indians.[100] His reputation was built not in spite of his self-interested behaviour but on the way he acted on his self-interest. He gained others' trust because they knew that they were dealing with a man who was more honest and fairer than others.

One aspect of Johnson's reputation calls for special attention, insofar as it differentiates Johnson from others described. As a military leader, he chose men whom he considered loyal to command his troops and who were prepared to master the Iroquois language. Officers were commanded to eat and camp with their Aboriginal allies, as well as fight alongside them.[101] These subordinates, in turn, demonstrated unusual loyalty. During the French and Indian War, they refused Governor Shirley's and Lydius's attempt to bribe them to join the Niagara campaign at twice the salary Johnson was paying them.[102] The vast majority of Six Nations warriors likewise turned down the offer. Consequently, Shirley, with his regulars, never reached Niagara. To add insult to injury, Johnson and Six Nations warriors later took Niagara. On numerous other occasions, including Hendrick's appeal to have Johnson reinstated, Johnson inspired loyalty, and fortunately for him, his ability to inspire outstripped his tendency to create jealousy and resentment among his foes.

Johnson's sense of loyalty and readiness to sacrifice also had a darker side. Since Johnson so strongly focused his loyalties and commitments, he tended to slight and ignore others. He did not always give credit where credit was due and accepted the glory others deserved. At the battle at Crown Point, for instance, Johnson was assigned command over General Phineas Lyman of Connecticut, who resented being made a subordinate to Johnson. Unlike Johnson, Lyman was trained as a soldier and knew how to command. After Johnson was shot and confined to his tent, Lyman became the principal commander in the field. It was under Lyman's command, then, that "victory" was gained. Johnson might have rationalized that, without his being on the front lines, the allied warriors would not have been mobilized, and the battle would have been lost. He likely would have been right. For whatever reason, Johnson never gave Lyman credit for his role. Had he given credit where credit was due, it is questionable whether he would have risen through the military and political ranks as he did. This incident may reinforce Jennings's and Wallace's view that Johnson was quite familiar with the darker aspects of the moral economy, but it also helps demonstrate that agents often used their reputation to exert force on public morale and to persuade their superiors.

Reputation also influenced family ties and sense of belonging. Molly Brant, the sister of Joseph Brant, a Mohawk captain and sachem, came to Fort Johnson in 1759, when the French and Indian War was coming to a close in North America. Jennings, who argues that Johnson never really became Indian, says he merely "mistressed Molly Brant." Lois Huey and Bonnie Pulis, by contrast, draw on evidence to show that Brant was far more of a wife and partner to Johnson than Catherine Weissenberg, the mother of Johnson's three white children, ever was.[103] According to those at the Johnson Hall Museum, Brant was Johnson's wife in all but name and eventually became a pillar in Johnson's relationship with Aboriginal people. Officially, however, Johnson avowed that Weissenberg was his wife, although not in a legal sense. For instance, he passed on his legacy and title to his son John, Weissenberg's first child. This does not mean that Johnson merely used Brant, as Jennings suggests. He did not neglect her children in his will. After his death, the four children received significant estates, albeit smaller ones than those given to his three children by Weissenberg. How much of this differential treatment was shaped by social and other external pressures remains unknown. As Huey and Pulis note, Johnson's guests often asked that he send their warmest greetings to Brant. They took note of her in a way that was not extended to Weissenberg.

Brant's status as clan mother clearly shaped her role in Indian affairs,[104] although her status was somewhat suppressed in records taken during Johnson's life. Following Johnson's death in 1774, however, General Frederick

Haldimand, Guy and John Johnson, Daniel Claus, and others left no doubt in their correspondence that Brant had become deeply involved in Indian affairs. Her advice was frequently sought by these men. That Johnson became a supporter of and mentor to Brant's younger brother, Joseph, who would go on to become a dominant war chief in the War of Independence, strongly suggests that the partnership was politically significant. Johnson and Brant's relationship was no doubt complicated, being built on expediency, mutual advantage, affection, and respect, among many other factors.

Brant's status raises the issue of the role of women in the moral economy, a matter about which the record is mostly silent. However, women made important contributions to the process of recognizing others as part of community, particularly in their role as clan mothers. Had clerks realized the importance of this role, and had they been privy to proceedings in Aboriginal communities, historical records would contain more details about this aspect of the moral economy. Even though I do not pursue this issue further, raising it reinforces the argument that other moral factors, for instance, his marriage to Brant and the links it gave him to the Mohawk community, likely shaped Johnson's reputation and enabled it to become as effective as it did. However much Johnson might have wanted to simply "mistress" Brant, he had to take into consideration that she was not merely attached to his reputation symbolically. As a clan mother, she had considerable social capital in the Mohawk community and, consequently, with Johnson and Indian affairs. Even if Johnson married simply to exploit familial bonds in Aboriginal culture, he would still have been subjected to the normative pressures of those bonds. To have Brant as a wife or mistress was to enter a world of deepening normative commitments, commitments influenced not only by cultural forces but also by gender relations and the principles that operated among the clan mothers.

Johnson's reputation brought him both status and responsibility. This double-edged sword cut two ways in the years following Brant's arrival at Fort Johnson. Pierre Pouchot surrendered Niagara to Johnson, Fort Frontenac had also fallen, and Wolfe's siege of Quebec virtually ended the French and Indian War. Although it took four more years before Canada was officially handed over to the British in the Treaty of Paris, British dominance on the eastern side of the continent was established. The termination of the war correlated with a growing sense of confidence or impatience, even arrogance, in Johnson's demeanor. Whether it was the effect of receiving so many accolades in a skyrocketing career, his success at just about everything to which he put his mind, his political victories over many a superior, his growing influence over Aboriginal people, his relationship with Brant, all of the above, or something else entirely, the records describe a man transformed by power and reputation.

This is not to say that Johnson wantonly abused his power. On more than one occasion, he complained, "I have ... every Room and Corner of my House constantly filled with Indians."[105] After Johnson Hall was built in 1763, Johnson served as the host of a constant stream of meetings, appointments, and treaty councils. The British victory did not diminish Johnson's involvement with Aboriginal people; it increased it. The Far Indians or western Indians were happy neither with the French, whom they believed had abandoned them to the British, nor with the British, whom they had been fighting because of advancing settlement. The end of the war with the French marked the beginning of the war in the west. The western nations around Detroit and in the Ohio Valley (the Illinois Confederacy, the Three Fires Confederacy, and the Wyandot, Mingos, western Delaware, Shawnee, and others) were shocked that the French had abandoned them. The western Delaware and Shawnee had relocated from Pennsylvania in the face of advancing settlement and were experiencing it yet again. The Mingos had been formed from discontents among the Six Nations, mostly Seneca, who had grown weary of empty British promises. Thus, although the French had been defeated, the same could not be said of the western nations, and Johnson was at the centre of the controversy.

Recall that, according to the British, nineteen or twenty sachems from the Six Nations had, in 1701 at Albany, surrendered title to a tract of land eight hundred miles long and four hundred miles wide, including Detroit (the Canagariachio Treaty).[106] The treaty council had been called because the Six Nations could no longer protect the area from French (read "Far Nations") incursions. The Six Nations' use of the right of conquest, based on victories during the Beaver Wars, could now be turned against them. Johnson was caught in the middle. This region, as well as the Ohio Valley, was now controlled and claimed by an Algonquian-Huron alliance, which Johnson had recognized by kindling a council fire at Detroit in 1761, despite complaints by the Six Nations. For most of its history up to 1761, the region had been subjected to even more internal conflict than the Six Nations' region in the east. Internecine warfare was common (especially between the Fox and everyone else). With the closing of the Seven Years' War, Pontiac (Ottawa) rose to enjoy considerable influence in the region, although he was never able to unify the tribes in the same way that the Six Nations were unified. The pressures placed on Johnson to act as go-between for the British and the Six Nations were now exacerbated by the opening of a new diplomatic arena. On numerous occasions, Johnson, like Weiser, indicated how fatigued he had become of Indian affairs. His health became so poor that he had to take periodic vacations. His impatience with constant visitors, both Aboriginal and white, is understandable. His shift in character, then, was not entirely the result of a growing arrogance.

During this period, Johnson also had to undo the damage caused by blundering military officers. First, the British never buried the hatchet (that is, conducted a peace and friendship treaty) with the western nations after the defeat of the French, which constituted a diplomatic blunder.[107] Second, men such as General Braddock held views similar to Thomas Lee – the best Indian policy was to crush insurgencies and to dominate by threat of military force – views that exacerbated the mistrust between the British and Aboriginal nations. Braddock paid a heavy price for acting on his views: he was ambushed and killed on his way to attack Fort Duquesne. His replacement, Jeffrey Amherst, was no better. Warriors trusted neither man and would not fight for them, leaving Johnson once again responsible for bringing warriors on side.

It is not difficult to understand why Johnson was not a particularly happy or even hopeful Crown agent when he began the arduous task of treating with the western nations. Conrad Weiser had died and Johnson was perhaps the only Crown agent (with the exception of a couple of his subordinates) whom Aboriginal people trusted. On 6-12 April 1760, Johnson, together with his appointee George Croghan, travelled to Fort Pitt to deal with the anger of the western nations by holding a conference with a large contingent of Far Indians and Six Nations representatives.[108] After opening the wood's edge ceremony by using a string of wampum to wipe the sweat, dust, and briars from the feet of the British and to clear their eyes, these nations gave a string to wipe the blood from the council seat in preparation for treaty negotiations. After reciting an origin story, one of the Shawnee delegates spoke. He identified himself as a member of the Silver Covenant Chain and, with an exchange of peace belts, buried the hatchet. The results of the conference are not clear, however, partially because the conference was not one of Johnson's more brilliant diplomatic moments. The British contingent proclaimed that they had become the most powerful people on the continent, implying that Aboriginal people would be crushed if they did not comply with the conditions of peace set out.

Although all parties agreed to an official peace, both sides viewed the peace as tenuous, as subsequent records indicate. More had to be done to cement a peace. Johnson was particularly worried about Amherst, who harboured little or no affection for Aboriginal people. On 10 March 1761, for instance, Johnson wrote to Daniel Claus about Amherst's disaffection for Aboriginal people, which could have dire consequences for Indian and domestic affairs.[109] Claus was instructed to stabilize relations in the west by maintaining a friendly correspondence with the western nations, especially in anticipation of a forthcoming conference. Johnson prepared well for the conference, sending out wampum belts to remind various nations of the treaty of peace they had signed in 1760.[110] During the period from July through September

1761, he travelled from Fort Johnson to Niagara and Detroit, sending emissaries to Michilimackinac in an effort to solidify the Covenant Chain relationship with the various western nations.

Given this context, the description of Johnson's journey to the west is particularly revealing of the moral economy.[111] Records provide an exceptionally clear view of attitudes and the dynamics between the British and Aboriginal people. Prior to his departure, Johnson met with the Mohawk at Fort Johnson. Things had not changed much since the earlier meeting with Hendrick in 1753. Encroachments onto Mohawk land (probably the Kayoderossera patent) continued to be the main focus of meetings, although the Six Nations also complained that they were being hemmed in on every side and had scarcely anything left to hunt. Johnson repeated the typical British response, namely, that the governor would prevent all further unauthorized encroachments. He said this even as settlement was advancing in direct contravention of instructions by the Lords of Trade to put an end to it. Indeed, the Crown continued to promise to end settlement throughout this period, a fact expressed in the Royal Proclamation of 1763 by George III. The proclamation stated that a line dividing the colonies from Indian land was to be set roughly at the Allegheny Mountains. No one was to settle or negotiate a land cession except through the Crown.[112]

Exacerbating the problem, Jeffrey Amherst explicitly instructed Johnson on 24 June 1761 to use the same approach with Indians that Amherst wanted to use with encroaching settlers. Those who continued to ignore the dictates of the Crown would find a powerful and heavy hand falling on their heads. Amherst added that the Indians would not be so blind as not to see the protection they enjoyed from the king. He sent instructions to Captain Campbell through Johnson to take possession of all posts in the west as quietly as possible in order to defend and protect the Indians and to keep the entire country subject to the king.[113] Amherst's commands directly contravened promises made to the western allies before and during the war.

Johnson's already complicated situation became even more complicated, and he seems to have capitulated to Amherst's commands. After a brief visit to Canajoharie, Johnson met an Oneida party coming to Fort Johnson to address a murder case and other concerns.[114] He held what appears to have been an impromptu council at which Conoghquieson, speaker for the Oneida, expressed condolences and brought a number of items to Johnson's attention. On the matter of murder, he argued that the killing of a white settler had been balanced by the murder of Oneida people by settlers. He intimated that alcohol had been the cause. Johnson replied that Amherst would not accept this form of justice or the alcohol defence (although Montgomerie had done so in 1730). The Oneida presented this proposition with a belt of black wampum with seven rows and added that their system of justice was a condition of maintaining the Covenant Chain; therefore, not accepting the proposition was tantamount to loosening the Chain. Not surprisingly, the Oneida also complained about settler (German) encroachment, which they promised to handle by giving the settlers a kick and expected the British to do the same. This statement was accompanied by a belt of six rows. They also complained about the inflation of prices for various goods and about Britain's failure to tear down all of the forts in their territory after the war. The forts were being repopulated by British soldiers, again, contrary to the Crown's promises.

The council's proceedings offer a general picture of Crown-Aboriginal relations in the period. The Oneida raised the same issues of betrayal and injustice as had been raised all during Johnson's tenure as Indian agent, as well as from the inception of the Chain. Rather than repeating the typical promises and reciting the typical lines of assuagement, however, Johnson warned the Oneida that a break in the Covenant Chain would be fatal to them. He stated that the encroachments by settlers must be the Oneida's fault, because the king had instructed the governors not to sell any land without his permission, implying that they themselves must have given permission since settlers would not violate the Crown's dictates! He also suggested that, given that there were many traders in the area, prices must be fair. Johnson also shifted the blame for the forts' still standing to the Oneida and claimed that their conflicts with officers must have been due to their drunkenness and the differences between cultures. His tone of impatience is obvious in the record, but he still gave a belt of wampum to legitimate his words.

Johnson's out-of-character behaviour, although consistent with Amherst's commands, did not end with the Oneida. On 17 July of the same year, he received a message concerning a Six Nations belt that had come to the attention of Captain Campbell at Detroit.[115] The belt had been circulating among the Six Nations in an effort to unite Aboriginal people to eliminate the British. Some Mohawk castles allied with them. The belt became a point of contention at each of the council meetings along the way. At Onondaga on 21 July, Johnson warned the Six Nations against having any hand in the rebellion.[116] The Onondaga sachems, like the Oneida, were subjected to his arrogant tone when they complained about Johnson going to Detroit to kindle a new council fire with the western Indians. The sachems rightly argued that, according to the Covenant Chain agreement, theirs was the council fire to which all western nations were supposed to come. But their argument fell on deaf ears. When the Onondaga sachem presented a belt that recorded British promises made before the war, Johnson said that the belt was not necessary, since he had all the promises on record. He then constructed a lame excuse for broken British promises. He blamed Britain's failures on the Six Nations' drunkenness. He treated the fire keepers of the Six Nations in the same manner that he had treated their younger brothers, the Oneida, a few days earlier.

Johnson's Amherst-like behaviour and language, his question-begging sophistry and blame-the-victim attitude, was an almost complete reversal of former modes of communication. He abandoned the use of communicative speech acts in favour of purely strategic ones, bad ones at that. He resorted to question begging, which communicated disdain for his interlocutors, because using the device suggested that he felt his interlocutors were either stupid or too powerless to respond. He used his status to belittle both the Oneida and Onondaga and, in so doing, silence them. Given his former relationship with the two nations, his speech acts not only prevented the Oneida and Onondaga from appealing to the intersubjective world of mutual understanding, they were also aimed at neutralizing that world by making it irrelevant. By refusing to admit the intelligibility and legitimacy of his interlocutors' claims, Johnson also removed them from the intersubjective lifeworld of rational interlocutors, thereby denying them access to the levers of argument and intelligent discourse they had once enjoyed.

One explanation for Johnson's actions is that he had become disappointed in his allies. Their reputation as strong and dignified warriors had become badly tarnished as they became increasingly impoverished. Records describing the events following Johnson's encounters with the Oneida and Onondaga support this theory. At the Onondaga council, the Mississauga, or one of their representatives, promised to meet Johnson at Niagara. On 30 July at Detroit, Johnson told Wabbicommicot, a Chippewa sachem, that the Chippewa (likely part of the same Anishnaabek people as the Mississauga) were the only powerful nation left on the continent.[117] He also expressed admiration for the Wyandot, whom he viewed as the principal leaders among the western nations. He believed that the Chippewa and others would follow their lead.[118]

During the council with the western nations, Johnson's former diplomatic skills and language returned. On 9 September 1761, the Detroit conference opened with the "Wiandots (Wyandots), Saguenays, Ottawa, Chipeweighs, Powtewatamies, Kickapous, Twightwees, Delawares, Shawanese, Mohiccons, Mohocks, Oneidas, and Senecas" (Guy Johnson's spellings). After the condolence ceremonies and an agreement to remove the hatchet, Johnson stated:

> This fire (council fire at Fort Johnson) yields such a friendly warmth that many Nations have since assembled thereto, and daily partake of its influence – I have therefore now brought a brand thereof with me to the place with which I here kindle up a large Council fire made of such Wood as shall burn bright & be inextinguishable, whose kindly Warmth shall be felt in, and shall extend to the most remote Nations, and shall induce all Indians, even from the setting of the Sun to come hither and partake thereof – Gave a Belt of nine Rows.

After purifying the council chambers with a belt of six rows and requesting, with a belt of twelve rows, that they send the circulating war belt to him, Johnson presented the Covenant Chain belt and stated:

> Brethren:
> With this belt In the name of his Britannick Majesty I strengthen and renew the antient Covenant Chain formerly subsisting between us, that it may remain bright and lasting to the latest Ages, earnestly recommending it to you, to do the same, and to hold fast thereby as the only means by which you may expect to become a happy & flourishing people. Gave a belt of the Covenant Chain containing 20 Rows of Wampum.

With a belt of fifteen rows, Johnson extended "His Majesty's intentions of good will in most Equitable terms between his Subjects & all Indians who are willing to enter into alliance." This clear distinction between His Majesty's subjects and Aboriginal allies re-emerged later when he corrected Bradstreet for making certain blunders during a treaty negotiation. Johnson had returned to using communicative speech acts.

A bit of confusion that took place at this treaty council is noteworthy for what it reveals about Johnson's reputation. After Anáiása of the Hurons (Wyandot) received the Covenant Chain belt and performed "the usual ceremonies," Macátepilesis of the Ottawa and all of the confederacy (probably the Three Fires) called the covenant an iron chain with the English and Mohawk: "We have it not in our power to make a Silver Chain, it is you that can make such, therefore, we beg you make it so strong that nothing can break it & you may be assured we will hold fast thereby to the latest Ages."[119] Why Macátepilesis said this is not clear. If earlier interpretations are correct, the Ottawa had conducted a long-standing, albeit intermittent, trade relationship with the English, which, if exclusively trade-oriented, would have constituted an iron chain. They might not have been able to forge a more robust Silver Covenant Chain because, as origin stories tell the tale, it had been initiated by the British in relation to the Five Nations. Perhaps, it was considered improper to forge a silver chain when the right to do so belonged to the Six Nations. Or perhaps they did not understand what elements were needed to forge a silver chain. Wabbicomicott (Chippewa), on behalf of the Ottawa Confederacy, indeed said that they were ignorant of much of what was being talked about but would in time say more. He gave green wampum to dispel darkness and to lead Warraghiyagey through the darkness. He then brought out a pipe for all to smoke, an act intended to bring the nations together. Whatever the problem was, it was not viewed as insurmountable because Johnson could be trusted to work the matter out. The Chippewa trusted him to interpret the silver version of the Chain for them and to ensure that all proper procedures were followed.

Johnson's council with the western nations illustrates how the parties established an atmosphere in which communicative actions were used once again to ensure proper understanding. Throughout these exchanges, Johnson acted and spoke as he once had with the Six Nations. Johnson could have used Macátepilesis's and Wabbicomicott's admissions more to his advantage. He could have exploited them as opportunities to demonstrate his noblesse oblige. Or he could have used their admission to establish superiority over his interlocutors, as he had done earlier. The records, however, indicate only that he left Detroit on 18 September, explaining little else until he arrived back at Fort Johnson. What follows provides a better picture of his attitude.

Recall that the Six Nations had insisted on having Johnson reinstated to Indian affairs, because he had big ears and other admirable communicative qualities.[120] They had also reported a French Indian who had taken an intelligence report about Fort Johnson to the governor of Canada. They urged the governors and commissioners collected at Albany to arrange affairs quickly, because Johnson's life was, as a consequence, in danger. They said that the French "will take more than Ordinary pains either to kill him [Johnson] or take him prisoner, upon Account of his great Interest among us, and being also one of the Five Nations (Collo Johnson is one of their sachems)."[121] Johnson was more to the Six Nations than a go-between or honest friend: he had earned recognition as a sachem, one who could speak for the Six Nations, even before marrying Brant. By 1761, his reputation had spread far and wide, but the Six Nations were broken, impoverished, and diminished militarily. This was not yet the case with the western nations.

Although the Six Nations had assigned Tanaghrisson as a half king to oversee the confederacy, the nations acted independently. When Johnson lit a separate council fire at Detroit, he acknowledged this independence. Indeed, Richard White's account of French operations in the Ohio, which is supported by Francis Jennings, shows that, by the 1750s, Six Nations' jurisdiction over the Ohio was in name only.[122] When Johnson ignored the Onondaga's claims and established a separate council fire at Detroit, he knew full well that political and military reality demanded such action. His impatience with the Oneida and Onondaga, then, is even more understandable, given the gravity of the situation he was about to face at Detroit. He knew that the Six Nations had often appealed to the British for protection from these Far Indians, since he had heard many of their requests and complaints. He also knew that he did not have the same influence or authority among the western nations as he did with the Six Nations and River Indians. In fact, before his 1764 trip to Niagara, he wrote to Colonel Bradstreet, requesting that he be allowed to take up to thirty soldiers from various garrisons for a show of force and to protect him, since there were a number of Delaware and Mississauga who intended to kill him.[123] Johnson had received constant intelligence reports of attacks on British soldiers and forts; for example, Jean Baptiste de Couagne from Niagara had sent some in 1763 concerning the loss of forty and fifty troops at a time.[124] Thus, while he could rely to some extent on his reputation, the Six Nations' influence, and the western nations' familiarity with the Covenant Chain, it would have been foolish to rely heavily on them. In addition, his reputation had made him a target to his enemies.

The western nations were also in a state of shock. They were bewildered and angry that the French had surrendered to the British and ceded their lands. Indeed, independent of Pontiac, a war belt had been circulating among the Seneca, Delaware, Shawnee, and Miami until it was intercepted by the British commander at Fort Miami, Ensign Holmes.[125] In a series of correspondence between General Amherst, Major Gladwin, and William Johnson, Amherst received intelligence reports from Gladwin about this belt, forwarded the belt and messages (with some embellishments) to Johnson, and instructed him to do what was necessary to put a stop to such treacherous behaviour: "[A]nd for Shewing the Indians the Contemptible Figure they must make in our Eyes, by violating the least Provocation on our Side; I mention the Contemptible Figure, as it certainly is not in their Power to Effect any thing of Consequence against Us."[126]

Owing to his bravado and blindness to the injustices of settler encroachment, Amherst asserted that the British had had nothing to do with provoking the war and that the western nations needed to be taught a lesson in gratitude. He was not alone. His subaltern, Ensign Holmes, thought he had prevented war from breaking out by intercepting the belt, which he believed signified only a minor complaint. He had, however, only caught a glimpse of the extent to which discontent in Ohio was based on a long history of abuse, false promises, and mistrust. And as both he and Amherst would soon find out, the western nations' military force was far from insignificant. That spring, Pontiac, utilizing the religious fervour that the prophet Neolin had ignited among the tribes, mobilized the warriors of the Ohio to attack the British and laid siege to British forts, including Fort Detroit. Although unable to take Detroit, Pitt, and Niagara, they successfully took the rest of the forts and undermined British confidence in their ability to control the region. Amherst's use of infamous germ warfare tactics – using smallpox-infected blankets against Pontiac – indicates just how serious the Pontiac threat had become.[127]

With this setting, Johnson's actual relationship with Amherst becomes more apparent, along with the reasons for his change of attitude toward the Oneida and Onondaga. On 10 November 1763, Johnson wrote a memorandum for his own private use. In it, he considered strategies, such as asking Indians, possibly from Canada, to help rangers defend the Mohawk River inhabitants, who would otherwise likely be destroyed by Pontiac and other raiding parties. He told himself that these Indians, who were yet Britain's friends, should be "kindly used and make it their Interest to continue so, untill we are better able to do without them." Believing that Pennsylvania and New Jersey could crush the Delaware in their region, he turned his attention to using the southern nations to battle northern ones and believed it would not be difficult to engage them because of their long-standing enmity. He mused that not more than a third of the British force should be made up of them, however, until they were well engaged. The value of engaging the southern Indians was that "it will not only prevent us from being surprised, but enable us to find our Enemys Haunts, & places of retreat, their Magazines &ca. and certainly intimidate the Enemy as much as it will animate our Troops whom ye frequent losses Sustained by them, begin to despair of Success anst. Such an Enemy in the Woods. wh. Should by all means be removed."[128] Johnson was obviously aware of the continued importance of courting Aboriginal allies and how he could gain their support by appealing to their long-standing rivalries. He was also quite aware of declining soldier morale, since he knew that the British soldiers were no match for the warriors in forest warfare. The declining morale of the troops, in fact, became a major issue. In the memorandum, he considers various ways to reinforce officers' authority over the troops.[129] Jealousy, anger, and the need for revenge were quite clearly forces that had to be acknowledged and could be exploited in Johnson's mind.

To Johnson, the trip to the west was to the domain of a potentially hostile people who, were they to unite, could still conceivably push the British back over the Alleghenies, if not farther. Although he did not mention the rise of a new Aboriginal religious movement, he must have been aware of the emergence of prophets such as Neolin, men who were attempting to rally the Algonquian nations to return to traditional ways and adding a religious motivation for eliminating the British.[130] Therefore, when he departed for the west in 1764, he was well aware of the moral economy operating in the western nations.

And so too were the Lords of Trade, it would seem. Indeed, it is more than plausible that they were aware of the difficulty of Johnson's task and that Amherst both misunderstood the situation and had adopted the wrong attitude. They recalled Amherst to England and condemned him for his Indian policies, as reported by George Croghan.[131] In his place, they sent General Thomas Gage. We can now begin to see how Johnson's former behaviour had largely been due to the suppression of his actual beliefs and attitudes.

With the new commander, confused and confusing, irrational and impulsive communications give way to clear and carefully explained communications. The tone and, indeed, substance of the correspondence between Indian agent and commander-in-chief changed dramatically, and this change was especially evident in Gage's reactions to a report from Colonel Bradstreet that described a treaty he had negotiated at Detroit. Gage wrote to Johnson, enclosing a copy of Bradstreet's report. In it, Bradstreet claimed that, upon hearing of his march, the Indians of the area had recalled their warriors and requested a council at Detroit. At the council, they agreed to several articles or conditions: a return of prisoners, a peace that was to last forever, the renunciation of any claims to the British forts, and the transfer to the English of all the land around them as far as a canon ball could be shot.[132]

If Amherst had still been in command, he would have likely read Bradstreet's report with relish. Gage, however, was a different man. He sent Bradstreet's report to Johnson in a not-so-well-hidden fit of anger. Gage, somewhat cautiously, wrote that he was concerned that most of Bradstreet's signatories, with the exception of a few Huron and Chippewa deputies, were those who had taken up arms against the English on 15 August.[133] On 2 September, he directly questioned the legitimacy of the treaty since Johnson, as sole superintendent of Indian affairs, was the only agent through whom the Crown was to treat with Aboriginal groups.[134] He expressed incredulity at Bradstreet's belief that he was empowered to dictate articles of peace. To Gage, it was "derogatory to the Honour and Reputations of his Majesty's Arms amongst the Indian Nations and is the basis of future massacres." In an almost identical letter, written on the same date because he believed that the first had somehow been stopped, Gage more forcefully condemned Bradstreet for his presumption and asserted that he would annul the treaty.[135] Just two days later, still not having heard from Johnson, Gage once again wrote to cast further doubt on the Bradstreet treaty and on Bradstreet.[136] He argued that if the Aboriginal groups had genuinely treated for peace, they would have been at Niagara, where Johnson was located, and they would have provided belts, not just strings, although he deferred to Johnson's opinion on the matter. He went even further and cast doubt on Bradstreet's competence in military intelligence, since it was likely that the warriors had come to watch the movement of troops, rather than treat for peace. Gage cited evidence to back his criticism. On 14 and 22 September, the nations represented at the Bradstreet treaty had killed English soldiers and settlers and continued to do so. Moreover, the tribal deputies who were at the treaty did not have the "appearance of Authority or with knowledge and consent of the Nations."[137] Gage then repeated that he would not ratify or confirm the treaty. Indeed, he was concerned that he could not get his orders to Bradstreet to cease this activity soon enough.

On 28 August 1764, Bradstreet wrote to Johnson, stating how effectively Bradstreet and Major Gladwin had communicated their ability to cut up the "Outawas, Petewatamas Chippewas" and that he expected that this had forced the Indians to comply with all demands, including giving up Pontiac

("Bondeac").[138] Bradstreet had even sent Captain Morris to the Illinois and Mississippi country to make the Indians there take an oath. On 7-10 September, he held a congress with the western nations at which they accepted, he claimed, subjecthood to George III, the king's sovereignty over all their lands, and the designation "children."[139]

Johnson's response to Bradstreet's treaty was a series of reproaches. He took particular aim at Bradstreet's claim in the same letter that the Indians had agreed to the following statement:

> By The power to us given by the Nations we represent, we do in their Name together with our selves most gratefully accept the terms above Granted, and we do most Solemnly bind ourselves and them to the true performance of each Article in every respect, In Witness whereof we have hereunto Affixed the Arms of the Nations we represent at Detroit this Seventh Day of September One Thousand and Seven Hundred and Sixty Four and in the reign of our Sovereign Lord George the third, King of Great Britain, France and Ireland &ca. &ca.[140]

Johnson wrote to Gage:

> Altho the words of the late Treaty may at first appear extraordinary, yet, I am not at a loss to Acct. for them, as I know it has been verry customary for many People to Insinuate that the Indians call themselves Subjects, altho I am thoroughly convinced they were never so called, nor would they approve of it. – tis true that when a Nation find themselves pushed, their Alliances broken, and themselves tired of War, they are verry apt to say many civil things, and make any Submissions which are not agreable to their intentions, but are said meerly to please those with whom they transact Affairs as they know we cannot enforce the observance of them. but you may be assured that none of the Six Nations, Western Indians &ca. ever declared themselves to be Subjects, or will ever consider themselves in that light whilst they have any Men or open Country to retire to, the very Idea of Subjection would fill them with horror. – Indeed I have been Just looking into the Indian Records, where I find the Minutes of 1751 that those who made ye. Entry Say that Nine different Nations acknowledged themselves to be his Majesty's Subjects, altho I sat at that conference, made entrys of all the Transactions, in which there was not a word mentioned, which could imply Subjection, however, these matters (notwithstanding all I have from time to time said on that Subject) seem not to be well known at home, and therefore, it may prove to be of dangerous consequence to persuade them that the Indians have agreed to things which (had they even assented to) is so repugnant to their Principles that the attempting to enforce it, must lay the foundation of greater Calamities than has yet been experienced in

this Country, – it is necessary to observe that no Nation of Indians have any word which can express, or convey the Idea of Subjection, they often say, "we acknowledge the Great King our Father, we hold him fast by the hand, and we shall do wt. he desires" many such like words of course, for which our People too readily adopt & insert a Word verry different in signification, and never intended by the Indians without explaining to them what is meant by Subjection. – Imagine to yourself Sir, how impossible it is to reduce a People to Subjection, who consider themselves independent thereof both by nature & Situation, who can be governed by no Laws, and have no other Tyes amongst themselves but inclination, and suppose that it is explained to them that they shall be governed by the Laws Liable to the punishments of High Treason, Murder, Robbery and the pains and penaltys on Actions for property of Debt, then see how it will be relished, and whether they will agree to it, for without the Explanation, the Indians must be strangers to the Word, & ignorant of the breach of it.[141]

Johnson wrote not principally to undermine Bradstreet's authority but to expose his lack of understanding of Aboriginal culture. He did not say that Bradstreet ought to have sent the representatives to him (Johnson), although he could have; rather, he corrected the assertions and underlying assumptions in Bradstreet's statement. Owing to Gage's already well-articulated anger at Bradstreet, Johnson likely did not need to communicate anything of prescriptive intent. He did, however, intimate that Bradstreet had endangered the Crown's interests and had potentially undermined its ability to maintain peace with the western nations.

To demonstrate Bradstreet's lack of understanding, Johnson took the opportunity to elaborate on what he considered to be the Aboriginal personality and culture. He used this and his history with them to paint a picture of a people who deeply valued freedom, so much so that their language contained no words for *subjection*. He could have, as many, including Amherst, did, described Aboriginal people as ignorant savages intellectually incapable of understanding Bradstreet's language. Instead, his explanation conveyed his belief that Crown agents had to understand and express respect for the underlying value systems and worldviews of Aboriginal people if treaty negotiations were to have a chance of being successful. He understood how important it was for agents to appreciate these systems and to communicate their understanding to their Aboriginal interlocutors.

After rejecting Bradstreet's claim as inauthentic, Johnson repeated his concern about the language of the treaty to Colonel Bouquet in a letter dated 6 December 1764:

I fear for the Consequences of the Words, *Subjection* And *Dominion* said to be Acknowledged by the Ottawas and Chipiweighs, they have no words to

Express any thing like either; so that Whenever they discover it, then Jealousy and Resentment must be Renewed, for my part I should rather covet to bring them to terms, which I had Reason to Expect they would keep, than such as they have an Invinceable Aversion to the thoughts of, And which must only tend to impose on those who are Ignorant of the State & Disposition of the Western Indians, or indeed of the Northern Indians in General.[142]

The same criticisms were communicated to Lieutenant Governor Colden in an attempt to prevent an even worse war from erupting.[143]

Johnson knew immediately that Bradstreet's treaty report was inauthentic, a misrepresentation of what had actually been said or agreed to, because he understood certain central aspects of the western nations' lifeworld. By implication, he knew that whatever intersubjective world had been established at the Bradstreet treaty, it was not one built upon communicative speech acts but rather on strategic speech acts. The western nations, since they continued to attack soldiers and settlers, were likely attempting to provoke Bradstreet into making an aggressive move so that the other nations would have reason to unite against the British. The difference in language between Bradstreet's and Johnson's treaty records reveal just how differently Aboriginal people dealt with those who had a reputation for committing themselves to developing a good understanding versus those who did not. The different outcomes of the two treaty negotiations indicate just how significant the differences were.

Bradstreet's treaty actually threatened to undermine Johnson's work and the prospects of a general peace. Johnson expressed as much in a letter to Gage, in which he reaffirmed Gage's conclusion.[144] After expressing concern over the absence of belts and the fact that the number of deputies had been too few to count as a treaty council, Johnson predicted that the Aboriginal signatories would not act as Bradstreet predicted. Johnson predicted that the western nations would claim that the prisoners they had agreed to return were with distant tribes and that returning them before winter would be impossible. He also predicted that, were Bradstreet to try to enforce the treaty articles and march to Sandusky to meet with Pontiac, he would be hindered severely by the onslaught of winter (which the warriors understood) and would discover that Pontiac was not there. In other words, he claimed that Bradstreet had been manipulated, possibly to lure the British into a vulnerable position. Johnson's correspondence with Gage offers one of the clearest indications that key Crown agents were keenly aware of the need to establish a shared lifeworld based on communicative acts in which the force of the moral economy was recognized.

In another letter, dated 16 September, Gage informed Johnson that he had given Bradstreet orders "to invite the Deputys of the Tribes who were not at Niagara to come to You & ratify their Peace. And that they would at the same Time lay before you all their Grievances and tell you plainly, the true Causes of their Complaints against Us, and that every Thing which was just and reasonable should be remedied."[145] The order was a grave reprimand to Bradstreet. Gage did not recognize any of the Detroit treaties or the terms that Bradstreet had arranged. At best, he recognized them as preliminaries to a genuine treaty negotiation. He also made clear that he had sent invitations with belts to these tribes through proper persons. In doing so, he not only reprimanded Bradstreet, he sent a clear message to Aboriginal people that he was well aware of their manipulations. He also made it clear that he and the superintendent of Indian affairs would not adopt an Amherst-like approach. By commanding Bradstreet to tell the western nations that Johnson would listen to their complaints, rather than threatening them with annihilation, Gage used the device of public reprimand to re-engage Aboriginal people in communicative actions.

As Gage and Johnson worked toward a peace with Pontiac, blunders by their colleagues and subalterns continued, all of which involved mishandling of the moral economy. Another report, written by Captain Montgomery on 8 November 1764, was ignored for reasons outlined by Johnson: "As I was pretty well convinced the whole of it proceeded from a Mistake, and a want of due knowledge either of the Situation, Interests, or Manners of the Indians, & this often occasions us to commit to Writeing not only Sentences but Sometimes whole Speeches different from the Meaning of the Indians, for Instance the late Treaty at Detroit, & that wth the Sandusky Wyendats."[146]

In his efforts to correct his colleagues, Johnson also attempted to attune them to Aboriginal perspectives and value systems. Following this initial exchange, Bouquet began a series of treaty councils in October, refusing to treat with any nations who did not comply with the Detroit and Niagara treaty agreements.[147] He demanded that all prisoners be delivered up and that the two war chiefs of the Delaware whom Bouquet considered the instigators (Squash Cutter and Attiatawitsera) also be delivered. He used shame to motivate the nations to comply. But after all was said and done, Johnson was none too relieved, as he indicated in his correspondence with Gage. He advised Gage that the Indians were interpreting the treaties as trifles and explained that this attitude was a consequence of Bradstreet's and others' blunders.[148]

In the same set of communications, Johnson took the opportunity to explain another mistake; this time it had to do with Bradstreet's failure to take his allies' advice. At one point, Seneca allies had wanted to attack the enemy at Sandusky, but Bradstreet had refused to allow it. He had also prevented the Seneca from going to battle against ten hostile Shawnee, even after they had danced the war dance in preparation. According to Johnson,

Bradstreet's refusal violated the principles of the intersubjective normative world established by the war dance. Curiously, Johnson does not even name Bradstreet in this letter, even though he had met with Bradstreet earlier and explained why he thought his actions during the campaign had been entirely wrongheaded. But Johnson's intent was clear. He wanted Gage to understand that the western nations would not respect the treaties, including those made by Bouquet, because they saw the English as weak, duplicitous, and cowardly. Owing to his own experience convincing Six Nations warriors to enter the battle at Crown Point by dancing the war dance with them, he also respected the Seneca's anger at Bradstreet for not allowing commitments made through the war dance to be carried out.

Johnson then took the opportunity to bring out more of the complexities of Indian affairs in his communications with Gage. By suggesting, if not insisting, that political, social, and conceptual value systems had to be understood to be competent in Indian affairs, Johnson was attempting to convince Gage that the Crown had to gain the respect of Aboriginal groups to bring about a peace, just as the Lords of Trade had expressed earlier. They had to demonstrate respect for their interlocutors' values of freedom and autonomy and to recognize the importance of their reputation as warriors, as it pertained to the intersubjective world.

Conclusion

Placed within a larger context, Johnson's earlier ill treatment of the Oneida and Onondaga reveals the deep ties between reputation and the moral economy. Exchanges among Crown officials about commands, reprimands, and policy reveal the important role that reputation, the moral economy, and the shared lifeworld played, even at the highest levels of Crown authority. Whereas a cursory reading of the records from 1761-67 might leave the impression that Johnson was being hypocritical in giving advice to his colleagues and superiors that he himself had not followed, a closer examination brings to light a portrait of a man who saw the necessity of recognizing and respecting warrior values and who genuinely respected these values. By the 1760s, as Johnson reports, many of the Six Nations had lost the warrior culture and rituals of crowing over the fallen. War, alcohol, and disease had taken their toll.[149] Warriors had become unruly, and sachems could no longer control them through the levers of honour and shame. It would not have been out of character for Johnson to take this decline in the honour of the warriors as an affront to his own moral sensibilities. His behaviour at Onondaga was likely precipitated not only by his focus on the powerful western nations but also by his disappointment in and possible disenchantment with his once dignified and powerful brothers. His speech acts likely reflected his sense of disenchantment with the Onondaga and Oneida as much as they reflected pressure from his superiors and other fronts. The decline in the Six Nations' warrior culture made the development and maintenance of a good understanding between the two peoples increasingly difficult because Johnson could no longer rely on the operation of the once robust moral economy in negotiations and treaty relations.

The Crown's reputation was critical to Aboriginal people, but Johnson's responses to the Onondaga and Oneida indicate that Aboriginal peoples' reputation was also important to the British. The moral economy was based on mutual respect for warrior values, which had as much to do with honour, dignity, independence (self-sufficiency), courage, and the like as it did with compassion and concern. It had as much to do with values held dear by hard-nosed negotiators and battle-hardened warriors as it did with those that reflected familial ties. These were the values that grounded Johnson's respect for Aboriginal people and that grounded Aboriginal peoples' respect for key Crown agents. They were the values that gave substance to the shared normative lifeworld.

The historical record reveals that members of the Chain viewed people with good reputations as resources in their efforts to defend freedom, autonomy, unity, and compassion. When these resources were destroyed by alcohol, disease, social upheaval, and betrayal, members could no longer rely on the internal (subjective) and intersubjective systems of governance to protect their relationship. The intersubjective world turned into one of disappointment, anger, and mistrust. It became a burden and a threat to both the subjective and objective normative worlds.

A continuing narrative of key agents could include Guy Johnson (Uraghquadirha, "Rays of the Sun"), Daniel Claus, T.G. Anderson, and others. This part of the narrative would indicate how the historical moral economy was held in high esteem, even as it unravelled. I mention this here to highlight the centrality of key agents and the importance of moral agency in maintaining the Covenant Chain relationship and its underlying ethic. The sensibilities, concepts, and principles governing a moral economy can remain in the imaginations and lives of people, even when the political and economic realities in which a moral economy is situated change. A moral economy can be recognized and practised even when intercultural sensibilities have shifted and one cultural group has come to dominate the other. As previously intimated, the significance of the Chain's moral economy and the role of key agents declined as bureaucratic procedure replaced them.

This chapter shows how moral agency enabled the moral economy to govern the early treaty relationship. A discourse ethics framework has been employed to bring certain features of the moral economy to light, most notably the procedural principles expressed in communicative speech acts. The focus on proper persons and moral agency discloses the central role that reputation played in enabling the procedural principles to operate. This procedural description, however, does not entirely explain how the ethic worked and does not exhaust the significance of reputation in the moral economy. I have noted references to underground chains and indicated that religious values pointed to some underlying force. Something in the complex array of historical, communal-identity, and high-context language use shaped that force and helped establish a common ground. This development, as Chapter 4 explains, proves problematic.

4

The Transcultural, Transhistorical Ethic of the Covenant Chain

The Covenant Chain's structure and function articulated and advanced a moral economy that operated as an ethic; that is, it provided a set of moral values and principles that guided speech and action, operating though key agents such as William Johnson. Conflicts within the moral economy were the most obvious modes of interaction that moved parties to recognize a common ground. The moral economy emerged from the evolutionary process of the complexification of the Covenant Chain; it was embedded in the development of economic, military, and political relations. Within this process, in which interlocutors used communicative actions to reach mutual understanding and agreement, the ethic guided both speech acts and expectations, judgments, and the way the parties responded, especially when the terms of the treaty agreement were broken. In this way, the common ground to which members appealed involved an intersubjective lifeworld.

The ethic clearly had some transcultural legitimacy, but I have not yet shown that it was not merely idiosyncratic, a cobbled together set of moral sensibilities, ideas, and principles. I have not shown that it was a universal ethic. A central concern of this book is to counter various forms of reductionism and skepticism by addressing this issue. Proving universality is perhaps too ambitious a goal in a study so focused on a historically situated ethic. Yet, given that I hope to establish the relevance of this ethic to contemporary debates concerning Aboriginal peoples, it is necessary at least to show that it is not of a sort that is necessarily confined to the particular historical Covenant Chain relationship. Rather than arguing that the ethic is universal, this chapter focuses on certain aspects of the ethic that compelled the Chain's members to seek increasingly wider grounds of legitimacy. It advances a weaker formulation of universality and shifts the burden of proof onto the detractor. When I use terms such as *universal* or *universalizable*, then, I do not mean to infer an *a priori* universality in the Kantian sense of being truly independent of empirical evidence.

Universalizability and Discourse Ethics

The aim of council fires – to reach agreement through dialogue and mutual understanding – fits within the framework of discourse ethics.[1] The core principle of discourse ethics is that "a norm can command the rationally motivated assent of all only if everyone involved or potentially affected has taken into consideration the consequences and side effects of the general observance of the norm for himself and others."[2] Council meeting protocols satisfy this criterion because they presupposed participation by rational interlocutors while requiring that all present be able to speak and take responsibility for understanding the consequences of decisions for others. "Opening eyes," "having big ears," and the practice of repeating propositions were formalized expressions of this requirement. The protocols of the Covenant Chain drew members away from their culturally relativistic positions so they could reach agreement. Procedural principles precluded either side's idiosyncratic and cultural premises from dominating and controlling the treaty process, however much both sides might have tried to dominate. To the extent that council meetings were governed by the moral economy, then, they were governed by a procedural ethic. As rational agents, members recognized that, even as individuals striving to satisfy their interests, they were accountable to others by virtue of their membership in the institutional arrangement. None were recognized as commanders who dictated right and wrong; rather, they were recognized as negotiators who would enter into a dialogue to form agreements about what would count as right and wrong.[3] In this respect, the ethic was coherent and consistent with discourse ethics.

The Chain's ethic evolved over the course of the historical relationship; it was historically emergent. Habermas explains how an ethic can be both historically emergent and committed to universalizability. Although he develops this idea in a number of works, I concentrate on the two-volume *Theory of Communicative Action* and *Moral Consciousness and Communicative Action*.[4] His work on how language-based communities developed into moral communities parallels my work on language use in the intercultural community of the Covenant Chain. Accordingly, his explanation offers a framework in which to explain how the emergence of a historically situated ethic can be connected to universalizing forces.

Habermas describes how rational language users come to develop three spheres of legitimacy: objective truth, normative rightness, and subjective truthfulness.[5] He stipulates that criteria of legitimacy can be recognized only by those committed to being open to criticism when making claims. He contrasts those capable of making validity claims that can be criticized with those of savage mind, people who cannot allow for distinctions between their worldview and the objective world, against which beliefs about the nature of reality or claims about right and wrong can be compared and evaluated.[6] Only a mind that has evolved beyond the savage stage is capable of making criticizable (defeasible) validity claims on matters regarding right and wrong or of judging whether a claim is legitimate. The dialogical framework of the Covenant Chain clearly satisfies this condition.

One of the first tasks Habermas sets for himself is to show that language develops in communicative exchanges between agents; it does not develop independently in agents, who then use language to communicate.[7] That is, language develops only because language users are social beings who need to communicate for various reasons. Individuals, insofar as they can treat themselves as individuals and value themselves as individuals, are first and foremost members of a group who develop their sense of individuality through communicative engagement within the group. One's sense of individuation (of being an individual) depends on language development, which, in turn, depends on living in a social context. Furthermore, language use presupposes a triangulation of conditions: an individual subject (the subjective world); an interlocutor (an intersubjective world); and an objective world that exists independent of these subjects. The objective world is that about which interlocutors speak (e.g., the food to be gathered, the predators to avoid, the materials to gather for shelter). Thus, once people come to use language to communicate, a complex triangulated world has already been established. The ability to use criticizable validity claims arises when speakers realize (explicitly or implicitly) that this triangulated world exists. The core of Habermas's framework, then, is the idea that interlocutors, in order to communicate, must not take their own subjective worlds to be the totality; they must accept that others have a subjective world and that both worlds are subject to correction by reference to an objective world.

The Crown-Aboriginal relationship, even before it took on the form of the Covenant Chain, was a triangulated world because the communicative demands of early trade and military alliances demanded both sides to be open to correction and criticism (e.g., over the fairness of transactions and the reliability of military allies). When members argued over matters of fairness, justice, loyalty, and the like, they assumed a triangulation of conditions, which enabled the relationship to be governed by ideas and principles to which both sides could appeal. Despite their cultural differences, the British and their Aboriginal allies, like people just learning to communicate, had to have developed a reliance on an intersubjective and objective world. They would have had to overcome the tendency to rely exclusively on their subjective (or even culturally confined) worlds and instead adopt criticizable validity claims as the mode of communication, even if only to get what they wanted from the other side. However culturally diverse the Chain's interlocutors were at the start of their relationship, their use of and response to criticizable validity claims (e.g., relative fairness or reliability) implies that the development of their triangulated world involved an objective normative world. However inchoate it was, they would have shared a sense of how the normative world (expressed in the moral economy) was constituted with respect to beliefs about human nature and the potential of human relationships (the shared lifeworld). They would have developed shared values, ways of perceiving each other, and ways to detect a sincere adherence to or violation of principles. Belonging to the Covenant Chain therefore demanded a suspension of idiosyncratic and culturally relativistic stances.

The triangulated world of the Covenant Chain relationship was, to some extent, governed by principles conceived as constituting an objective normative order to which all who considered themselves members of the Chain were bound. What might have begun as a mere intersubjectively agreed upon normative order (it might have been temporary and negotiable) eventually became an objective normative order entrenched institutionally in protocols, bodies of law, and codified agreements (e.g., land titles). Although members, in some sense, created the objective world, that world stood in relation to the subjective and intersubjective worlds as an independent world, against which subjective and intersubjective judgments and actions could be measured and evaluated. When engaged in arguments to justify themselves to each other, members appealed to this objective normative world. In this way, members were subject to the force of logic.

The idea of a triangulated world helps explain the Chain's unifying function. In the process of socialization, initial attempts at negotiation between disparate cultures may initially produce a sense of alienness; over time, however, negotiations produce a sense of a common world (e.g., common interests, a common enemy, common experiences) as interlocutors learn how to communicate. Once they learn how to use criticizable validity claims that enable them to reach mutually satisfying agreements, they produce a sense of a common normative order. In the learning process, each side appeals to ideas and norms contained in the other's worldview (much like Richard White describes) to bring about agreement. Even in the attempt to infuse their own cultural expectations into the relationship, the process of defining ideas and norms demands that interlocutors learn to subject their claims, values, and perspectives to the scrutiny of their interlocutors. In doing so, they subject their values and perspectives to a comparative procedure, according to which their interlocutors either accept or reject the claims being made, based on the values and perspectives they hold. If the process is successful, in the sense that interlocutors are able to reach agreements, a common standard and set of values are produced and an objective world of ideas and norms emerges in the form of a shared normative lifeworld.[8] This world can then be used to bridge other culturally bound expectations, enabling both sides to become critically reflective with respect to their separate and culturally bound conceptions of rightness, fairness, justice, honour, and so on. An ethic, insofar as it is conceived as a set of standards to which all sides in a debate can appeal, is possible, therefore, only because interlocutors assign it the status of an objective world. All interlocutors who appeal to the objective world treat one another as insiders united under a common normative ground.

The evolutionary character of the Chain's ethic is anticipated in the discourse ethics framework. Habermas utilizes Lawrence Kohlberg's developmental psychology to claim that all civilized cultures have proceeded through stages of moral development.[9] When people become cognitively capable, they recognize the validity of certain rational thought processes (procedural rationality) as a means for reaching agreements over ethical issues. This claim, Habermas argues, is based on a study of how rational beings developed into language-using societies. His developmental approach takes the analysis of language use all the way back to its evolution from gestures and grunts to articulated symbols.[10] I do not, and of course cannot, draw a strict parallel to explain the origins of the Chain's ethical features. I must begin at the point where the interlocutors came together as trading partners and were already members of societies with sophisticated language systems. Initial communications between the two sides, however, would indeed have been little more than gestures and grunts until they developed translation skills. Although the parallel is not perfect, it can be argued that the language of the Covenant Chain's intercultural relationship underwent a process of development similar to that of a single cultural group developing its own language. As the British and Aboriginal people learned to communicate to make deals and resolve disputes, the conditions necessary for a discourse ethic also were established.

My use of the term *evolution* to describe the transformative process of development in the Covenant Chain, then, includes the members' coming to acquire a linguistic capacity to communicate and, consequently, a procedural rationality to handle conflicts. This capacity enabled them to develop adaptive responses to conflict in a learning process that moved them to discover common ground for maintaining the relationship. I use the term *discover* because the interlocutors were not forced to accept a common ground, an objective world or set of values. As Habermas describes such a community: "In this way the necessary presuppositions of communicative action constitute an infrastructure of possible communication constructed around a moral core – the idea of unforced intersubjectivity."[11] However much interlocutors might try to force, cajole, and manipulate the other to accept their cultural norms, they feel the force of having to act in accordance with this moral core once they try to communicate with each other to justify their positions. Interlocutors come to see that they must allow their arguments to move freely toward establishing common points of reference if their agreements are going to be viewed as legitimate.

The developmental framework also helps explain how radically different cultural groups who stay the course of developing and maintaining a complex relationship can transform into an intercultural moral community. The first point Habermas makes is that two people engaged with each other, for whatever reason (to fight, hunt, or mate), use gestures to send a message, and these messages call for an adaptive response from the other.[12] Such gestures are oriented toward reaching mutual understanding and success, as determined by whatever desire or motivation that moves the interlocutors to gesture.[13] In other words, for gestures to work, there must be a common understanding between the one who gestures and the one to whom the gesture is directed. Both must understand what a gesture means with respect to the agent's intention and what actions and consequences understanding it entails. Hence, even at this primitive level of communication, the shared lifeworld that interlocutors form enables their gestures and grunts to *represent* objects, feelings, intentions, and so on in a way that is representative for all in the communicative community. Habermas spends considerable time explaining how gestures become symbols and how the use of symbols leads interlocutors to establish rules to ensure that the symbols have universal meaning and that the rules are subject to evaluation. Of special significance to the analysis of the ethic of the Covenant Chain is that certain symbolic expressions eventually become thematically criticizable and subject to criteria of validity.[14] When symbolic representations become criticizable, the inter-subjective validity of the use of representations is determined by how well people's individually and subjectively formulated understandings and statements conform to an objective world.

Habermas makes similar claims for the use of normative language. In cases of war, for instance, interlocutors develop expectations (symbolized by terms such as *loyalty, courage,* and *trustworthiness*) that they apply to all community members. Interlocutors must not only know what the symbols mean, in order to use them, they must also share a common understanding of what it means to succeed, fail, be loyal, and so on in regard to the expectations that the symbols represent.[15] These symbols, then, are expressions of a group will in the sense that they express a common endeavour.[16] The ability to use normative symbols (language) implies a communal understanding of meanings and expectations. These expectations orient how people feel toward one another and how those feelings direct behaviour. The feelings, in turn, contribute to the further development of a sense of community, which unites those who use the language in a way that those who are unable to use the language cannot be united, namely, according to a shared lifeworld.

It is worth mentioning that people who have developed only a minimal set of symbols to communicate – where symbols emerge, for instance, as a result of fighting alongside each other or in response to acts of good will, sacrifice, and the like – can achieve a stronger sense of unity and solidarity than those who have developed extremely sophisticated communicative symbols (e.g., scholars) and a shared sense of an objective world (e.g., of a political and economic system). Their objective normative world can be more effective in governing relations in an intercultural community than in a single-culture community. Depending on circumstances, cultural differences can actually be relatively minor impediments to the development of an intercultural ethic.

Applying the discourse ethics framework to the Covenant Chain, particularly its procedureal elements, draws out the features of its ethic that transcended cultural boundaries. Although the Chain's protocols and symbols were Aboriginal in origin, the underlying procedural expectations arose whenever people, of both cultures, found sufficient reasons to form agreements. While this focus on procedure shows that the Covenant Chain's ethic was aimed at universalizability – at drawing people from their individual, culturally relative stances – it also raises problems.

Procedural versus Substantive Ethics

Although it appears that the Covenant Chain's ethic satisfied at least one condition of universalizability – that is, it was not culturally bound – it is also clear that two substantive elements were central to the ethic: a common ground or good (as expressed by unity, freedom, and autonomy) and a set of virtues. This raises two problems. First, a plethora of critics (including Nietzsche) have characterized moral goods or substantive moral values as being ineluctably culturally biased and historically bound. Since they are not universalizable, the substantive elements of the Chain's ethic are incompatible with its procedural aspects. To the extent that appeals to a common ground were fundamental to the Chain's ethic, and to the extent that the virtues of key agents (as proper persons who were sincere, compassionate, and the like) were indispensable to its operation, the structure and function of that ethic was idiosyncratic, incoherent, and historically bound. Indeed, Habermas's reason for developing a procedural ethic is to obviate the need to appeal to substantive goods or virtues as the grounds for ethics (morality). Insofar as a fundamental function of the Chain's ethic was grounded in a common good and depended on the exercise of certain virtues, critics can claim that the Chain's ethic was cobbled together in an ad hoc manner and workable only under the peculiar intercultural and historical conditions of the period.

It is tempting, then, to focus on the procedural aspects of the Covenant Chain rather than its substantive elements to salvage the attempt at universalizing its ethic. Yet, as the description and analysis of the Chain's ethic discloses, the substantive elements were integral to the ethic. Charles Taylor, however, offers a way to address this problem. He criticizes Habermas for rejecting substantive moral goods because, he argues, the role of the good in moral life is ineluctable.[17] In fact, the procedural force of discourse ethics presupposes a commitment to some good. Taylor argues that procedural approaches to ethics presuppose some good, for without such a presupposition, a procedural ethic cannot even get off the ground.[18] Taylor does, however, agree with Habermas on the need to extract culturally biased values or goods (e.g., those derived ultimately from religious authority or political ideologies) from moral theory. The problem of eliminating cultural determinations is, admittedly, a deeply serious one. But Taylor argues, all the same, that procedural principles alone cannot constitute an ethic. Some conception of the good must ground procedure, because no argument in favour of a procedural ethic would convince skeptics to obey procedural injunctions.[19] If correct, Taylor's argument demonstrates why appeals to a common good by members of the Chain were no accident. Such appeals could not have been purely idiosyncratic or optional but had to have been involved in all procedures aimed at reaching agreement. The real problem, then, is not to choose between procedural and substantive ethics but to show how (under what formulation) a common good can be articulated in a manner that is not culturally bound and in such a way that it coheres with the procedural principles it is supposed to ground.

Taylor is no less concerned with the problem of universalizability than Habermas and is equally concerned with the problem of cultural and historical relativism. His debate with Habermas helps to reframe my attempt to show that the Chain's ethic was coherent and universalizable. Taylor uses the term *hypergood* to distinguish between second-order goods, which are qualitatively distinct from lower-order goods (i.e., goods defined by individuals and groups in terms of their desires, cultural practices, and norms). Hypergoods can be used to discriminate between lower-order goods and to attribute differential worth to them. For example, the concept of freedom can be used to differentiate between one person's desire to enslave people (the good associated with dominance) and another person's desire to help others flourish (the good associated with compassion). Freedom, as a hypergood, can be used to judge the first as morally wrong and the second as morally right. (Indeed, Habermas himself, according to Taylor, presupposes freedom as just such a good.) Hypergoods are of incomparably greater importance than lower-order goods and provide a standpoint for weighing and judging lower-order goods.[20] This distinction suggests a strategy. If the explicitly identified goods and virtues of the Covenant Chain ethic can be formulated as first-order goods and the common ground as a second-order good, then there may be a way to formulate a coherent procedure-substance relationship.

Taylor's next step is to recognize that historical debates in ethics have been over competing hypergoods (e.g., freedom, obedience to God, and so on), a fact that skeptics have used to undermine the possibility of ever determining which goods can count as universal.[21] In other words, appealing to hypergoods does not provide an escape from cultural or historical relativism. Since people from different cultures can define freedom, or just about any proposed hypergood, differently, according to their particular cultural heritage and systems, the challenge is to formulate a hypergood in sufficiently generalized terms. The price of doing so, however, is to make the hypergood increasingly rarified and devoid of content. Appeals to the good can become empty and without power to compel.

Not only do we need a conception of the good with the power to compel, Taylor argues, but "articulation is a necessary condition of adhesion; without it, these goods are not even options."[22] With an appropriate formulation of the hypergood and use of effective speech acts, articulations of the good can inspire others to recognize a good and empower them to act. "To come closer to them [hypergoods], to have a clearer view of them, to come to grasp what they involve, is for those who recognize them to be moved to love or respect them, and through this love/respect to be better enabled to live up to them."[23] To articulate the hypergood, then, is to give it definition or explicit meaning. "All this speaks strongly in favour of the attempt to articulate the good in some kind of philosophical prose."[24] For the reasons that Taylor sets out, I accept that the good needs to be articulable in a way that enables conflicts among competing hypergoods to be resolved.

All of this spells trouble for the task at hand. Appeals to the good or common ground of the Covenant Chain were not articulated in the manner Taylor demands but were made through metaphor, origin stories, and wampum. When members of the Covenant Chain failed to come to agreements, as in the Joseph Brower case in which the two sides argued over the proper conception of justice, procedure failed because the conception of justice they thought they had agreed upon had failed to satisfy both sides' cultural expectations. This and other culturally based disagreements were mediated by appeals to underground chains, origin stories, and wampum protocol. These appeals were not to clearly defined concepts of the good but rather to common sensibilities that seem to have remained inchoate. It would appear, then, that unless appeals to underground chains and the like can be shown to be articulations of a sort that led to judgment, decision, affirmation, and condemnation, the Covenant Chain's ethic cannot be universalized. Although the Chain's ethic lacked a philosophical articulation of the hypergood, I argue that references to underground chains and appeals to origin stories and wampum use were articulations of a sort of hypergood. Even though these articulations were not used to justify or condemn in the systematic way Taylor demands, they were used to support or frustrate certain lower-order goods in ways that could be compelling and possibly more compelling than justificatory procedures are. They did so through the process of shifting emphasis away from justification and toward healing and unification.

The Structure of the Chain's Ethic Revisited

To respond to this challenge, it is necessary to reframe the Covenant Chain's ethic within a philosophically oriented rather than a sociologically oriented conceptual structure. By doing so, the conceptual relationship among the various elements of the Chain's ethic can be distinguished and made more precise, revealing the relationship between the common ground–hypergood and lower-order goods, moral rules, and principles. At the same time, doing so helps draw clearer distinctions between factors of the moral economy that were clearly historically or culturally bound and those that are difficult to analyze as such. This reframing offers a categorial device to systematize discussion of the unification-healing process and distinguish it from the justification process. At the same time, it indicates that unification and healing were rationally connected to justification. I use four categories to capture what I have been calling ethical factors and the moral economy to facilitate the transition from the sociological to the philosophical.

First, formal ethical factors are guiding principles, as expressed, for example, in ceremonial protocols, institutional mission statements, codes of ethics, constitutions, and the like. In the Covenant Chain records, references to "pure hearts," the "clearing of throats," "wiping tears away from eyes," and "opening ears" can be considered formal in the sense that they are stylized, institutionalized expressions of moral expectations. Such expressions, when considered in and of themselves, are defined relative to cultural and historical contexts because they develop in relation to those contexts.

Second, moralistic ethical factors are doctrinaire impositions of moral values and rules, that is, externally imposed norms, as in cases of inculcating religious virtues such as chastity or standards of civility. These rules operate like orders dictated by an authority, be it church, social institution, parent, and so on. They tend to be indoctrinated norms and values and are viewed as external to what people would otherwise value. Holding values of this sort can, in the end, be explained as the product of psychological and social manipulation (e.g., fear of divine judgment or social sanction). They are resistant to critical reflection. These values tend to be exercised irrespective of the demands and complexities of a situation.

People who conceive of and practise morality in this way utilize strategic speech acts to manipulate others to behave according to moral norms; a commitment to arrive at mutual understanding is contrary to the assertion of authority. Citing examples of moralistic behaviour would not convince the skeptic or reductionist that moral values and principles are anything more than facades that mask underlying psychological, social, economic, and political forces. They cannot count as anything more than culturally bound rules and values.

Third, reflective ethical factors emerge from the process of reflecting critically on the norms and values that shape decision making and judgment. Subject to critical and self-critical examination, these norms and values are treated as obligations to be considered and weighed in a process of coming to a decision or agreement; they are not treated as non-negotiable absolutes to be imposed dogmatically. When these norms and values come into conflict, people weigh their relative force through acts of deliberation. The ability to reflect, weigh, deliberate, and decide presupposes moral agency, in the sense that people assume responsibility for deciding the values and principles upon which they will act. People who practise and think in terms of reflective morality use communicative speech acts in the course of their dialogue with others. People who engage in reflective morality seek agreement by subjecting their culturally bound norms and values to critical reflection in an attempt to convince others of the reasonableness of their approach and position. They use reflective morality to transcend cultural bounds. This category in and of itself does not refer to a substantive moral value and is best described as representative of a procedural ethic.

Fourth, spiritual ethical factors (for lack of a better term) are a type of morality similar to that of Buddha or Jesus. Those said to practise this type of morality are responsive to the suffering and ultimate aspirations of others. They hold compassion, and possibly benevolence (love for others), as a central moral concern. Compassion is also typically associated with a commitment to enabling others to achieve a higher state of awareness and peace. People operating along these lines often view the moral state as an intermediary, or perhaps lower, state than the spiritual. For the purposes of this study, I make no such claim, mostly because the idea of operating with a sense of compassion, responsibility, and a deep connection with others simply seems to be a moral idea. I see no reason to draw a distinction between the spiritual and the moral in regard to these motivations and orientations. Introducing this category recognizes substantive goods that are not readily reducible to the goods captured under formal and moralistic morality. It makes room in the analysis for what may be considered deeper moral connections between people. As Tom Birch suggests, we seem to be capable of this deontic response, the internally compelling sense that moral agents feel when they respond to a need to bring benefit to others or to recognize their moral worth.[25]

The spiritual category also helps frame the role of religious and community factors, insofar as they form part of a shared lifeworld. I have suggested, for instance, that it is too facile a move to dismiss Aboriginal peoples' demands for missionaries as the consequence of psychological manipulation (fear of damnation) or social pressure. It is conceivable that some members of the communities were motivated by a genuine spiritual quest, as Robert

Livingston observed. Although I do not make use of this particular notion of the religious, I do use the awareness of deeper motivations and needs to bring attention to intangible factors, especially implicit and complex motivations that operate in a shared lifeworld. Among these intangibles are senses of the good.

A brief examination of the clash between moral commitments illustrates how these four categories can be used to draw distinctions among different aspects of the moral economy operating in the Covenant Chain relationship. The moral motivations of agents such as Governor Winthrop, who used the concept of vacuum domicilium to declare Indians bereft of any natural right to the land they used, could be said to be formal and moralistic. A study of the religious dimension of the relationship would reveal enormous amounts of evidence in support of the view that religious authorities, both English and French, used similar arguments when they converted Aboriginal people to Christianity for religious and political reasons. Their language when they described Aboriginal peoples and cultures as backward and heathen was strategic and designed to justify an imposition or inculcation of Christian religious and moral belief systems. In the record of Indian Affairs itself, the moral stance of men such as Bradstreet, Braddock, and Amherst is moralistic. This kind of morality stands out in the dominant historical narrative. But it was also a kind of morality criticized by men such as Roger Williams and William Johnson, sometimes at great personal expense (e.g., Williams's exile). These criticisms, especially as expressed in the relationship between Johnson, Gage, and Bradstreet (see Chapter 3), draw on the contrast between moralistic and reflective morality, revealing how the imposition of moralistic attitudes can evoke the capacity of reflective morality. In Johnson's case, Bradstreet's and Amherst's moralistic attitudes evoked Johnson's reflective capacity, as if to compel him to criticize their approaches, by drawing on his commitment to communicative ways of understanding his Aboriginal interlocutors' values, sense of freedom, and autonomy. The relevance of reflective morality is also evident in Gage's criticism of Bradstreet as foolish and a danger to the treaty relationship. This was, in effect, a criticism of Bradstreet's moralistic orientation and his failure to be sufficiently reflective.

The Johnson-Gage-Bradstreet incident not only draws attention to the fact that key Crown agents were moved to become more reflective, it also shows how the language used among these agents changed, becoming more communicative than strategic, as they became more reflective. Both Johnson's and, to a surprising degree, Gage's criticisms of Bradstreet were based on a reflective awareness of their own people's failings and, as a consequence, of Aboriginal people's values, conceptions, norms, and cultural practices. Both withdrew from using strategic speech acts to cajole Aboriginal people into agreements and even accepted that their own English-based values and norms could be critically assessed by Aboriginal people. Johnson's remarks about Aboriginal people's sense of freedom and aversion to subjecthood can be interpreted as an awareness of the need to reflect on his own culture's ethic in order to respond properly to that of his Aboriginal interlocutors. In being able to compare the two, he, in effect, reflected on the shared normative lifeworld. The initial trade relationship's potential to become a relationship based on a moral economy can now, in part, be explained as the consequence of reflective awareness engendering the evolution of a shared normative lifeworld. A relationship that was at first purely utilitarian evolved to incorporate a moral economy, not because the parties shared or had even invented moralistic rules and sensibilities, but because they engaged in dialogue aimed at establishing a reflective mutual understanding.

The language of unity and the Covenant Chain's unity function, once understood within this framework, indicate that reflective, communicative actions (using wampum to open eyes, clear throats, purify hearts) could have at least two consequences. They made interlocutors who might initially have been restricted to their own cultural sensibilities open to and able to acknowledge the moral sensibilities of their interlocutors. They also created the potential for innovation and creativity in attempts to reach a common understanding and ground. Once the rational, reflective communicative procedure had been established, it was possible to value dogmatic and strategic communicative acts negatively and to establish a different order of moral standards. The implementation of reflective morality, as a result, introduced hypergoods into the moral economy in a way that allowed people to systematically condone, reject, or reorder lower-order goods and moral principles, even though there was no appeal to explicitly articulated hypergoods.

Re-examining the role of compassion reveals other means by which reflective morality introduced hypergoods to the moral economy. Expressions of condolence, framed in the way they were during ceremonies, fostered an awareness of the suffering of others because considerable energy and investment of wampum was involved. This awareness was expected to help build trust and solidarity. The communicative speech acts required to build this kind of relationship depended on interlocutors demonstrating that they had some understanding of the other's subjective world and a willingness to build an intersubjective world. Formal and moralistic morality demand no such awareness and tend strongly to proscribe it. Through this process, people invest some of their identity in the community being built. They expect to benefit from membership and also come to expect deontic responses from others in the community – that is, they expect others to respond automatically (without calculation) to threats to their safety and well-being. In turn, they recognize that they are expected to have deontic responses to the suffering of other community members and the community as a whole. By this I do not mean that members are expected to act altruistically. Rather, since members are expected to act on the basis of a shared understanding and shared identity, deontic responses to external threats are expected as natural expressions of reciprocity. Deontic responses are not necessarily acts of heroism, either; they arise as a consequence of having a sense of belonging to a community, which generates a sense of being owed protection and recognition by the community, and being committed to the same in return. Just as high-context languages enable rich descriptors to convey meaning, there is a connection between expected benefits, a sense of belonging, and debts owed that creates and enables expectations of deontic responses to operate as part of a shared normative lifeworld.

Spiritual morality now becomes more clearly relevant to the Covenant Chain's ethic. The Covenant Chain was structured to promote the development of deontic responses since it constantly made members aware of the need for oneness. The explicit use of the language of one heart, mind, and body (when one part is harmed, all parts are harmed) in renewal ceremonies constantly reminded members of their obligation to protect each other and committed them to performative actions (e.g., wampum use) to indicate that they had done so and would continue to do so.[26] These deontic responses are not the sort of responses that result from reasoned argumentation and negotiation about what should be done; rather, they indicate the type of attitude members of a moral community are expected to have toward one another. Unifying protocols and practices demanded that Covenant Chain members act and speak as people who belonged to a community. In situations of unresolvable conflict, this demand moved dialogue beyond argumentation and negotiation toward healing or the recognition of unity. The idea of healing was connected to acts of remembering and, therefore, to a sense of a common history. Remembering promoted a sense of identity and belonging more fundamental than could have been brought about by adhering to explicit rules and values. This sense would, for the most part, be taken for granted and operate at a deeper level of the relationship. Insofar as wampum was the primary vehicle through which this deeper ground was recognized, it can be said that it formed one mode (along with origin stories and the Three Bare Words) of articulating a common ground. It was by virtue of invoking sensibilities related to reflective and spiritual morality and awareness, then, that hypergoods were introduced into the Covenant Chain relationship. Insofar as applying formal and moralistic morality brought out the capacity to think and act reflectively, the latter was a latent potential, normally hidden, that could be evoked when some higher-order good (e.g., justice or freedom) had been violated or threatened.

The Function of Wampum Revisited

How did these ways of articulating the common ground result in judgments, decisions, and the like if they were not used directly to justify or condemn lower-order goods? Wampum – as the medium through which speeches were made, agreements recorded, authority acknowledged, and legitimacy carried into treaty negotiations – was more than a procedural device. Its binding force cannot be explained solely in terms of the forces that bind, say, a contract (fear of external enforcement agencies) or even the integrity and faithfulness of members. Wampum was not used merely symbolically in the sense that it represented something else, like a country's flag represents its nationhood. Its use was connected to an intention to draw members into an attitude of recognizing an underlying order; it brought the idea of an implicit and ultimate legitimating force to bear on proceedings and negotiations by embodying that force, but not in the sense that people were moved to worship as they would before an idol.

When the evolution and complexification of the Covenant Chain is kept in mind, the spiritual factor of its moral economy becomes clear. Wampum took on more of the burden of authority in all arenas of the relationship, from ceremonies to expressing condolences and from recording agreements to healing wounds, as the relationship became more complex. It acquired a metafunction of sustaining awareness of and sometimes acting as an ultimate legitimating force, but not in the sense that the person holding wampum could exercise authority willy-nilly. All functions, including the recording of treaty agreements, had something to do with framing, reminding people of, or restoring unity.

A description of how wampum came into prominence will bring this aspect of its character into bolder relief. Initially, the Aboriginal-Crown relationship was held together by individual agents such as Edmund Andros. During this early era, the number of colonies and Aboriginal groups in the Chain was small, and the Chain's function was less complex. The role of wampum, although still significant, was less pronounced. Andros was able to serve as governor, magistrate, and commander-in-chief. His reputation seemed to provide most of the force behind decisions reached. As increasing numbers of colonies and Aboriginal nations entered the Chain and as its functions grew more complex, however, it became more difficult for one person to perform all core functions. A division of labour developed. As trade relations evolved into military alliances and legal relationships, wampum continued to be integral to all procedures. In fact, it became more central. Articulations of a common ground (articulated at first in terms of fair trade practices) became increasingly obscure and indeterminate as the relationship became more complex.

Explaining why the British continued to show respect for wampum for so long and in so many arenas (when they did not do so for other practices) is difficult, unless we assume that its use resonated with their own cultural sensibilities. To some extent, this has already been established. Richard White's explanation of the middle ground – the consequence of each side justifying its claims in terms that referred to the other side's cultural norms – introduces the idea of crosscultural justification. That British agents came to master wampum protocol and sometimes used it to chastise their allies and even referred to it in correspondence among themselves indicates that the meanings conveyed by wampum use could be mastered and incorporated into the assumptions and values of the shared normative lifeworld. Mastering wampum enabled the British to use its normative force within a shared language and in their own (intra-Indian affairs) high-context language. The expectations that wampum carried into proceedings became readily recognizable and utilizable; wampum was recognized as an intercultural source of authority and legitimacy.

Certain agents might even have been drawn to wampum protocol because it allowed them to carry on a discourse with Aboriginal people and among themselves without abandoning their own culture's fundamental moral sensibilities, which some (e.g., Baron de Lahontan and Rousseau) saw as having been occluded by the corrupting forces of European society. Not only did some European writers exploit Aboriginal culture to criticize their own, the correspondence and behaviour of key agents (e.g., Weiser, Croghan, and Johnson) also suggest that they identified with and deeply respected their allies' values (e.g., honour and integrity) because they expressed what they believed their own culture should have protected, but had failed to do so. Their acceptance of wampum protocol was neither an act of submission to Aboriginal expectations nor a mere diplomatic nicety; it was an act of recognizing a source of authority they themselves wanted to recognize. At the same time, they leveraged the values represented by that authority to gain compliance from their allies. Wampum use, then, drew attention to and evoked awareness of deeply hidden motivating forces.

The intent and perhaps effect of continually reinforcing unity was to evoke shared experiences and memories, expectations of loyalty and honour that, in turn, reinforced commitments to act on deeply held (implicit) shared values. The high-context linguistic features of wampum protocol helped maintain awareness of the logic of the intersubjective world, in which these shared values could be recognized and exert force. As the socialization effects of wampum use took hold, members did not simply act as if they shared political, legal, and moral values and sensibilities, they also had to have shared them, otherwise they would not have been able to use wampum as a means for expressing authority in the way that they did.

Wampum users consequently invested some of their identity in the shared normative lifeworld. The sharing of values and sensibilities and the sense of unity, community, belonging, and identity that resulted constituted a kind of power that, for the sake of brevity, I will call the power of identity or identification. This power is well illustrated through the case of child soldiers. Reshaping children's minds to create child soldiers is a process we call brainwashing, especially if those children have their sense of identity altered to such a degree that they will turn against and exterminate their own people. Likewise, propagandists can more readily appeal to common values to unite a group or nation if their propaganda constructs a common identity in opposition to that of another group characterized as evil. By creating or manipulating this common identity, a sense of a common good (destruction of the enemy) is also created. Since identity manipulation exploits forces that affect behaviour, the way people identify can be said to empower them to act one way and disempower them to act in other ways. This, of course, is an extreme and negative example of how and why we – as members of families, communities, cities, and nations – attempt to build identities to reinforce certain types of behaviour and ways of interacting. At the same time, it helps show how the structure and function of the Covenant Chain were aimed at utilizing this power of communal identification to reinforce certain commitments and behaviours.

The power and authority of wampum led interlocutors to focus on common goods and compelled members to check (evaluate) their actions and subjective worlds against the intersubjective world of shared sensibilities and the objective shared world of mutually recognized norms. Accordingly, wampum became the physical expression that represented – or, better, embodied – the good that held together the subjective, intersubjective, and objective worlds. This good embodied in wampum use was recognized, not because both sides happened to identify the good it represented in the same way, but because members had engaged in a history of communicative actions in an attempt to establish unity and a common identity.

Charles Taylor's analysis of how the good inevitably enters into moral evaluation helps explain why this power of identity develops. In *Sources of the Self*, Taylor argues for the centrality of the good in moral life. After examining and defending appeals to the good against attacks from many fronts (including those from Nietzsche, Hume, and the existentialists), Taylor argues that a substantive sense of the good is absolutely necessary for a sense of a moral self to develop.[27] For my purposes, Taylor's concept of the moral self can be equated with moral agency and identity. He states, "By contrast, the notion of self which connects it to our need for identity is meant to pick out this crucial feature of human agency, that we cannot do without some orientation to the good, that we each essentially are (i.e., define ourselves at least *inter alia* by) where we stand on this."[28] To be a person – that is, a moral agent engaged in social life – is to have a sense of the good. As members of a moral community (defined by Taylor, as by Habermas, as a language community), we must conceive of our sense of the good in relation to a common good.[29] It is to this common good that we must refer when attempting to convince others of the rightness and legitimacy of our claims.[30] At the same time, we subject ourselves to criticism on the basis of this good when we wish or need to be recognized as rational members of a moral community. Taylor's analysis, then, helps explain why identity, unity, common good, and wampum use were tied together so intimately in the Covenant Chain relationship. Wampum use reinforced the recognition of interwoven goods, which generated a sense of a common good in which both sides, as political entities and as individuals, had invested to shape a common identity under the treaty relationship. The hypergood was, accordingly, a complex good, the articulation of which could not be simple or straightforward. How it operated to produce judgment or justifications could not (because it cannot), likewise, be explained in a straightforward manner. Nor could its referent (the common good) be straightforwardly defined or delimited in the sense that the boundaries of what counted as good could be clearly established.

Yet appeals to the hypergood and how it could direct behaviour and result in the suspension of certain principles and conceptions (e.g., justice) have in part been described. Furthermore, we have determined that, however commitments to lower-order goods were woven together to form a hypergood, the process could not have been completely arbitrary and capricious. Ironically, perhaps, Habermas's description of how a procedural ethic arises helps explain this determinable and logical characteristic of the hypergood. Since a community of communicators must be presupposed in any rational discourse aimed at decision or judgment, there is already "the idea of the unlimited communication community," which serves to replace any metaphysical grounding *from within the world* (Habermas's phrase).[31] People who communicate to make mutually acceptable decisions implicitly recognize that they belong to a larger or more comprehensive community of potential participants, each of whom could bring their own arguments and statements of relevant facts to a decision-making forum. Any one of their contributions could show a particular claim or decision to be false, weaker than claimed, or in need of modification. However clear people initially are about their own positions, and however convinced they are of their rightness as rational interlocutors, they must become open to correction or falsification; otherwise, they risk placing themselves outside the dialogical community and, consequently, the resources and advantages of belonging to the community. So, to be open to falsification in this way is to be undogmatic in relation to some yet-unanticipated grounding (e.g., insight) that one might assert or come to rely on for justification at any particular point in time. Being so open is to accept universalizability as a general principle for negotiating agreements. The hypergood that emerges in this process, as a result, is, in part, subject to evaluation as a universal ground. By the same token, it is recognized as a candidate for a universal ground. It has undergone a process in which certain hypergoods have been eliminated or overridden, not necessarily because they have been explicitly rejected but because they were not suitable and, consequently, not used. For example, the good of fair trade might have been a sufficient good to order the relationship in the early days, but with complexification, it became insufficient as a hypergood.

As difficult as it is to explain the way in which the hypergood was articulated, the conditions upon which it was established, and how it was recognized, it is clear that it operated. Even if it did not operate systematically, in the philosophical sense, it did not operate arbitrarily either. Using terms such as *evolution* and *complexification* has helped show that the hypergood was embedded in the forces of unification and identification. As noted earlier, the way the hypergood operates is sometimes best observed in cases where it is violated. In the case of a trade relationship that evolves into a military alliance, for example, the cessation of the trade relationship will result in a sense of betrayal and a desire for retaliation, senses and desires that make no sense where no such evolution happens. A more complex, higher-order good emerged in the more complex relationship than could have developed in the purely trade-based relationship. Members of a more complex relationship are expected to recognize a greater number of goods as pertinent to the protection of the relationship and to carry on a discourse that recognizes the good of the relationship as a whole. When a violation occurs, consequently, it has ramifications for many areas of the relationship because the threat to one good is a threat to all goods that the relationship is committed to protect. In this negative way of determining the fate of lower-order goods, we can see that there was a logic to the operation of the Chain's hypergood. This partially explains how wampum came to be part of a high-context language.

Virtues, Agency, and the Common Ground

The Covenant Chain's emphasis on the virtues and the importance of reputation suggests that the goods pertinent to the virtues were not necessarily culturally and historically bound but were somehow based on the hypergood. When the Lords of Trade recognized how crucial people such as William Johnson and Conrad Weiser were to British interests because of their reputation as proper persons, they recognized just how critical the virtues were, even at the highest levels of Crown authority. Reputations were not based simply on whether agents were viewed as clever negotiators but on whether their virtues were exercised as members and protectors of an intercultural community as well. The failure of men such as Braddock and Amherst, dishonest traders and encroaching settlers, in contrast, underscores how threats to and the failure to protect the relationship could bring out the relevance of the hypergood. The contrast between the two types of people helps clarify the deontic nature of belonging to community. Men such as Amherst did not speak or act according to a shared sense of the good of the community. Consequently, they were not obeyed. Aboriginal people felt no moral compulsion to protect the likes of these men. Men such as Johnson and Weiser, in contrast, were capable of bringing deontic feelings of obligation to bear on their treaty negotiations, enabling them to appeal to implicit debts owed them as community members, debts of solidarity.

Like family members or members of a group who have shared experiences and who have sacrificed for the benefit of others, Johnson and Weiser could demand loyalty, just as they were expected to demonstrate it in return. They expected Aboriginal members of the Chain to defend and support the institution and give preferential treatment to its members. When warriors failed to protect the British, or when the British failed to protect their Aboriginal allies, they were accused of betrayal and were viewed as having failed to give the proper response. Since none of these demands and expectations are possible among strangers (certainly not among enemies) and were tenuous at best between Aboriginal allies who wavered between the British and French, it is clear that the Crown's key agents, the "proper persons," were effective because they protected and nurtured the good of the whole by exercising a certain set of virtues. Thus, like following procedural principles, individuals were expected to exhibit the virtues because they predisposed them to protect the relationship as a whole.

In the sense that the hypergood binds lower-order goods into a unity and orders them, the virtues (e.g., honesty, honour, sincerity, and courage) formed part of a more comprehensive set of goods that emerged in the evolutionary development of the military and legal functions of the Covenant Chain. Recognizing and practising these virtues protected a plethora of other goods related to trade, national security, and community order. The virtues were not simply added willy-nilly to the number of goods fostered and recognized by the Covenant Chain, making the relationship a hodge-podge of ethical forces. Nor did the centrality of the virtues undermine the Chain's evolutionary direction toward universality. Rather, their centrality functioned to motivate members to recognize and defend the community as a whole. Their importance was derived from the unity function of the treaty relationship.

Freedom and Autonomy

Thus far, I have offered only indirect explanations of how hypergoods were articulated, but the discussions of freedom and autonomy indicate that attempts were made to articulate a hypergood directly. When Johnson identified freedom and autonomy as core Aboriginal values in an attempt to convince his superiors of the wrongness of Bradstreet's thought and actions, he was identifying values that were understood, at least in some ways, across cultural boundaries. Johnson identified hypergoods to convince his superiors that certain kinds of ideas, actions, and principles should be abandoned because they were either unintelligible to Aboriginal people or violated the Aboriginal values of freedom and autonomy, which of course, were hardly foreign to European intellectuals of the time, who were discussing justifications for people giving up their freedom in exchange for the protection of a sovereign. Johnson relied on his superiors' participation in the intersubjective and objective normative worlds to generate an understanding of the consequences that would follow Bradstreet's attempt to subject the western nations to the Crown's authority. Johnson appealed to freedom and autonomy, in effect, to condemn and proscribe.

When comparing Bradstreet's treaty record against Johnson's record for the same period (1761, 1764, and 1766), the glaring differences can now be explained in terms of hypergoods and their support for a shared lifeworld upon which policies and practices were based. When both Gage and Johnson saw that Bradstreet was being manipulated, despite Bradstreet's claim that he had been in control of the treaty negotiations at Detroit, they clearly understood that he had failed, because he had failed to understand the hypergoods that had come to operate in the Covenant Chain relationship. He had been, as a result, blind to the true meaning of his interlocutors' statements and actions. Failing to appreciate the hypergoods blinded him to the subjective worlds of his interlocutors and the intersubjective world established by key agents. Both Johnson and Gage understood that a failure to recognize and honour these hypergoods would result in feelings of resentment, betrayal and anger – hence, the systematic character of the hypergood–lower-order good relation.

Critics might still object at this point by claiming that the concepts of freedom and autonomy are ambiguous. They could argue that the definition and conceptual framing of freedom were not the same between the two cultures and that they certainly were not the same as they are today, being defined predominantly in accordance with liberalism. Neither side could have framed freedom in accordance with the modern sense of individualism. Even Europeans at the time were in fact only just being exposed to liberal conceptions of freedom. Thus, the idea of freedom that Johnson articulated was not transhistorical. Nor was it transcultural, since the two sides' different cosmological and epistemological frameworks would have produced unresolvable differences in interpretation. The apparent understanding that Gage and others demonstrated, then, was based on a superficial understanding of freedom and nothing more than a calculated evaluation of the behaviour of the western nations in response to Bradstreet's treaty. They were simply responding to the fact that inappropriate people had signed Bradstreet's treaty and to the fact that aggressive actions continued. Their condemnation of Bradstreet, therefore, had nothing to do with a shared intersubjective or objective normative lifeworld.

Given Johnson's history and experience with Aboriginal people, however, it is not reasonable to conclude that his understanding and explanations were merely strategic. Moreover, given that the Lords of Trade recognized the importance of employing proper persons who had earned the respect of their Aboriginal allies, sharing a lifeworld and understanding the hyper-goods that operated in that lifeworld were indeed accepted as crucial elements in the treaty relationship. Johnson's abilities in this respect gave him an advantage as a negotiator, which was seen as a valuable resource by the Lords of Trade. Hence, it would be incorrect to argue that Johnson's (or, for that matter, Gage's) understanding of freedom and autonomy had no substantive and operative significance. Yet it is obvious that the concepts of freedom and autonomy vary, and have varied, between cultures, making it difficult if not impossible to claim that any specific articulation is either culturally or historically neutral. The most that can be claimed at this point is that articulations of freedom and autonomy were attempts at voicing a transcultural, transhistorical hypergood. These articulations were aimed at universality, even if they did not fully succeed.

Perhaps all attempts to define freedom and autonomy explicitly and clearly would have generated conflicts about interpretation, as critics argue, resulting in the dissolution of the relationship. This is not, however, the way articulations were implemented, at least not so long as the Aboriginal allies remained militarily and economically strong and the British remained dependent on them. When agents such as Johnson and Weiser attempted to advise or instruct their superiors and subordinates on how to understand Aboriginal allies and how to conduct themselves (e.g., when Weiser instructed Lee about Haudenosaunee religion), they drew on an intercultural hypergood without which the treaty relationship would not have been possible. Weiser distinguished between dogmatic beliefs and "union of the soul with God" (see Chapter 3) to indicate that the Haudenosaunee system of beliefs was not entirely unlike that of Europeans who freely pursued spiritual quests. The second formulation pointed to something more fundamental, even though less clearly articulable. The responses of men such as Lee and Gage can be viewed as acts of learning how to acknowledge a set of difficult-to-articulate sensibilities related to a shared lifeworld. Men such as Weiser and Johnson acquired reputations as masters at building intersubjective lifeworlds based on appeals to concepts such as freedom, autonomy, and spiritual quests. In doing so, they could shift discourses and attitudes away from the logic of dominance and control to one of mutual understanding and community, much like skilled interlocutors could shift council proceedings away from justification toward healing.

Sufficient reason, then, has not been identified to deny that freedom and autonomy operated as hypergoods, albeit in an opaque manner. This raises a problem of ambiguity. The hypergood is supposed to be a single higher-order good that orders lower-order goods. Yet it is clear that there was more than one obvious candidate for the hypergood in the Covenant Chain relationship. While it is tempting to suggest that there was a third order that united the plurality of second-order hypergoods, it is more reasonable to assume that the higher-order goods belonged to a network that constituted the hypergood. This assumption makes sense since I have suggested all along that the relationship's complexity produced a unity that comprised a plurality of factors and that the hypergood was somehow determined by this unity.

In light of the way in which the hypergood emerged and the complex nature of the context in which it did so, it is now arguable that demanding a clear and formal articulation of the hypergood is inappropriate. Appealing to the usual grounds and criteria used to deny crosscultural and transhistorical relevance, as set out by Taylor, is not then entirely appropriate for judging the relevance and universalizability of a moral theory. In an attempt to show how the Chain's mode of articulation was effective as a means for drawing attention to the network of goods that constituted the hypergood, I will examine the Chain's ethic in its ability to meet the demand for universalizability. I begin by responding to a seemingly unrelated question posed by Wade Wells at the Johnson Hall historical site in Johnstown, New York, in 2005: "What would have happened had William Johnson not died in 1774 but rather lived through the War of Independence?" Wells's question raised the possibility of using a counterfactual analysis to disclose a further set of conditions that operated in the moral economy. Almost certainly, Johnson would have sided with the British, since he was a Tory through and through. He developed the Mohawk Valley (Tryon County) in accordance with his monarchical commitments and resisted attempts at democratization throughout his tenure. As a Crown loyalist, Johnson organized political, legal, and social arrangements according to patronage, familial loyalty, and ethnicity: the English and Irish enjoyed privileges, whereas Dutch Germans, Aboriginal peoples (except the Mohawk), and others were treated as second-class citizens. Furthermore, as noted earlier, Johnson evoked contrary judgments about his character. Where some viewed Johnson as loyal and fair, others saw him as calculating, shrewd, and unfair. Johnson played many roles and had many facets to his personality. He was a complex man living in complex relationships.

Given Johnson's influence with the Six Nations and others, it is likely that the Six Nations would have remained united during the War of Independence, since Johnson would have done everything in his power to maintain a single warrior force against the rebels. It would not have been difficult for him to demonstrate to the sachems and warriors that he, on behalf of the Crown, had attempted to protect them from settler encroachments and illicit trade, which he could blame on rebel forces. It could be argued, then, that the war might have turned out quite differently had Johnson lived and remained healthy.

Since Johnson was a man whom both the British and Aboriginal people trusted and looked to as a go-between, he became an insider to both sides. He spoke to and sometimes represented both sides as a proper person. Accordingly, he was the embodiment (not always a good one) of the values and principles of the intersubjective lifeworld of the Covenant Chain. As much as the Crown and Aboriginal people depended on him, however, he depended on the Crown and Aboriginal people for his reputation and the opportunity to embody their values. Without this dual role, his reputation would have been no more than a good friend or decent fellow. The system of dual dependency had a dialectical form. On the one hand, his role was to acquire land and settle disputes in favour of the Crown. On the other hand, he was to protect his Aboriginal allies from settler encroachments. More fundamentally, as a sachem, he was responsible for protecting and employing Aboriginal conceptions of justice while exercising British law in the territories he superintended. His role and, therefore, his political identity as a proper person were defined in terms of opposing responsibilities. Johnson's effectiveness, as a result, relied heavily on his ability to maintain dual identities and find ways to manage conflicting responsibilities. This conclusion also applies to agents such as Weiser, Croghan, Schuyler, and even Andros.

This counterfactual scenario brings to light another facet of the Covenant Chain's complexity. Johnson's multiple roles and the dual responsibilities they created suggest that the moral effectiveness of agents depended on the ability to weave a course through complex situations and contradictory demands rather than an ability to clearly justify decisions. Johnson excelled at making interlocutors recognize that the complexity of the relationship or situation demanded a certain capacity for making judgments. Moralistic men such as Braddock and Amherst would have certainly failed to keep the Six Nations on side during the war, not only because they were resented but because they were single-minded in their attempts to justify their actions. Similarly, had the Quakers succeeded in determining the course of Pennsylvania's actions with their single-minded moral commitments, less morally justifiable but effective means of keeping the alliance together would have been rejected. It is likely that even Conrad Weiser would have failed to keep the Six Nations on side because he was morally predisposed to protect them from harm by encouraging them to remain neutral while the British and Americans fought among themselves.

The tension an effective go-between faced would have been similar to that of contemporary moral agents who play dual roles as public agents and as private citizens. According to Thomas Nagel, there is no easy way to balance expectations between private and public morality, since one's public responsibility will almost inevitably come into conflict with one's private commitments.[32] As institutional arrangements become greater in number and complexity, role-differentiated responsibilities create more and different kinds of tensions. Moral life today is rife with tensions created by role differentiation, which demands that one balance opposing expectations and opposing responsibilities. It makes sense, then, to accept that, when adopting multiple roles in complex contexts, there may be no clear line of justification for decisions, whether one acts as a moral agent today or hundreds of years ago.

This situation is not exclusive to public officials or military commanders. Any parent, professional, or adult in some other decision-making role can find him- or herself in a similar situation. It is the nature of moral life. Moral life, whether in intra- or intercultural contexts, is typically complex and dialectical. Moral agents, who are expected to play multiple roles, find themselves, in effect, having to apply multiple principles and conceptions of the good, which are sometimes incompatible, to resolve conflicts and tensions. In resolving the tensions between their roles, they cannot simply choose to apply one theory (or frame of reference) and ignore others. The more intercultural relationships are institutionalized – complete with institutional goals, values, principles of interaction, and so on – the more likely these role-related tensions will become entrenched, that is, become systemic. As a consequence, the primary responsibility of moral agents' participating in such institutions will be to make judgments that weave together the various concerns, forces, and principles that weigh on them. William Johnson, at the time of the war, was one of the few remaining British agents who had been placed in the role of go-between and who had proven that he was capable of performing to both sides' satisfaction. Upstate New York, at least, would have remained much more cohesive during the war than it was.

If moral life is inescapably dialectical, in the way described, and if moral agents such as Johnson can and must judge what they are to do, all the same, it is inappropriate and even wrong-headed to expect moral life and the moral economy to always comprise clear and consistent articulations of hypergoods, principles, basic concepts, and lines of justification. Indeed, it is likely that Johnson would not have been recognized as a proper person and one with big ears had he adopted this approach to moral life. His ability to weave contrary and even contradictory expectations and goods would have been undermined; his commitment would have been a misplaced demand for logical rigour.

James Tully's concept of strange multiplicities to some extent indicates where Johnson's moral sensibilities and sense of the good, those of the Covenant Chain's ethic and those I am trying to capture, might have lain.[33]

Even though Tully's theory is framed to address issues of constitutionality in political philosophy, it is relevant to ethics because of its handling of fundamental normative sensibilities. Tully considers two basic kinds of constitutionality – ancient and modern. He distinguishes between constitutions whose common ground is discovered versus those that are imposed.[34] The latter define citizens as equal (the same) with respect to rationality and culture. Cultural and gender differences are ignored because they are deemed irrelevant, and citizens are considered homogeneous. These modern constitutions are governed ultimately by abstract rules. The ancients, in contrast, were governed by procedures that required dialogue to reach a common ground. Differences were protected, in effect, by not assuming that culture was irrelevant or that citizens were homogeneous. The ancients had to weave together various strands of discourse to find a common ground in a way that allowed cultural differences to shape outcomes. Diverse and incompatible interests and values were somehow brought into a unity.

For the ancients, finding a common ground was conceivable only if a dialogue with those who had a stake in the outcome of negotiations was opened. The ancients were more concerned about the dynamics of becoming attuned to one another, in order to reach agreements, than about finding an ultimate justification for agreements based on a pre-established common ground. Tully argues that the Covenant Chain was an ancient rather than a modern constitution. Its dialogical character of keeping channels of communication open was the principal and perhaps only means of establishing a common ground. Just as it made sense to the ancients to expect multiplicities of all sorts to arise, so too did members of the Covenant Chain expect a multiplicity of moral sensibilities to emerge in the course of negotiations. Indeed, if my analysis of complexity and community is correct, the British and Aboriginal allies had no choice but to expect it. Consequently, it was only through dialogue aimed at mutual attunement that a community and institutional arrangement for this strange multiplicity could emerge and be sustained. If we are to find the hypergoods of the relationship, then, they would be in the process of opening and maintaining a dialogue driven by this commitment to mutual attunement.

According to Tully , rational dialogue is a higher-order process that integrates multiplicities according to a common ground that is reached by accident. Ancient constitutional dialogues succeeded through a process of trial and error, period. Yet they were coherent in the sense that each side could understand the agreement and could give an account of it, at least to each other. What Tully describes in Chapter 4 of *Strange Multiplicity* is an arrangement between sovereign nations who identified as self-governing collectives and who spoke to one another in their own voices. As they struggled to understand one another and to reach agreements, they found that they could reach common ground on conditions of peace, friendship, and respect. Tully considers this process – and Tully is not as reluctant as I am to describe this process as emanating from the spirit of the Two Row Wampum – one of mutual recognition.[35] This move disengages him from the Habermasian approach. In fact, he criticizes the Habermasian approach to constitutionality for its insistence on the universality of principles, suggesting that the Covenant Chain was constituted to handle differences in a unique way without any appeal to universalizability.[36] There simply was no commitment to universalizability, just a cobbling together of efforts to communicate and reach mutual understanding. Tully does not, however, want to go the full distance in admitting that such a constitutional arrangement left members with little mutual understanding; to him, this conclusion would be overly pessimistic. He is willing to say that although much remains opaque, "the everyday mastering of the criss-crossing, overlapping and contested uses of terms is not different in kind (but of course in degree) from the understanding demanded by constitutional dialogue."[37] Nevertheless, although the two sides discovered many commonalities, there was no universe to which members could appeal to establish universality – in fact, they belonged to a multiverse.[38]

What Tully explains with regard to agreement formation parallels what I am trying to explain with regard to moral judgment. It is possible to account for a moral judgment that all interlocutors understand and accept as reasonable without that judgment being forced by an appeal to some explicit moral principle or ground. As Tully argues, this is quite possible in a crosscultural context. Furthermore, it is by virtue of the dialogical process that a shared sense of the good and the legitimacy of outcomes are determined. However, by my lights, Tully goes too far in denying that the Chain was based on a substantive common good and in asserting that common grounds reached through dialogue had nothing to do with a commitment to universalizability. If my analysis of the hidden and implicit factors of the Covenant Chain's ethic is correct, Tully's analysis cannot be a complete explanation of how the Chain's normative elements worked. Much of what Tully sees as opaque, I see as having to do with these hidden and implicit factors. These factors guided the dialogical process and the Covenant Chain's procedures. Agreements were not entirely cobbled together and arrived at accidentally. If I am correct about each side's ability to appeal to an implicit common ground, it cannot be the case that agreements relied exclusively on dialogue. There may not have been an explicit *telos* to which both sides appealed, but it was something more than dialogue, negotiation, and agreement that enabled the two sides to establish alliances, legal proceedings, and other forms of treaty making, as my discussion of wampum, origin stories, and the Three Bare Words indicates. If Tully had focused as much on wampum as on dialogue and on the linking-of-arms wampum belts as much as on Guswenṭah (his spelling, *Kahswentah*), he would have had a much more difficult time drawing his conclusion.

Despite my disagreement with Tully, his framing of the context of the Covenant Chain as a strange multiplicity is, nevertheless, vital to my explanation of the articulability of the Chain's ethic and to my defence of its universality. The ethic was the product of genius. In fact, the strangeness of the multiplicity ran deep. What initially appears to be an accidental matching of sensibilities in the crosscultural interactions of the Covenant Chain begins to look more like a kind of hidden logic once the significance of underground chains, wampum, and so on to the Chain's ethic are acknowledged. It was a logic that enabled interlocutors to refer to the forces of unity and identity to direct or redirect the course of dialogue when they encountered conflicts of interest, perspective, or principle. I use the term *logic* because there was an element of being compelled cognitively by the Chain's unity function and wampum protocol to move from justification to healing.

The systematic nature of the Covenant Chain's procedures implies that dialogue was governed; it did not stand alone in enabling the parties to reach agreement. Some of Gottfried Wilhelm Leibniz's observations are useful at this point because they indicate how we might even expect an implicit, unarticulated sense of a shared good to develop, even among strange multiplicities. Leibniz observes that all societies with developed legal systems could be characterized in accordance with a similar ethic. As he went about researching various societies' legal systems, Leibniz found that all such societies were committed to three basic moral principles. All had a version of the harm principle, which states that an unjustifiable harm perpetrated on community members (that is, innocent victims) is sufficient grounds for exacting some kind of consequence (e.g., punishment). The second principle, to "give what is owed," is an obligation of reciprocity while the third held up honesty and integrity as key values.[39] Curiously, both procedural and substantive elements are included in these three principles. If each principle is of a sort that typically arises in any developmental, socialization process by which people seek to establish some kind of rule-governed society, then it is reasonable to assume that these principles and their corresponding values (goods) express universally embedded principles and hypergoods. It can be argued that to have a law-governed society is to have a society that is governed by some underlying good, which the three moral principles make operational.

Leibniz's observations indicate, first, that some goods may in fact be universally recognized. Second, as norms governing a civil society, the three principles express how people, in fact, judge whether a society is a good one. They, therefore, express how a universal good is and can be recognized through recognizing a plurality of goods. The procedural principles of the Covenant Chain (the virtues and possibly even the values of freedom and autonomy) can then be seen as operative expressions of the hypergood. Freedom (freedom from harm and oppression) is closely connected to the harm principle. Reciprocity is typically viewed as a condition of a free and open society, and integrity is typically viewed as a necessary condition of such a society. Thus, Leibniz's principles and those of the Chain can be connected as expressions of a civil society's hypergood.

On the matter of undetectability, Leibniz's principle of infinitesimality suggests why the hypergood and any tendency toward universalizability can, in principle, remain hidden.[40] It states that certain kinds of developments and changes are owing to indiscernible increments. It tells us not to look for points at which things of type x come into being but to examine processes within which x comes to exist. For instance, in biomedical ethics it is sometimes necessary to determine when a human organism becomes a person. For those who believe that personhood is complex (those who do not simply assume that they are eternal souls, etc.), the emergence of a person occurs at some point during a process of physical, mental, and social maturation. Although p, as a zygote, may not qualify as a person, p, as a twenty-year-old student would. Therefore, p became a person at some point between these two points. Asking at what precise point this happened or what precise set of conditions applied to create the person is to ask the impossible because personhood is not of a type that its existence or emergence can be strictly determined, owing to the complexity of the relationship between the conditions upon which personhood depends (e.g., brain development and the capacity for thought and decision making, certain kinds of feelings and emotions, self-identity, and socialization). Dating and detecting when all of these conditions are present and integrated in just the right way to constitute a person is impossible because the development of personhood occurs in accordance with interconnections among conditions – indiscernible increments of degree and complexity. When persons emerge from this complex array of factors, new properties come to exist that could not have existed at earlier stages. For example, the capacity to perceive, conceive, argue, choose, and so on emerge as complexity increases, and they could not have existed at earlier, simpler stages.

Similarly, and despite the looseness of the analogy, it can be argued that the emergence of a common ground in the Covenant Chain, as a hypergood, emerged indiscernibly through the process of complexification and was only inchoately recognized quite late in the relationship (e.g., by Johnson and Gage). The hypergood, then, arose through infinitesimal increments of complexity, allowing community members to recognize when a principle was appropriate (or not) and when a judgment was competent. This hypergood operated as a universal. Leibniz, then, does help to explain how a hypergood can arise in a hidden manner, but he does not explain how it remains hidden yet operative.

The direction in which I am attempting to steer analysis of the Covenant Chain is hardly new. Many ethicists (e.g., James Rachels, Barry Hoffmaster, Alisdair MacIntyre, Annette Baier, and Nancy Davis) and even some recent textbooks in practical or applied ethics (e.g., James Liszka's *Moral Competence*) conceive of ethics as the integration of a complex network of factors that constitute moral life.[41] They are coming to understand that many of our moral dilemmas cannot be resolved by justificatory approaches alone and that explanations of moral life cannot be constructed in a straightforward manner. Moral competence is needed and must be factored into the properties of moral life. This competence demands that moral agents weave together the array of factors that contribute to the complexity of moral life and that they understand how to order them appropriately so that their decisions produce a communal good.

If the primary pursuit of moral life and theorizing is to achieve moral competence, it makes more sense to conceive of the hypergood as that which underlies judgment and action as a guiding force to which the morally competent are attuned and which, as a result, they follow. Indeed, it is the satisfaction of this hypergood that convinces a community of the decision maker's moral competence. Attunement to this good enables lower-order goods to be identified and judged as appropriate or inappropriate by virtue of their ability to draw on people's recognition of the hypergood. The particular genius of the Covenant Chain is that it promoted the recognition of moral competence over and above justification by ensuring that a strange multiplicity was maintained and by maintaining the dual functions of justification and unity healing.

Accessing the Implicate Moral Order

Although I offer evidence for the existence of a hypergood that operated in the Covenant Chain relationship and to which members appealed to synthesize the procedural and substantive elements of the Chain's ethic, it could still be argued that this hypergood was simply something conjured (like Plato's myth of Ur) because of a felt need for an ultimate grounding. I have, after all, relied on the notion of an objective normative lifeworld to make my case, and this lifeworld does not persist unless people remain actively engaged in communicative actions. In other words, it does not exist independently of people committed to community building and protection. Since I accept that no explicit, formal articulation of the hypergood is genuinely free of cultural bias or historical limitations, the Chain's hypergood remains a presupposition expressed only analogically, indirectly and metaphorically through wampum use and origin stories. This suggests that the hypergood is itself a fabrication designed to give the appearance of a coherent system of moral relations. Hence, something more needs to be done to at least show that the hypergood was not fabricated by the collective imagination or will but was recognized through metaphor.

Thus far, the hypergood has been analyzed as logically prior to both the principles of the procedural and the values of the substantive ethics of the Covenant Chain. Although it is not prior to the socialization process, because it emerges in the process, it can be said to be prior in the sense that appeals to it must be made in order to make sense of the array of moral factors that together constitute moral life. It is not prior in the sense that Kant claims the categorical imperative is prior to empirical determinations of moral rules: it is not determined a priori through an act or pure practical reason. But it is prior in a quasi-logical sense because it must be presupposed in order to view both procedural and substantive elements as belonging to a single normative lifeworld. To make sense of this situation, we must be prepared to accept the possibility that not everything about moral life is explicable and cognizable. At the same time, however, those inexplicable elements need to be approachable, otherwise we are left with a mystery that makes appealing to a universal hypergood vulnerable to accusations of arbitrariness and caprice.

By drawing on the distinction between the normally hidden and the hidden-in-principle, it is possible to take the analysis of the hypergood further to show that it might be grounded in something more definite than imagination and will, such that its universalizing tendencies are indicative of a genuine universalizability. Goods that are hidden because they are part of the taken-for-granted intersubjective world (e.g., goods associated with histories of personal sacrifice, trust, and integrity) are examples of the normally hidden. Those that are hidden-in-principle are factors that develop through the process of socialization and are conceptualized as the background or storehouse of assumed concepts, values, and sensibilities that make communication possible. I have drawn on the idea of the implicit throughout this description of the Covenant Chain's ethic to frame descriptions and explanations of such hidden-in-principle aspects. I have also used the category of the spiritual as a placeholder to ensure that certain kinds of intangible grounding factors are not overlooked simply because a way to articulate and take account of them has not yet been found. "The spiritual" represents a kind of binding force, much like the concept of reality grounds various descriptions and theoretical frameworks in physics. By drawing a parallel between ethics and physics, utilizing David Bohm's notion of the implicate order, I argue that the appeal to the hidden-in-principle is not an act of fabrication but rather an act of recognition.[42] A summary account of Bohm's theory must suffice.

Bohm views the conflict between different explanatory schemes in physics as presupposing a more fundamental order of reality. The conflict itself presupposes a more fundamental order. Bohm develops his argument by describing how physicists recognize a need for a grand unifying theory to integrate Newtonian (or Einsteinian) and quantum physics. If we include developments in string theory, the theory of dark matter and energy, the problem of unification is exacerbated, insofar as each theory is viewed as irreducible to the others, which remain mutually incompatible as descriptions of reality. The irreducibility of, say, Newtonian (descriptive of macro-level phenomena) to quantum (descriptive of subatomic-level phenomena) physics presupposes a third implicate order. The parallel in ethics is this: just as no physicist today would jettison either Newtonian or quantum physics, no ethicist would jettison either substantive ethics (goods and the virtues) or procedural ethics just because the tension between them appears irreconcilable. Just as physics as a whole would be seriously limited in its ability to inform us about the physical world if Newtonian physics were abandoned, ethics would be seriously limited in its ability to inform us about how to deal with moral life if substantive ethics were abandoned in the interest of establishing a more philosophically coherent ethical theory. Just as the tension between Newtonian and quantum physics points to a totality of the physical world, so too does the tension between procedural and substantive ethics point to a totality of moral life. Although neither explicit order fully captures the totality, the necessity of accepting both implies the existence of some third underlying, implicate moral order.

To extend the parallel further, in physics, the shift in scientific paradigms over the course of history was largely due to the emergence of new paradigms that could better explain phenomena. That there can be better explanations implies that an underlying order to the experienced and theorized (or thematized) reality exists. It is against this order, indeed, that theories are tested. If theorizing can be improved by shifting perspective, or by introducing new concepts and altering methods of inquiry, then the underlying order is a totality against which proposed new explicit orders are compared and judged for adequacy. This totality is an implicate order because it is never made entirely explicit. The explicit orders (systems of properties, laws, and so on) we rely on are attempts to capture the totality; however, because they fail to do so, we distinguish between theory and reality. Once an implicate order is acknowledged, it calls for a suspension of belief in the absolute truth of explicate orders, because we acknowledge that these explicit orders are incomplete. By acknowledging theoretical incompleteness, we accept that theories can be wrong and misleading. To acknowledge an implicate order, then, is to accept the view that theories and explicit orders are nets that we construct and cast to capture some of the totality, not all of it.

Theoretical frameworks, therefore, should be viewed as more or less valuable or useful relative to a particular domain or field of inquiry. Maintaining the tension between irreducible and incompatible theoretical frameworks, as in physics, is a precursor to understanding more about the implicate order. Insofar as the structure, function, and dynamics of the Covenant Chain were attempts to hold two disparate moral frameworks in tension, they can be seen as predisposing members to recognize the implicate moral order. Just as the totality of the implicate order stands prior to any explicit attempt at ordering it, so too does the implicate moral order stand prior to the particular moral theories we use to articulate descriptions and explanations of moral life, including theories about the hypergood. The hypergood, therefore, insofar as it is related to and grounded in the totality of the implicate moral order, cannot be thematized, articulated, or explained in its totality. In Spinozistic terms, every determination is a negation. To determine (define) a good and its specific relation to lower-order goods is to negate (fail to define) the hypergood in its totality. Recall that the hypergood is defined in terms of the complex network of goods that animate moral life. If formal, explicit articulations cannot capture the hypergood qua network, however necessary attempts to construct them may be, then such attempts should be viewed as heuristics that prepare us to shift to a different mode of articulation.

Re-examining references to underground chains, wampum use, and the like in light of this conclusion exposes something of the genius of the Covenant Chain. Despite never being articulated through clear and explicit concepts, the implicate moral order was, nevertheless, articulated through indirect references, through symbols such as "underground chain." Jan Zwicky's work on metaphor and how good metaphors aim at the truth helps characterize how these references worked to maintain awareness of the implicate moral order so that appeals could be made to it when necessary. Zwicky states, "By 'metaphor' I mean the linguistic expression of the results of focussed analogical thinking."[43] References to underground chains or even above-ground chains, for that matter, employed metaphors in a focused way to develop an analogue for an implicate binding force or moral order. By setting the metaphor beside the referent, we can see that they have the same form, while, at the same time over-riding "calcified gestures."[44] I take attempts at developing explicit, technical language to capture the hypergood and common ground to be one kind of calcified gesture.

Returning to the discourse of the Covenant Chain – to the language of polishing, wiping tears from the eyes, keeping the chain inviolable – it is now clear that this metaphorical language does, in fact, point to the logic of morally ordered relationships in ways that technically precise articulations cannot. One begins to see that technical articulations can, in fact, freeze or ossify communication in and understandings of moral relationships because they fix meanings that must remain fluid in the interactions between people if they are to enable interlocutors to be attuned to and respond to one another and the hypergood. In Spinozistic terms, technical moral language negates the possibility of becoming attuned to one another and to the implicate moral order that constitutes the common ground of the community. Good metaphors, in Zwicky's view, do the opposite by releasing our understanding and communicative actions from those limitations and bonds. In the Covenant Chain, although the metaphor of the chain or linking arms was initially and explicitly associated with formal agreements and codifications, it also had the potential to release members from the conceptual bonds those associations produced. It pointed out the logic of relationships that were aimed at developing mutual understanding. That is, to achieve the end of mutual understanding, interlocutors had to open their point of view and attitudes to optimize, or even maximize, their capacity to use communicative speech acts and to resist becoming reliant on strategic ones. Communicative speech acts, therefore, were more than simply necessary conditions for rational negotiation: they were the means to disclose the implicate moral order.

Zwicky's observations about the relationship between good metaphors and truth also help situate the role of the implicate moral order. According to Zwicky, "A good metaphor is no more a clever artifact than is an intelligently musical use of language. Both, in different ways, are attempts to tell the truth."[45] The function of origin stories and wampum use, then, was to tell the truth about the objective normative lifeworld according to which the relationship had evolved. These devices were, in fact, truth-oriented and drew their users into a truth orientation, however intangible, hidden, and formally inarticulable that truth was. Such truths could be contrasted with fallacies and falseness. Hence, once interlocutors shared an understanding of the context in which high-context languages and rich descriptors were employed, they had to orient themselves to the truth at which metaphors (origin stories and wampum use) were aimed. Thus, to know what the metaphors signified was to have engaged with a communicative community oriented toward normative truth.

Zwicky continues, "The truth of the implicit 'is not': this suggests that the positive assertion in a metaphor is always an act of overcoming. – As though 'calcified' uses must in fact precede metaphorical gestures; as though it were characteristic of language that it first conceal the world – be non-metaphorical – before the metaphor reveals it to us."[46] In this statement, she, in effect, describes the process of trying to articulate the common ground, both as it is described in the record and as I have tried to describe it in this work. Adhering to a certain mode of ethical thought (procedural or substantive) may be a necessary first step in becoming aware of the implicate moral order. Becoming more fully aware of how the implicate moral order operates, then, requires having some reason to suspend reliance on that particular mode. My attempt to formulate the Covenant Chain's ethic at first led to an articulation of two incompatible frameworks. In the attempt to resolve the tension between these two frameworks to show that they could together constitute a coherent theory, they became calcified. In responding to demands for clear definition and logical coherence, I removed the analysis from the dynamic context of the intersubjective world, possibly by necessity (as expected by both Zwicky and Geertz). My analysis, therefore, omitted the dynamic and critical factor – engagement or participation – that enables us to understand how an integration of the seemingly incompatible theories of moral life is possible.

It can be argued that, as moral theorists, we must acknowledge the inarticulable, hidden-in-principle hypergood of the implicate moral order as a grounding for ethics. This ground is not fabricated: it can be approached adequately (but not completely) through the use of good metaphors. Through the use of such metaphors, the tension between incompatible theoretical frameworks can be maintained and should be maintained when those frameworks are irreducible and necessary. Furthermore, this grounding is conceivably universal since it arises wherever moral agents engage in communicative actions to form a moral community. If the Covenant Chain's hypergood is not a true universal, in the philosophical sense, neither is it merely a generalizable good. It was not a good that is culturally bound to either European or Aboriginal traditions. There are also reasons to believe that it was not a historically bound ethic. Insofar as it was based on conditions that evolved through the process of socialization, the details of which describe such processes across temporal periods, the burden of proof now rests with the skeptic who would deny the relevance of the Chain to the contemporary First Nations–Crown relationship.

Conclusion

While historical treaties were certainly formal agreements, they were also commitments to community or to relationship, to being open to ever deepening disclosures of what communal (hence, moral) life is about. Treaties were at one and the same time diplomatic agreements between sovereign nations, legally mediated relationships between members of an institution, and morally governed relationships of solidarity. Seen from a moral point of view, they were formal relationships that had a tendency toward ossification, which was checked by constant reminders to recognize and act on the basis of an underlying common ground. They were arrangements that enabled members to become and remain creatively attuned to the implicate moral order and the good it defined for the human community.

Was there, at any time, a mutually recognized and respectful Crown-Aboriginal relationship? There are two ways to answer this question: one straightforward, one not so straightforward. Mutual respect was demonstrated in straightforward manner through the negotiation process. Discourse ethics describes the principles of this kind of respect: treating all involved in the negotiation as free interlocutors, whose perspective and positions are deserving of attention and critical understanding. But in attempting to show that the ethic underlying the negotiation process was coherent, I identified more complex ways of exercising mutual respect. One was becoming attuned to the other's suffering and spiritual aspirations, among other elements, thereby becoming attuned to the shared lifeworld, raising it from the level of the taken-for-granted to that of explicit appreciation. Compassion was the central means through which this mode of respect was expressed. At a fundamental level, however, mutual respect was demonstrated and grounded in the dynamics of the intersubjective lifeworld (the use of wampum, the appeal to origin stories, and so on) through which interlocutors became attuned to the workings of the implicate moral order.

Much of the contemporary debate about the relationship between Aboriginal and non-Aboriginal people has been about problems generated by the epistemological, metaphysical, and possibly psychological differences between the two cultures. John Clammer, Sylvie Poirier, and Eric Schwimmer's view is that the different ontologies presupposed by the two sides make coming to a common understanding of a hypergood extremely difficult, even impossible.[47] This is no doubt true if by *common understanding* they mean making explicitly formulated cultural expectations and sensibilities compatible. If we accept the implicate moral order as a more fundamental order, different cultural expectations do not pose an insurmountable problem. They can, in fact, serve as devices to move us into awareness of deeper commonalities and deeper modes of mutual respect.

Epilogue

As far as I can tell, the Covenant Chain was never formally extinguished as a treaty-negotiating forum by the likes of an act of Parliament or a Supreme Court decision. Rather, it died a gradual death as Aboriginal peoples' military power was dwarfed by British and American military forces and as proper persons were replaced by bureaucracies. Today, some member nations of the Haudenosaunee continue to appeal to the Chain as the core of their treaty relationship with the Canadian Crown. Some Anishnaabek nations also appeal to belts from the 1760s, as they did in 1817, to call on the Canadian Crown to honour the peace and friendship arrangement formally ratified in 1761, 1764, and 1767. The ethic of the Covenant Chain appears not to be dead. It, at least, has not been entirely forgotten.

In my attempt to carry the relevance of the historical Covenant Chain's ethic forward to inform current debates about Aboriginal rights and related issues, I anticipate the argument that historical developments have changed the political, economic, and legal character of the relationship so radically that the conditions that compelled the evolution of the Covenant Chain ethic no longer apply. In the absence of those compelling factors, the contemporary relevance of origin stories and wampum is severely diminished, if not made virtually irrelevant. But does the absence of the conditions that enabled an ethic to emerge obviate the need to recognize that ethic?

One of the better approaches to answering this question, I think, is to argue that the very fact that the Crown–First Nations relationship is a historical one should form the basis of any attempt to reinstate the ethic of the Covenant Chain. Since its contemporary irrelevance can be traced back to various events – such as the Indian Act, the War of 1812, and the shift from peace and friendship treaties to surrenders and the like – the current relationship can be said to be the consequence of intentional one-sided modifications to the original relationship. Those intentional modifications gradually eroded the Crown's commitment to the Chain's ethic, certainly not by mutual consent but by ignoring the voices of those with whom they had once shared a normative lifeworld. How we tell the story of these intentional modifications, in part, determines how we interpret the contemporary relationship and evaluate the terms of reference currently being employed. If we tell the story as one of uncontrollable economic and political forces causing the shift in conditions, then we will conclude that carry-forward attempts are indeed futile. But if we identify acts of human agency in setting new conditions, then we can say that people were responsible for these shifting conditions. We could then argue that these acts were acts of betrayal because the Crown ignored the conditions that had once generated mutual trust and respect. If the latter interpretation is correct, it would appear that the proper course of action would be to rectify this betrayal in an act of reconciliation.

Great caution needs to be exercised in carry-forward efforts. As much as I support the efforts of Aboriginal scholars to carry various historical practices and ideas forward into current debates, such carry-forward efforts are fraught with danger. Dale Turner's *This Is Not a Peace Pipe,* for instance, cites the use of wampum, especially Guswentah (the Two Row Wampum), in arguing for the need to recognize reciprocity and respect as principles of intercultural exchange.[1] Turner's purpose in writing is to encourage a division of labour among Aboriginal peoples and Aboriginal scholars. Aboriginal scholars, he argues, should consider themselves word warriors who will bring Aboriginal concerns forward in terms that are understandable, both conceptually and methodologically, to that society: "I contend that a community of indigenous intellectuals – word warriors – ought to assert and defend the integrity of indigenous rights and nationhood *and* protect indigenous ways of knowing within the existing legal and political practices of the dominant culture."[2] Presumably, Turner would have indigenous intellectuals bring the historical material of wampum belts and ethical expectations, including the focus on mutual understanding, to contemporary debates about Aboriginal rights and sovereignty.

Through a critique of Canada's 1969 White Paper, which laid out a policy of assimilation; Alan Cairns's doctrine of citizens plus; and Will Kymlicka's doctrine of multiculturalism, Turner attempts to blaze a path through the maze of problems that word warriors will encounter as they try to carry their traditional practices and ways of knowing forward to contemporary debates.[3] Before criticizing this strategy, let me re-emphasize that I support Turner's ambition. It begins where it must, not in some ideal-world construction, but where thought and practice actually reside. Through critical evaluation of the status quo, he attempts to move beyond its assumptions to create a more inclusive context in which an enriching dialogue can proceed.

The danger in Turner's call to word warriors is that the Crown, from the beginning and in both of its renditions (British and Canadian), has striven to make First Nations dependants, children, and subjects. Even though military and political realities militated against this political aspiration, there is continuity in the Crown's aspiration. Once it could, the Crown attempted to transform treaties from peace and friendship agreements into surrenders. This intent, then, needs to be factored into our understanding of the historical forces that have shaped the current situation. What is carried forward can become a target for extinguishment or reinterpretation to suit some purpose other than genuine reconciliation (e.g., appropriation or cooptation). Historically, the Crown has argued that Aboriginal rights, titles, and modes of recognition have been virtually extinguished because the Crown's regulatory schemes have made them irrelevant. Aboriginal rights have been regulated away. Both Dale Turner and James Tully are well aware of this history. Extinguishment of Aboriginal and treaty rights in exchange for individual rights and title to land (held in fee simple) is another strategy that has been used. What Turner seems to downplay, but Tully does not, is the Crown's commitment to extinguishment as a morally legitimate means for achieving political and social order.

A crucial factor in these attempts to undermine Aboriginal claims and the relevance of Aboriginal perspectives is the demand for clarity, definition, and the formal articulation of Aboriginal claims – in other words, an ossification of the symbols used to order the relationship. If word warriors were to bring the wampum tradition and, by implication, the ethic of the Chain forward for explicit recognition, they would make them a target for ossification. As a result, historical devices that fostered communicative actions would be transformed into tools for strategic action. Word warriors would be asked to define the Two Row Wampum and set out the principles entailed in accepting it. In effect, they would be asked to provide representations of the treaty relationship, which would deny the relevance of a shared lifeworld (or what remains of it). To the extent that this ossification would be determined by legal and political powers, the power and authority of the implicate moral order (once carried by wampum and origin stories) would be buried. In the current situation, the power imbalance and the lack of strong Aboriginal institutions to represent and sustain the Aboriginal voice and carry traditions forward, especially those that are as complex as wampum, would render this a poor strategy. Success would depend on re-establishing an intersubjective lifeworld, moral economy, and objective normative lifeworld in response to the implicate moral order. This can only be done in a fluid, non-ossified manner.

A first move for word warriors committed to carrying traditions forward must, I think, first of all, entrench the history of the Crown–First Nation relationship and origin stories (including that of the Covenant Chain, with all of its strangeness) into the collective memory of North American society. Such strange stories would help neutralize power imbalances by shifting the focus away from legalistic and political justifications toward mutual understanding and an open dialogue on what the relationship could be in light of what it once was.

Notes

Preface
1 Queen Victoria, "Declaration by Her Majesty in Favour of the Ojibway Indians Respecting Certain Lands on Lake Huron," 1847, Library and Archives Canada (LAC).
2 See Will Kymlicka, "American Multi-Culturalism and the 'Nations Within,'" in *Political Theory and the Rights of Indigenous Peoples*, ed. Duncan Ivison, Paul Patton, and Will Sanders (Cambridge: Cambridge University Press, 2000).
3 John Clammer, Sylvie Poirier, and Eric Schwimmer, "Introduction: The Relevance of Ontologies in Anthropology – Reflections on a New Anthropological Field," in *Figured Worlds: Ontological Obstacles in Inter-Cultural Relations*, ed. Michael Lambek (Toronto: University of Toronto Press, 2004).
4 Olive Dickason, *Canada's First Nations: A History of Founding Peoples from Earliest Times* (Toronto: McClelland and Stewart, 1992) and *The Myth of the Savage and the Beginnings of French Colonialism in the Americas* (Edmonton: University of Alberta Press, 1984). For examples of Bruce Trigger's work, see "Brecht and Ethnohistory," *Ethnohistory* 22, 1 (1975): 51-56, and *Children of Aetaentsic: A History of the Huron People to 1660*, Carleton Library Series 195 (Montreal and Kingston: McGill-Queen's University Press, 1976); Bruce G. Trigger and Wilcomb E. Washburn, eds. *The Cambridge History of the Native Peoples of the Americas*, vol. 1, *North America* (New York: Cambridge University Press, 1996); Wilcomb E. Washburn and Bruce G. Trigger, "Native Peoples in Euro-American Historiography," in Trigger and Washburn, *The Cambridge History of the Native Peoples*, 61-124.
5 Alan R. Emery and associates, *Guidelines for Environmental Assessments and Traditional Knowledge* (Ottawa: Centre for Traditional Knowledge to the World Council of Indigenous People, 1997).
6 See the Scientific Panel for Sustainable Forest Practices in Clayoquot Sound, *First Nations' Perspective: Relating to Forest Practices Standards in Clayoquot Sound* (Victoria: Government of British Columbia, 1995).

Introduction
1 The argument is similar to the one Jeremy Webber, a legal philosopher, develops in "Relations of Force and Relations of Justice: The Emergence of Normative Community between Colonists and Aboriginal Peoples," *Osgoode Hall Law Journal* 33, 4 (1995): 623-60. Webber argues that an intercommunal normativity developed over time. My argument advances the idea that an ethic evolved over time as the relationship became more complex. I attempt to show that this ethic can be thematized and potentially universalized.
2 Robert A. Williams Jr., *Linking Arms Together: American Indian Treaty Visions of Law and Peace, 1600-1800* (New York: Oxford University Press, 1997), 5.
3 See, for instance, Daniel Francis, *The Imaginary Indian: The Image of the Indian in Canadian Culture* (Vancouver: Arsenal Pulp Press, 1992), and Shepard Krech III, *The Ecological Indian: Myth and History* (New York: W.W. Norton and Co., 1999).

4 Although his poetry lamented the loss of the Noble Savage, Scott was at the helm of one of the twentieth century's most vicious assimilation projects. The Canadian government and allied churches sought to remove the "Indianness" from the "ignoble savage." Whether they were romanticized or demonized, Aboriginal people were defined as uncivilized and not recognized as having a voice to which the civilized world needed to attend.

5 Washburn and Trigger, "Native Peoples in Euro-American Historiography."

6 *R v Van Der Peet,* [1996] 2 SCR 507. In this case, the Supreme Court attempted to define Aboriginal rights in terms of the practices of Aboriginal people before contact. This approach, sometimes called the "frozen rights" approach, implies that Aboriginal people have to establish that a practice (e.g., fishing in a certain area) had been in place before contact with Europeans in order for that practice to be considered an Aboriginal right.

7 Samuel Eliot Morison, ed., *The Francis Parkman Reader* (Cambridge, MA: Da Capo Press, 1998), 18.

8 Even the Iroquois, whom Parkman believed to be far superior to the Algonquians, were described as follows: "That the Iroquois, left under their institutions to work out their destiny undisturbed, would ever have developed a civilization of their own, I do not believe. These institutions, however, are sufficiently characteristic and curious." Ibid., 41.

9 Ibid., 32.

10 Washburn and Trigger, "Native Peoples in Euro-American Historiography," 114.

11 Bernard W. Sheehan, "Indian-White Relations in Early America: A Review Essay," *William and Mary Quarterly,* 3rd series, 26 (1969): 267-86.

12 James Axtell, "A Moral History of Indian-White Relations Revisited," in *After Columbus: Essays in the Ethnohistory of Colonial North America,* ed. James Axtell (New York: Oxford University Press, 1988), 9-33.

13 Washburn and Trigger, "Native Peoples in Euro-American Historiography," 81-85.

14 Ibid., 86.

15 Ibid., 95.

16 Georges E. Sioui, *For an Amerindian Autohistory,* trans. Sheila Fischman (Montreal and Kingston: McGill-Queen's University Press, 1992), xxii, 101.

17 Michael Foster defines upstreaming analysis as taking descriptions of protocol as practised today and comparing them to the historical record. When the two match, there is reason to believe that a genuine, historically grounded Aboriginal practice or use of a concept has been found. Moreover, the two can be mutually informing. Using this technique, Foster concludes that one of the core functions of wampum was to open and maintain channels of communication. He argues that wampum was, and continues to be, a communication device designed to promote the establishment of good minds and good relations. The circularity of this technique makes it unsuitable for my purposes, but I wish to acknowledge its influence. I had reached the same conclusion (before reading Foster) in response to Eric Johnston's comments about going back to the wampum (see Preface).

18 E. Richard Atleo (Umeek), *Tsawalk: A Nuu-Chah-Nulth Worldview* (Vancouver: UBC Press, 2004), 3.

19 Clifford Geertz, *The Interpretation of Cultures* (New York: Basic Books, 1973).

20 Ibid., 27.

21 Ibid., 6-7.

22 Ibid., 19.

23 Ibid., 5.

24 See, for example, Donald Davidson, "Actions, Reasons and Causes," *Journal of Philosophy* 60, 23 (1963): 685-700; "Causal Relations," *Journal of Philosophy* 64, 21 (1967): 691-703; "Freedom to Act," in *Essays on Freedom of Action,* ed. Ted Honderich (London: Routledge and Kegan Paul, 1973), 139-56; and "Thinking Causes," in *Mental Causation,* ed. John Heil and Alfred Mele (Oxford: Clarendon Press, 1993), 3-17. See also John Searle, "Minds, Brains, and Programs," *Behavioral and Brain Sciences* 3 (1980): 417-24.

25 Lawrence C. Wroth, "The Indian Treaty as Literature," *Yale Review* 17 (1928): 766.

26 William N. Fenton, "Structure, Continuity, and Change in the Process of Iroquois Treaty Making," in Jennings et al., eds., *The History and Culture of Iroquois Diplomacy: An*

Interdisciplinary Guide to the Treaties of the Six Nations and Their League (Syracuse, NY: Syracuse University Press, 1985), 5.

27 Ibid.
28 See Robert A. Williams Jr., "Linking Arms Together: Multicultural Constitutionalism in a North American Indigenous Vision of Law and Peace," *California Law Review* 82, 4 (1994): 981-1049, and *Linking Arms;* Paul Williams, "The Chain" (master's thesis, Osgoode Hall Law School, 1982); and Mark D. Walters, "Brightening the Covenant Chain: Aboriginal Treaty Meanings in Law and History after *Marshall," Dalhousie Law Journal* 24, 2 (2001): 75-138.
29 Michael Pomedli, "Eighteenth-Century Treaties," *American Indian Quarterly* 19, 3 (1995): 319.
30 Williams, "Linking Arms Together," 984-85.
31 Pomedli, "Eighteenth-Century Treaties," 319.
32 Francis Jennings, *The Ambiguous Iroquois Empire: The Covenant Chain Confederation of Indian Tribes with English Colonies from Its Beginnings to the Lancaster Treaty of 1744* (New York: W.W. Norton and Company, 1984), 167.
33 Peter Nabakov, "Native Views of History," in Trigger and Washburn, *The Cambridge History of the Native Peoples of the Americas,* 1-59.
34 Sam D. Gill, *Mother Earth: An American Story* (Chicago: University of Chicago Press, 1987), 14.
35 Sioui, *For an Amerindian Autohistory,* xxii, xiv, 9.
36 Bruce Morito, *Thinking Ecologically: Environmental Thought, Values and Policy* (Halifax, NS: Fernwood, 2002).
37 Even Georges Sioui, who develops an Amerindian autohistory, sees value in the writings of the French author Baron Lahontan (see *For an Amerindian Autohistory,* Chapter 5), even though Lahontan translated speeches by his Aboriginal interlocutor (Adario or Kondarionk) in terms used by European philosophers of the day.
38 Peter Wraxall, *An Abridgment of the Indian Affairs, Contained in Four Folio Volumes, Transacted in the Colony of New York, from the Year 1678 to the Year 1751,* ed. Charles Howard McIlwain (Cambridge: Harvard University Press, 1915; repr., New York: Benjamin Bloom, 1968), 154.
39 Ibid., 155.
40 John Borrows, "Nanabush Goes West: Title, Treaties, and the Trickster in British Columbia," Chapter 4 in *Recovering Canada: The Resurgence of Indigenous Law* (Toronto: University of Toronto Press, 2002), 77-110.
41 Ibid., 102-3.
42 *Delgamuukw v British Columbia,* [1997] 3 SCR 1010.
43 Wraxall, *An Abridgment of the Indian Affairs;* Lawrence H. Leder, ed. *The Livingston Indian Records, 1666-1723* (Gettysburg: Pennsylvania Historical Association, 1956).
44 LAC, MG 21, Commission for Indian Affairs, Albany, "Schedule of propositions made by the Indians and answers given by the Commission at Albany, 1677-1719."
45 Wraxall, *An Abridgment of the Indian Affairs,* xcvii, xcix.
46 See Francis Jennings, *Empire of Fortune: Crowns, Colonies, and Tribes in the Seven Years' War in America* (New York: W.W. Norton and Company, 1988), Chapter 4.
47 LAC, RG 10, Commissions for Indian Affairs, Albany, reel C-1220, October 1729 and April 1730, 294a-315.
48 Jennings, *Empire of Fortune,* 337-38; Leroy V. Eid, "The Ojibwa-Iroquois War: The War the Five Nations Did Not Win," *Ethnohistory* 26, 4 (1979): 297-324.
49 Jennings, *Empire of Fortune,* 318.

Chapter 1: The Historical Context

1 Francis Jennings, *The Invasion of America: Indians, Colonialism, and the Cant of Conquest* (Chapel Hill: University of North Carolina Press, 1975), *The Ambiguous Iroquois Empire,* and *Empire of Fortune;* Stephen Saunders Webb, *1676: The End of American Independence* (New York: Alfred A. Knopf, 1984); Allen W. Trelease, *Indian Affairs in Colonial New York: The Seventeenth Century* (Ithaca, NY: Cornell University Press, 1960); James H. Merrell, *Into the American Woods: Negotiators on the Pennsylvania Frontier* (New York: W.W. Norton, 1999); and Richard White, *The Middle Ground: Indians, Empires and Republics in the Great Lakes Region, 1650-1815* (Cambridge: Cambridge University Press, 1991).

2 Jennings, *The Ambiguous Iroquois Empire*, 247.
3 See, for instance, Pomedli, "Eighteenth-Century Treaties," and Williams, *Linking Arms Together*.
4 Jean-Jacques Rousseau, "Discourse on the Origin and Foundations of Inequality," in *The First and Second Discourses: Jean-Jacques Rousseau*, ed. Roger D. Masters (New York: St. Martin's Press, 1964), 151.
5 Ibid., 128.
6 Jennings et al., *The History and Culture of Iroquois Diplomacy*, 164-68.
7 Leder, *The Livingston Indian Records*, 71-74.
8 Ibid., 70-71.
9 Jennings et al., eds., *Iroquois Indians: A Documentary History of the Diplomacy of the Six Nations and Their League*, microfilm collection (Woodbridge, CT: Research Publications, 1984), reel 3, 31 July–6 August 1684 (hereafter *Iroquois Indians: A Documentary History*). Original source, "Proceedings of a council at Albany between VA Governor Effingham and NY Governor Thomas Dongan and the sachems of the Mohawks, Oneidas, Cayugas and Senecas," Virginia Colonial Papers, folder 4, item 2a, Virginia State Library, Richmond, Virginia.
10 LAC, RG 10, reel C-1221, 23 June 1755, 28-53.
11 *Iroquois Indians: A Documentary History*, reel 12, 24 July 1744. Original source, "Proceedings of council at Lancaster, June 1744 (Lancaster Treaty)," Pennsylvania Provincial Council Minutes, vol. 4, 11.
12 Francis Jennings, "Iroquois Alliances in American History," in Jennings et al., *The History and Culture of Iroquois Diplomacy*, 51.
13 William Johnson, *The Papers of Sir William Johnson* (Albany: University of the State of New York, 1951), 1:158.
14 See especially pages 10-13 of the original record.
15 See, for instance, LAC, MG 21, file 2; E.B. O'Callaghan and John Romeyn Brodhead, eds., *Documents Relative to the Colonial History of the State of New-York ...* 15 vols. (Albany: Weed, Parsons, and Company, 1853-87), 13:510, 20 July 1677; *Iroquois Indians: A Documentary History*, reel 2, 20-21 July 1677, original source, "Col. Henry Coursey Addresses Mohawk and Seneca through Cootes on Behalf of Virginia and Maryland," Calvert Papers, MS 174 299, Maryland Historical Society; Leder, *The Livingston Indian Records*, 39-49.
16 Leder, *The Livingston Indian Records*, 43.
17 Ibid., 45.
18 LAC, MG 21, file 2, 113.
19 L.G. Van Loon, "Tawagonshi, Beginning of Treaty Era," *Indian Historian* 1, 3 (1968): 23-26.
20 Jennings, *Ambiguous Iroquois Empire*, 54.
21 Gunther Michelson, "The Covenant Chain in Colonial History," *Man in the Northeast* 21 (1981): 117.
22 Ibid., 104-5, 120.
23 Daniel K. Richter, "Ordeals of the Longhouse: The Five Nations in Early American History," in Richter and Merrel, *Beyond the Covenant Chain*, 11-27.
24 Ibid., 24.
25 Jennings et al., *The History and Culture of Iroquois Diplomacy*, 158.
26 Wraxall, *An Abridgment of the Indian Affairs*.
27 O'Callaghan and Brodhead, *Documents*, 13:529.
28 Leder, *The Livingston Indian Records*, 39.
29 O'Callaghan and Brodhead, *Documents*, 3:67-68.
30 Ibid.
31 LAC, MG 19, "Articles of Peace, Friendship and Alliance, concluded by Sir William Johnson Baronet, His Majesty's Sole Agent and Superintendant of Indian Affairs for the Northern District of North America & Colonel of the Six United Nations on Behalf of His Britannic Majesty with the Huron Indians of the Detroit," box F33, 18 July 1764.
32 LAC, RG 10, reel C-1220, 7-8 September 1733, 40a-42a.
33 Jennings et al., *History and Culture of Iroquois Diplomacy*, 165.
34 See *Iroquois Indians: A Documentary History*, reel 1, 13 December 1665. Original source, "Articles of treaty of peace proposed by six ambassadors from the Iroquois to the French," Les Archives Nationales, Paris, France, Series C A, vol. 2, 187-90.

35 See *Iroquois Indians: A Documentary History,* reel 3, 31 July–6 August 1684. Original source, Virginia Colonial Papers, folder 4, item 2a.
36 LAC, RG 10, reel C-1220, 28 June 1737, 112-14.
37 *Iroquois Indians: A Documentary History,* reel 5, 15-28 August 1694, 5-6.
38 Jennings, *The Ambiguous Iroquois Empire,* 8, 114, 249.
39 Williams, *Linking Arms Together,* 114.
40 William W. Warren, *History of the Ojibway People* (St. Paul: Minnesota Historical Society Press, 1984).
41 White, *The Middle Ground.*
42 Ibid., 145.
43 Jennings, *The Ambiguous Iroquois Empire,* 148.
44 Eid, "The Ojibwa-Iroquois War."
45 Jennings et al., *The History and Culture of Iroquois Diplomacy,* 127.
46 Wraxall, *An Abridgment of the Indian Affairs,* 15, 39.
47 Ibid., 52.
48 Ibid., 70-71.
49 LAC, RG 10, reel C-1220, 23 August 1746, 151-52.
50 Arthur H. Buffinton, "The Policy of Albany and English Westward Expansion," *Mississippi Valley of Historical Review* 8, 4 (1922): 334-35.
51 Ibid., 345.
52 Jennings, *Empire of Fortune,* 304.
53 Johnson, *Papers,* 1:338.
54 Ibid., 1:239.
55 O'Callaghan and Brodhead, *Documents,* 4:648-52.
56 Ibid., 4:747-48.
57 Ibid.
58 Habermas uses this term *lifeworld,* in part, to describe a common standard, an objective world of ideas and norms that emerges when people learn to subject their claims, values, and perspectives to the scrutiny of their interlocutors. If interlocutors are able to reach agreements, the process produces a shared lifeworld. See Jürgen Habermas, *The Theory of Communicative Action,* vol. 1, *Reason and the Rationalization of Society,* trans. Thomas McCarthy (Boston: Beacon Press, 1984), 137.
59 LAC, RG 10, reel C-1220, 4 June 1723, 36a-39a.
60 LAC, RG 10, reel C-1220, 13 March 1724, 112-13a.
61 See, for example, White, *The Middle Ground,* 149-52.
62 David Hackett Fischer, *Champlain's Dream* (Toronto: Vintage Canada, 2009).
63 Jennings discusses this ambiguous role throughout *Ambiguous Iroquois Empire.* See, for example, 45, 160-61, 263.
64 Ibid., 301.
65 E.B. O'Callaghan and Christopher Morgan, eds., *The Documentary History of the State of New-York* (Albany: Weed, Parsons, 1850), 2:585.
66 LAC, RG 10, reel C-1220, 11 September 1733, 43-45a.
67 LAC, RG 10, reel C-1220, 6 April 1737(?), 101a-102.
68 Jon William Parmenter, "Pontiac's War: Forging New Links in the Anglo-Iroquois Covenant Chain," *Ethnohistory* 44, 4 (1997): 617-54.
69 George III, Royal Proclamation, 1763, reprinted in RSC 1985, App. II, No. 1.
70 White, *The Middle Ground,* 260.
71 Parmenter, "Pontiac's War," 620.
72 White, *The Middle Ground,* 269.
73 Johnson, *Papers,* 4:466-88.
74 Parmenter, "Pontiac's War," 632.
75 Ibid., 635-39.
76 LAC, MG 19, box F29, 1817, 9-12.
77 Ibid.
78 See Jennings, *Empire of Fortune,* 78-81; O'Callaghan and Brodhead, *Documents,* 6:788, 799, 800-1.

79 Jennings, *Empire of Fortune,* 60.
80 Ibid., 82.
81 Ibid., 213-17.
82 Ibid., 221.
83 Ibid., 215. Jennings quotes from Louis Antoine de Bougainville, *Adventures in the Wilderness: The American Journals of Louis Antoine de Bougainville, 1756-1760,* ed. Edward P. Hamilton (Norman: University of Oklahoma Press, 1964), 36, 60.
84 Buffinton, "The Policy of Albany and English Westward Expansion," 344.
85 Daniel K. Richter, "Indian-Colonist Conflicts and Alliances," in *Encyclopedia of the North American Colonies,* ed. Jacob Ernest Cooke (New York: Charles Scribner's Sons, 1993), 223-36.
86 Webb, *1676: The End of American Independence,* 14.
87 Ibid., 14-15.
88 See O'Callaghan and Brodhead, *Documents,* 3:148, 1:77-78; Jennings, *The Ambiguous Iroquois Empire,* 132.
89 Jennings, *The Ambiguous Iroquois Empire,* 43.
90 Wraxall, *An Abridgment of the Indian Affairs,* 95.
91 See, for example, LAC, RG 10, reel C-1220, 72a-74.
92 Buffinton, "The Policy of Albany and English Westward Expansion," 337.
93 Jennings, *The Ambiguous Iroquois Empire,* 209.
94 White, *The Middle Ground.*
95 LAC, RG 10, reel C-1220, 10 October 1723, 114a-116.
96 Trelease, *Indian Affairs in Colonial New York,* 93.
97 Taiaiake (Gerald) Alfred, *Peace, Power, Righteousness: An Indigenous Manifesto* (Toronto: Oxford University Press, 1999), 52.
98 Atleo, *Tsawalk,* 23.
99 Trelease, *Indian Affairs in Colonial New York.*
100 Ibid., Chapter 4.
101 White, *The Middle Ground.*
102 Habermas, *The Theory of Communicative Action,* 82.
103 Ibid., 89.
104 Cornelius J. Jaenen, "The French Relationship with the Amerindians" (paper presented at the IV Convegno Internazionale dell'Associazione Italiana di Studi Canadesi, Universita di Messina, Messina, 25-28 March 1981).
105 Barbara Arneil, *John Locke and America: The Defence of English Colonialism* (Oxford: Clarendon Press, 1996), 33, 84.
106 Ibid., 82. This contradictory behaviour remains a topic of debate among historians. See Washburn and Trigger, "Native Peoples in Euro-American Historiography," 80, 84.
107 Arneil, *John Locke and America,* 82; Francis Jennings, "Virgin Land and Savage People," in *Indians and Europeans: Selected Articles on Indian-White Relations in Colonial North America,* ed. Peter Hoffer (New York: Garland, 1988), 112.
108 Arneil, *John Locke and America,* 81.
109 J. Holland Rose, Arthur Percival Newton, and E.A. Benians, eds., *The Cambridge History of the British Empire,* vol. 1, *The Old Empire from the Beginnings to 1763* (London: Cambridge University Press, 1929), 163-64.
110 Merrell, *Into the American Woods,* 196-97.
111 See, for example, Arneil, *John Locke and America,* 108, 14.
112 Ibid.
113 John Winthrop, "General Considerations for Planting New England," in *Chronicles of the First Planters of the Colony of Massachusetts Bay, 1623-1636,* ed. Alexander Young (Boston: C.C. Little and J. Brown, 1846), 277.
114 John Locke, *Two Treatises of Government,* ed. Peter Laslett, 2 vols. (New York: Cambridge University Press, 1960), 2: Part 3.
115 Arneil, *John Locke and America,* 84.
116 Ibid., 192.
117 Ibid., 194.

118 James Tully, *Strange Multiplicity: Constitutionalism in an Age of Diversity* (New York: Cambridge University Press, 1995), 71-72.

119 Ibid., 74.

120 Arneil, *John Locke and America*, 23.

121 Ibid., 16.

122 Ibid., 16, 23.

123 See, for instance, Jennings, *The Invasion of America*, 82; Chester Eisenger, "The Puritans' Justification for Taking the Land," *Essex Institute Historical Collections* 84 (1948): 131-43.

124 *Iroquois Indians: A Documentary History*, 536.

125 See, for example, Williams, *Linking Arms Together;* Kathy Butler, "Overcoming Terra Nullius: Aboriginal Perspectives in Schools as a Site of Philosophical Struggle," *Educational Philosophy and Theory* 32, 1 (2000): 93-101; Robert J. King, "Terra Australis: Terra Nullius Aut Terra Aboriginum?" *Journal of the Royal Australian Historical Society* 72, 2 (1986): 75-91.

126 Tully, *Strange Multiplicity*, 75.

Chapter 2: Structure and Function of the Covenant Chain Treaty Relationship

1 Richter, "Indian-Colonist Conflicts and Alliances," 225.

2 Merrell, *Into the American Woods*, 188.

3 Johnson, *Papers*, 11:576-77.

4 Richter, "Indian-Colonist Conflicts and Alliances," 225.

5 Fenton, "Structure, Continuity, and Change in the Process of Iroquois Treaty Making," 14.

6 Mary A. Druke, "Iroquois Treaties: Common Forms, Varying Interpretations," in Jennings et al., *The History and Culture of Iroquois Diplomacy*, 91.

7 Elizabeth S. Peña, "The Role of Wampum Production at the Albany Almshouse," *International Journal of Historical Archeology* 5, 2 (2001): 158.

8 Ibid.

9 Mary Maples Dunn and Richard S. Dunn, eds., *The Papers of William Penn* (Philadelphia: University of Pennsylvania Press, 1981), 2:243.

10 "Information about Pennsylvania Indian Affairs," 7 August 1755–3 December 1792, and at Easton, July and November 1756, Journal of C.F. Post, July-September 1758, and Charles Thomson's "Inquiry into Complaints of Delawares, 1757(?)-1758," in Jennings et al., *Iroquois Indians: A Documentary History*, reel 17, 29 July 1756. Original source, American Philosophical Society Library (APS), Philadelphia, Manuscripts, "Reports of Meetings with the Indians 1755-57, at Philadelphia and Easton; Journal of Christian Frederick Post, 1757; and Charles Thomson's enquiry, 1758," 970.4, M415.

11 Ibid.

12 Wraxall, *An Abridgment of the Indian Affairs*, 210. James Merrell also notes this event in pointing out the importance of wampum. See James H. Merrell, "Their Very Bones Shall Fight: The Catawba-Iroquois Wars," in Richter and Merrell, *Beyond the Covenant Chain*, 126.

13 Wraxall, *An Abridgment of the Indian Affairs*, 60-61.

14 Merrell, *Into the American Woods*, 191.

15 Ibid., 192. See also LAC, RG 10, reel C-1220, 88a-94, which describes a council between Governor Burnet and the Far Indians where belts were given with what appear to be acronyms on them, such as GR, GPW, and PF.

16 O'Callaghan and Brodhead, *Documents*, 2:625.

17 Merrell, *Into the American Woods*, 188.

18 Jennings, *Empire of Fortune*, 86.

19 See, for example, ibid., 317, and O'Callaghan and Brodhead, *Documents*, 10:574-75.

20 Merrell, *Into the American Woods*, 235.

21 Ibid., 183.

22 "Information about Pennsylvania Indian Affairs," 7 August 1755–3 December 1792, and at Easton, July and November 1756, Journal of C.F. Post, July-September 1758, and Charles Thomson's "Inquiry into Complaints of Delawares, 1757(?)-1758," Jennings et al., *Iroquois Indians: A Documentary History*, reel 17, 29 July 1756.

23 Johnson, *Papers*, 3:512.
24 Merrell, *Into the American Woods*, 103.
25 Ibid., 102.
26 Jürgen Habermas, *The Theory of Communicative Action*, vol. 2, *Lifeworld and System: A Critique of Functionalist Reason*, trans. Thomas McCarthy (Boston: Beacon Press, 1987), 122.
27 Ibid., 125.
28 Ibid., 126.
29 Strategic speech acts are instrumental, intended to help achieve some end, while communicative speech acts are aimed at developing mutual understanding. See Jürgen Habermas, *Moral Consciousness and Communicative Action*, trans. Christian Lenhardt and Shierry Weber Nicholsen (Cambridge, MA: MIT Press, 1990) and *The Theory of Communicative Action*, vol. 1.
30 Fenton, "Structure, Continuity, and Change," 6.
31 Ibid., 10.
32 William N. Fenton, "Sir William Johnson Carries the Ritual of Condolence over the Path to Onondaga, 1756," APS, William Fenton Papers, Series III, box set – Soc; "Condolence Ceremonies Involving Sir William Johnson," in *The Great Law and the Longhouse: A Political History of the Iroquois Confederacy*, ed. William N. Fenton (Norman: University of Oklahoma Press, 1998), 738-42.
33 Merrell, *Into the American Woods*, 211; Samuel Hazard, ed., *Minutes of the Provincial Council of Pennsylvania: From the Organization to the Termination of the Proprietary Government* (Philadelphia: T. Fenn and Co., 1851-52), 6:49.
34 Johnson, *Papers*, 2:238.
35 Reuben G. Thwaites, *The Jesuit Relations and Allied Documents: Travels and Explorations of the Jesuit Missionaries in New France, 1610-1791*, trans. Reuben G. Thwaites (Cleveland: Burrows Brothers Co., 1896), 27:247-53.
36 Jennings et al., "The Earliest Recorded Description: The Mohawk Treaty with New France at Three Rivers, 1645," in Jennings et al., *The History and Culture of Iroquois Diplomacy*, 139-42; Williams, "Linking Arms Together," 981.
37 Michael K. Foster, "Another Look at the Function of Wampum in Iroquois-White Councils," in Jennings et al., *The History and Culture of Iroquois Diplomacy*, 114.
38 Johnson, *Papers*, 3:208-9.
39 O'Callaghan and Brodhead, *Documents*, 3:321-28.
40 Ibid., 7:854-67.
41 Ibid.
42 Ibid., 4:492-95.
43 Ibid.
44 LAC, RG 10, reel C-1221, 29 March 1746, 349-50.
45 Jennings, *Empire of Fortune*, 60-62.
46 *Iroquois Indians: A Documentary History*, reel 17, 29 July 1756.
47 Johnson, *Papers*, 3:510-12.
48 Hazard, *Minutes of the Provincial Council*, 6:468-75.
49 Leder, *The Livingston Indian Records*, 36, 37, 45.
50 Johnson, *Papers*, 11:388.
51 Ibid., 1:512-13.
52 Ibid., 1:453.
53 LAC, RG 10, reel C-1220, 7-8 September 1733, 40a-42a.
54 LAC, RG 10, reel C-1220, 11 September 1733, 43.
55 Merrell, *Into the American Woods*, 217-20.
56 Hazard, *Minutes of the Provincial Council*, 7:689-91.
57 George S. Snyderman, "The Function of Wampum in Iroquois Religion," *American Philosophical Society Proceedings* 105 (1961): 475.
58 Ibid., 494.
59 For an Aboriginal reference to medicine, see LAC, RG 10, reel C-1220, 20 September 1725, 152.

60 See, for example, Marshall Joseph Becker, "The Vatican Wampum Belt: An Important American Indian Artifact and Its Cultural Origins and Meaning within the Category of 'Religious' or 'Ecclesiastical-Convert' Belts," http://www.cbu.ca/mrc/wampum.

61 William N. Fenton, "Wampum: The Magnet That Drew Furs from the Forest," in *The Great Law and the Longhouse: A Political History of the Iroquois Confederacy*, ed. William N. Fenton (Norman: University of Oklahoma Press, 1998).

62 Raymond Skye, *The Great Peace ... The Gathering of Good Minds* (Brantford, ON: Working World Training Centre, 1998), CD-ROM; Tehanetorens, *Wampum Belts* (Ohsweken, ON: Iroqrafts, 1983).

63 Williams, *Linking Arms Together*, 38.

64 Borrows, "Nanabush Goes West," and "Frozen Rights in Canada: Constitutional Interpretation and the Trickster," Chapter 3 in *Recovering Canada: The Resurgence of Indigenous Law* (Toronto: University of Toronto Press, 2002), 56-76.

65 Johnson, *Papers*, 3:709, 712.

66 White, *The Middle Ground*, 52.

67 Hazard, *Minutes of the Provincial Council*, 4:707.

68 Ibid.

69 LAC, RG 10, reel C-1220, June 1723, 33a-36.

70 White, *The Middle Ground*, 36.

71 Ibid., 145.

72 Thwaites, *The Jesuit Relations and Allied Documents*, 43:19.

73 Fenton, "Structure, Continuity, and Change," 10.

74 Ibid., 18.

75 Ibid., 19.

76 LAC, RG 10, reel C-1220, 7-8 September 1733, 40a-42a.

77 LAC, RG 10, reel C-1220, 4 July 1730, 320-24.

78 Ibid., 321.

79 Ibid., 321a.

80 LAC, RG 10, reel C-1220, 20 May 1731, 336-40.

81 Ibid., 340a.

82 LAC, RG 10, reel C-1220, 13 March 1724, 112-13a.

83 LAC, RG 10, MG 21, "Schedule of propositions."

84 *Iroquois Indians: A Documentary History*, reel 6, 20 July 1698, 4. Original source, Public Record Office, Kew, England, CO5/1041.

85 This is the fifty-reel repository titled *Iroquois Indians: A Documentary History*.

86 O'Callaghan and Brodhead, *Documents*.

87 LAC, RG 10, reel C-1220, 7 October 1723, 59-59a.

88 LAC, RG 10, reel C-1220, 27 June 1737, 110a-11a.

Chapter 3: Reputation and the Role of Key Agents

1 Hugh Shewell, *"Enough to Keep Them Alive": Indian Welfare in Canada, 1873-1965* (Toronto: University of Toronto Press, 2004), 20.

2 Ibid., 150.

3 Merrell, *Into the American Woods*, 32.

4 Ibid., 31.

5 Trelease, *Indian Affairs in Colonial New York*, 116.

6 Milton W. Hamilton, *Sir William Johnson and the Indians of New York* (Albany: University of the State of New York/State Educ. Dept., Office of State History, 1975), 5.

7 O'Callaghan and Brodhead, *Documents*, 13:112-13.

8 A.J.F. Van Laer, "Documents Related to Arent Van Curler's Death," in *Yearbook*, ed. A.J.F. Van Laer (Albany, NY: Dutch Settlers Society of Albany, 1927-28), 30.

9 Webb, *1676: The End of American Independence*, 319.

10 See O'Callaghan and Brodhead, *Documents*, 3:215, and ibid.

11 Jennings, *The Invasion of America*, 301.

12 Webb, *1676: The End of American Independence*, 332.

13 Ibid., 334.
14 O'Callaghan and Brodhead, *Documents,* 12:523-24.
15 Ibid., 12:542.
16 Ibid., 12:528.
17 Webb, *1676: The End of American Independence,* 352-53.
18 Ibid., 356.
19 O'Callaghan and Brodhead, *Documents,* 3:559.
20 Ibid.
21 Ibid., 3:360.
22 Webb, *1676: The End of American Independence,* 364.
23 See ibid., 366; W.H. Whitmore, ed., *The Andros Tracts: Being a Collection of Pamphlets and Official Papers* ... 3 vols. (New York: Burt Franklin, 1971), 1:100-13.
24 O'Callaghan and Brodhead, *Documents,* 13:509.
25 LAC, RG 10, reel C-1220, 14 July 1723, 82a.
26 LAC, RG 10, reel C-1220, 15 July 1724, 83-83a.
27 LAC, RG 10, reel C-1220, 7 August 1724, 85.
28 LAC, RG 10, reel C-1220, 10 June 1727, 188-88a.
29 LAC, MG 21, file 2, 28318, 28483.
30 Ibid., 28360.
31 Ibid., 28360.
32 Ibid., 28406.
33 Trelease, *Indian Affairs in Colonial New York,* 209.
34 Ibid., 311-12.
35 See ibid., 312. See also O'Callaghan and Brodhead, *Documents,* 4:222.
36 See O'Callaghan and Brodhead, *Documents,* 4:16, and Wraxall, *An Abridgment of the Indian Affairs,* 22.
37 See Trelease, *Indian Affairs in Colonial New York,* 336, and O'Callaghan and Brodhead, *Documents,* 4:362-64.
38 Trealease, *Indian Affairs in Colonial New York,* 315.
39 O'Callaghan and Brodhead, *Documents,* 2:576.
40 Jennings, *The Ambiguous Iroquois Empire,* 224-28.
41 Ibid., 240-48.
42 Samuel Hazard, *Annals of Pennsylvania from the Discovery of the Delaware, 1609-1682* (Philadelphia: Hazard and Mitchell, 1850), 532-33.
43 Jennings, *The Ambiguous Iroquois Empire,* 346-47.
44 Ibid., 241.
45 Paul A.W. Wallace, *Conrad Weiser: Friend of Colonist and Mohawk, 1696-1760* (New York: Russell and Russell, 1945), 96.
46 Ibid., 98.
47 Ibid., vii.
48 Merrell, *Into the American Woods,* 64.
49 Jennings, *The Ambiguous Iroquois Empire,* 313.
50 Wallace, *Conrad Weiser,* 32.
51 Ibid., 33.
52 Jennings, *The Ambiguous Iroquois Empire,* 356.
53 Wallace, *Conrad Weiser,* vii
54 Ibid., 46.
55 Ibid., 47.
56 Ibid., 189.
57 Ibid., 179.
58 Hazard, *Minutes of the Provincial Council,* 4:733.
59 Jennings, *The Ambiguous Iroquois Empire,* 379-87.
60 Horatio Hale, *Iroquois Book of Rites,* vol. 2 (Philadelphia: Library of Aboriginal American Literature, 1883; repr., ed. William Fenton, University of Toronto Press, 1963), 74.
61 Wallace, *Conrad Weiser,* 55.
62 Ibid., 184.

63 Ibid., 197-98.
64 Ibid., 199.
65 Ibid., 202.
66 Ibid., 248-49.
67 Ibid., 292.
68 Ibid., 300.
69 Ibid., 298.
70 Ibid., 247.
71 Jennings, *The Ambiguous Iroquois Empire,* 77.
72 Robert Moss, *The Firekeeper: A Narrative of the Eastern Frontier* (New York: Tom Doherty Associates, 1995).
73 Hamilton, *Sir William Johnson and the Indians of New York,* 10, 45.
74 Wraxall, *An Abridgment of the Indian Affairs,* xcix.
75 Jennings, *The Ambiguous Iroquois Empire,* 80.
76 O'Callaghan and Brodhead, *Documents,* 6:781-88.
77 Leo Francis Stock, ed., *Proceedings and Debates of the British Parliaments Respecting North America* (Washington, DC: Carnegie Institution, 1924), 2:437.
78 O'Callaghan and Brodhead, *Documents,* 6:799.
79 Ibid., 6:800.
80 Ibid., 6:805.
81 Ibid., 6:807.
82 Ibid., 6:797.
83 Ibid., 6:808-15.
84 John Christopher Guzzardo, "Sir William Johnson's Official Family: Patron and Clients in an Anglo-American Empire, 1742-1777" (PhD diss., Syracuse University, 1975). I have Wade Wells at the Johnson Hall historic site to thank for pointing out this unpublished dissertation to me.
85 Ibid., 54-56.
86 Ibid., 70.
87 Wallace, *Conrad Weiser,* 247-50.
88 Lois M. Huey and Bonnie Pulis, *Molly Brant: A Legacy of Her Own* (Youngstown, NY: Old Fort Niagara Association, 1997), 21.
89 Quoted in Wallace, *Conrad Weiser,* 350-51.
90 O'Callaghan and Morgan, *Documentary History,* 8:700-1.
91 Johnson, *Papers,* 1:465-66; Jennings, *The Ambiguous Iroquois Empire,* 117.
92 O'Callaghan and Brodhead, *Documents,* 6:897-99.
93 Johnson, *Papers,* 1:340.
94 Wraxall, *An Abridgment of the Indian Affairs,* cvi-cviii.
95 John Long, *Voyages and Travels of an Indian Interpreter and Trader* (1791; repr., Toronto: Coles, 1971), 88-89.
96 Wallace, *Conrad Weiser,* 151.
97 Ibid., 152.
98 Ibid., 247.
99 Ibid., 249.
100 Guzzardo, "Sir William Johnson's Official Family," 55.
101 Ibid., 107-8.
102 Ibid., 110.
103 Jennings, *Empire of Fortune,* 76; Huey and Pulis, *Molly Brant.*
104 Jennings, *Empire of Fortune,* 25-27.
105 See, Johnson, *Papers,* 12:370. See also 4:184 and 6:178.
106 Jennings et al., *The History and Culture of Iroquois Diplomacy,* 165.
107 White, *The Middle Ground,* 434.
108 Johnson, *Papers,* 3:203-16.
109 Ibid., 3:353-55.
110 Ibid., 3:395.
111 Ibid., 3:428-523.

112 George III, Royal Proclamation, 1763.
113 Johnson, *Papers*, 3:421.
114 Ibid., 3:428-37.
115 Ibid., 3:437-40.
116 Ibid., 3:442-48.
117 Ibid., 3:456.
118 Ibid., 3:450.
119 Ibid., 3:474-82.
120 Ibid., 1:339-40.
121 O'Callaghan and Brodhead, *Documents*, 6:876.
122 White, *The Middle Ground*, 226.
123 Johnson, *Papers*, 11:13.
124 Ibid., 4:134, 35, 37.
125 Ibid., 4:96-100.
126 Ibid., 4:99.
127 See White, *The Middle Ground*, 288; Parmenter, "Pontiac's War," 628. See also the letter from Bouquet to Amherst, 15 July 1763, LAC, Amherst Papers, MG 13, W034, B2693.
128 Johnson, *Papers*, 4:235-36.
129 Ibid., 4:231.
130 White, *The Middle Ground*, 279.
131 Johnson, *Papers*, 4:464.
132 Ibid., 4:503.
133 Ibid., 4:508-10.
134 Ibid., 4:522.
135 Ibid., 11:342-44.
136 Ibid., 4:524-25.
137 Ibid.
138 Ibid., 11:340-41.
139 Ibid., 4:526-33.
140 Ibid.
141 Ibid., 11:394-96.
142 Ibid., 4:610.
143 Ibid., 4:615.
144 Ibid., 4:534.
145 Ibid., 4:538-39.
146 Ibid., 11:399.
147 Ibid., 11:438-56.
148 Ibid., 11:491-95.
149 Ibid., 1:346-47.

Chapter 4: The Transcultural, Transhistorical Ethic of the Covenant Chain

1 Even though Habermas today uses the term *discourse morality* – because, for him, ethics (*Sittlichkeit*) is a culturally situated and relative normative system – I retain the term *discourse ethics* because it is the term with which most people interested in the Habermasian approach are familiar and because, in English philosophy, the distinction between ethics and morality is not as strong as it is in German philosophy. English philosophers sometimes use phrases such as "his moral beliefs constrained him to do x." They sometimes use *ethical theory* to refer to the theoretical debate over ultimate, universal grounding and moral theory to refer to the same. What is important for my purposes is not terminological consistency with Habermas but the distinction between being culturally and historically bound (the realm of relativistic ethics) and being crossculturally and transhistorically legitimate (the realm of universal ethics). I do not adopt Habermas' discourse ethics in total because of problems that inhere in it; consequently, I am not inclined to adopt his language in total.

2 Jürgen Habermas, *Justification and Application: Remarks on Discourse Ethics*, trans. Ciaran Cronin (Cambridge, MA: MIT Press, 1995), 129.

3 Habermas, *Moral Consciousness and Communicative Action,* 36.
4 Habermas, *The Theory of Communicative Action,* Vol. 1, Chap. 2, and Vol. 2, Chap. 5, section 1; and see, especially, Habermas, *Moral Consciousness and Communicative Action,* Chap. 2, "Reconstruction and Interpretation in the Social Sciences."
5 See Habermas, *The Theory of Communicative Action,* Vol. 1, 75, 307.
6 Ibid., Vol. 1, 44, 45, 51.
7 Ibid., Vol. 1, 69, 86, 117.
8 Ibid., Vol. 1, 137.
9 Habermas, *Justification and Application,* 114.
10 Habermas, *The Theory of Communicative Action,* Vol. 2, 9.
11 Habermas, *Justification and Application,* 130.
12 Habermas, *The Theory of Communicative Action,* Vol. 2, 7.
13 Ibid., Vol. 2, 9.
14 Ibid., Vol. 2, 18.
15 Ibid., Vol. 2, 19.
16 Ibid., Vol. 2, 38-39.
17 Charles Taylor, *Sources of the Self: The Making of the Modern Identity* (Cambridge, MA: Harvard University Press, 1989), 64, 86-87, 98.
18 Ibid., 88-89.
19 Ibid., 87.
20 Ibid., 63.
21 Ibid., 72.
22 Ibid., 92.
23 Ibid., 96.
24 Ibid., 103.
25 See Thomas H. Birch, "Moral Considerability and Universal Consideration," in *Environmental Ethics: Divergence and Convergence,* ed. Susan J. Armstrong and Richard G. Botzler (New York: McGraw-Hill, 1998), 380-90.
26 Only rare glimpses of other performative communications are indicated in the record, but even their limited presence is informative. As mentioned, the pipe ceremony and dancing were also significant in creating and sustaining a sense of unity.
27 Taylor, *Sources of the Self,* 8.
28 Ibid., 33.
29 Ibid., 35.
30 Ibid., 72.
31 Habermas, *Justification and Application,* 165.
32 Thomas Nagel, *Ruthlessness in Public Life,* ed. Stuart Hampshire (New York: Cambridge University Press, 1978).
33 Tully, *Strange Multiplicity.*
34 Ibid., 60.
35 Ibid., 127-28.
36 Ibid., 131.
37 Ibid., 133.
38 Ibid., 131.
39 Gottfried Wilhelm Leibniz, *Monadology, and Other Philosophical Essays,* trans. Paul Schrecker and Anne Martin Schrecker (Indianapolis: Bobbs-Merrill Co., 1965), xxiii.
40 Ibid., xiv, xxiii.
41 See James Rachels, "Moral Philosophy as a Subversive Activity," in *Applied Ethics: A Reader,* ed. Earl R. Winkler (Cambridge, MA: Blackwell Publishers, 1990); Barry Hoffmaster, "The Theory and Practice of Applied Ethics," *Dialogue* 30 (1991): 213-34; Alisdair MacIntyre, *After Virtue* (Notre Dame, IN: University of Notre Dame Press, 1981), 20-21; Annette Baier, "Trust and Antitrust of Moral Theorists," *Ethics* 96 (1986): 232-60; Nancy (Ann) Davis, "Moral Theorizing and Moral Practice: Reflections on Some of the Sources of Hyprocrisy," in *Applied Ethics: A Reader,* ed. Earl R. Winkler (Cambridge, MA: Blackwell Publishers, 1990); and James Jakób Liszka, *Moral Competence: An Integrated Approach to the Study of Ethics,* 2nd ed. (Upper Saddle River, NJ: Pearson Education, 2002).

42 For Bohm's notion of the implicate order, see *Wholeness and the Implicate Order* (New York: Routledge, 1980).

43 Jan Zwicky, *Wisdom and Metaphor* (Kentville, NS: Gaspereau Press, 2003), 5.

44 Ibid., 8.

45 Ibid., 9.

46 Ibid., 11.

47 See Clammer, Poirier, and Schwimmer, "Introduction," 3-22.

Epilogue

1 Dale Turner, *This Is Not a Peace Pipe: Towards a Critical Indigenous Philosophy* (Toronto: University of Toronto Press, 2006), 47-52.

2 Ibid., 74.

3 See Alan C. Cairns, *Citizens Plus: Aboriginal Peoples and the Canadian State* (Vancouver: UBC Press, 2000); Will Kymlicka, *Liberalism, Community and Culture* (Oxford: Oxford University Press, 1989).

Bibliography

Archival Sources

Archives of Ontario (AO), Toronto, Ontario

American Philosophical Society Library (APS), Philadelphia, Pennsylvania
William Fenton Papers

Library and Archives Canada (LAC), Ottawa, Ontario
MG 13, Amherst Papers
MG 19, Articles of Peace, Friendship and Alliance, concluded by Sir William Johnson Baronet ...
MG 21, Commission for Indian Affairs, Albany, "Schedule of propositions made by the Indians and answers given by the Commission at Albany, 1677-1719"
RG 10, Department of Indian Affairs

Published Sources
Alfred, Taiaiake (Gerald). *Peace, Power, Righteousness: An Indigenous Manifesto.* Toronto: Oxford University Press, 1999.
Arneil, Barbara. *John Locke and America: The Defence of English Colonialism.* Oxford: Clarendon Press, 1996.
Atleo, E. Richard (Umeek). *Tsawalk: A Nuu-Chah-Nulth Worldview.* Vancouver: UBC Press, 2004.
Axtell, James. "A Moral History of Indian-White Relations Revisited." In *After Columbus: Essays in the Ethnohistory of Colonial North America,* edited by James Axtell, 9-33. New York: Oxford University Press, 1988.
Baier, Annette. "Trust and Antitrust of Moral Theorists." *Ethics* 96 (1986): 232-60.
Becker, Marshall Joseph. "The Vatican Wampum Belt: An Important American Indian Artifact and Its Cultural Origins and Meaning within the Category of 'Religious' or 'Ecclesiastical-Convert' Belts." http://www.cbu.ca/mrc/wampum.
Birch, Thomas H. "Moral Considerability and Universal Consideration." In *Environmental Ethics: Divergence and Convergence,* edited by Susan J. Armstrong and Richard G. Botzler, 380-90. New York: McGraw-Hill, 1998.
Bohm, David. *Wholeness and the Implicate Order.* New York: Routledge, 1980.
Borrows, John. "Frozen Rights in Canada: Constitutional Interpretation and the Trickster." Chapter 3 in *Recovering Canada: The Resurgence of Indigenous Law,* 56-76. Toronto: University of Toronto Press, 2002.
–. "Nanabush Goes West: Title, Treaties, and the Trickster in British Columbia." Chapter 4 in *Recovering Canada,* 77-110. Toronto: University of Toronto Press, 2002.
Bougainville, Louis Antoine de. *Adventures in the Wilderness: The American Journals of Louis Antoine de Bougainville, 1756-1760.* Edited by Edward P. Hamilton. Norman: University of Oklahoma Press, 1964.

Buffinton, Arthur H. "The Policy of Albany and English Westward Expansion." *Mississippi Valley Historical Review* 8, 4 (1922): 327-66.

Butler, Kathy. "Overcoming Terra Nullius: Aboriginal Perspectives in Schools as a Site of Philosophical Struggle." *Educational Philosophy and Theory* 32, 1 (2000): 93-101.

Cairns, Alan C. *Citizens Plus: Aboriginal Peoples and the Canadian State.* Vancouver: UBC Press, 2000.

Clammer, John, Sylvie Poirier, and Eric Schwimmer. "Introduction: The Relevance of Ontologies in Anthropology – Reflections on a New Anthropological Field." In *Figured Worlds: Ontological Obstacles in Inter-Cultural Relations,* edited by Michael Lambek, 3-22. Toronto: University of Toronto Press, 2004.

Davidson, Donald. "Actions, Reasons and Causes." *Journal of Philosophy* 60, 23 (1963): 685-700.

–. "Causal Relations." *Journal of Philosophy* 64, 21 (1967): 691-703.

–. "Freedom to Act." In *Essays on Freedom of Action,* edited by Ted Honderich, 139-56. London: Routledge and Kegan Paul, 1973.

–. "Thinking Causes." In *Mental Causation,* edited by John Heil and Alfred Mele, 3-17. Oxford: Clarendon Press, 1993.

Davis, Nancy (Ann). "Moral Theorizing and Moral Practice: Reflections on Some of the Sources of Hyprocrisy." In *Applied Ethics: A Reader,* edited by Earl R. Winkler, 164-80. Cambridge, MA: Blackwell Publishers, 1990.

Dickason, Olive. *Canada's First Nations: A History of Founding Peoples from Earliest Times.* Toronto: McClelland and Stewart, 1992.

–. *The Myth of the Savage and the Beginnings of French Colonialism in the Americas.* Edmonton: University of Alberta Press, 1984.

Druke, Mary A. "Iroquois Treaties: Common Forms, Varying Interpretations." In Jennings et al., *The History and Culture of Iroquois Diplomacy,* 85-98.

Dunn, Mary Maples, and Richard S. Dunn, eds. *The Papers of William Penn.* 5 vols. Philadelphia: University of Pennsylvania Press, 1981.

Eid, Leroy V. "The Ojibwa-Iroquois War: The War the Five Nations Did Not Win." *Ethnohistory* 26, 4 (1979): 297-324.

Eisenger, Chester. "The Puritans' Justification for Taking the Land." *Essex Institute Historical Collections* 84 (1948): 131-43.

Emery, Alan R., and associates. *Guidelines for Environmental Assessments and Traditional Knowledge.* Ottawa: Centre for Traditional Knowledge to the World Council of Indigenous People, 1997.

Fenton, William N. "Condolence Ceremonies Involving Sir William Johnson." In *The Great Law and the Longhouse: A Political History of the Iroquois Confederacy,* edited by William N. Fenton, 738-42. Norman: University of Oklahoma Press, 1998.

–. "Structure, Continuity, and Change in the Process of Iroquois Treaty Making." In Jennings et al., *The History and Culture of Iroquois Diplomacy,* 3-36.

–. "Wampum: The Magnet That Drew Furs from the Forest." In *The Great Law and the Longhouse: A Political History of the Iroquois Confederacy,* edited by William N. Fenton, 224-39. Norman: University of Oklahoma Press, 1998.

Fischer, David Hackett. *Champlain's Dream.* Toronto: Vintage Canada, 2009.

Foster, Michael K. "Another Look at the Function of Wampum in Iroquois-White Councils." In Jennings et al., *The History and Culture of Iroquois Diplomacy,* 99-114.

Francis, Daniel. *The Imaginary Indian: The Image of the Indian in Canadian Culture.* Vancouver: Arsenal Pulp Press, 1992.

Geertz, Clifford. *The Interpretation of Cultures.* New York: Basic Books, 1973.

Gill, Sam D. *Mother Earth: An American Story.* Chicago: University of Chicago Press, 1987.

Guzzardo, John Christopher. "Sir William Johnson's Official Family: Patron and Clients in an Anglo-American Empire, 1742-1777." PhD diss., Syracuse University, 1975.

Habermas, Jürgen. *Justification and Application: Remarks on Discourse Ethics.* Translated by Ciaran Cronin. Cambridge, MA: MIT Press, 1995.

–. *Moral Consciousness and Communicative Action.* Translated by Christian Lenhardt and Shierry Weber Nicholsen. Cambridge, MA: MIT Press, 1990.

–. *The Theory of Communicative Action.* Vol. 1, *Reason and the Rationalization of Society.* Translated by Thomas McCarthy. Boston: Beacon Press, 1984.

–. *The Theory of Communicative Action.* Vol. 2, *Lifeworld and System: A Critique of Functionalist Reason.* Translated by Thomas McCarthy. Boston: Beacon Press, 1987.

Hale, Horatio. *Iroquois Book of Rites.* Vol. 2. Philadelphia: Library of Aboriginal American Literature, 1883. Reprint, edited by William Fenton, Toronto: University of Toronto Press, 1963.

Hamilton, Milton W. *Sir William Johnson and the Indians of New York.* Albany: University of the State of New York/State Educ. Dept., Office of State History, 1975.

Hazard, Samuel. *Annals of Pennsylvania from the Discovery of the Delaware, 1609-1682.* Philadelphia: Hazard and Mitchell, 1850.

–, ed. *Minutes of the Provincial Council of Pennsylvania: From the Organization to the Termination of the Proprietary Government.* 16 vols. Philadelphia: T. Fenn and Co., 1851-52.

Hoffmaster, Barry. "The Theory and Practice of Applied Ethics." *Dialogue* 30 (1991): 213-34.

Huey, Lois M., and Bonnie Pulis. *Molly Brant: A Legacy of Her Own.* Youngstown, NY: Old Fort Niagara Association, Inc., 1997.

Jaenen, Cornelius J. "The French Relationship with the Amerindians." Paper presented at the IV Convegno Internazionale dell'Associazione Italiana di Studi Canadesi, Universita di Messina, Messina, Italy, 25-28 March 1981.

Jennings, Francis. *The Ambiguous Iroquois Empire: The Covenant Chain Confederation of Indian Tribes with English Colonies from Its Beginnings to the Lancaster Treaty of 1744.* New York: W.W. Norton and Company, 1984.

–. *Empire of Fortune: Crowns, Colonies, and Tribes in the Seven Years' War in America.* New York: W.W. Norton and Company, 1988.

–. *The Invasion of America: Indians, Colonialism, and the Cant of Conquest.* Chapel Hill: University of North Carolina Press, 1975.

–. "Iroquois Alliances in American History." In Jennings et al., *The History and Culture of Iroquois Diplomacy,* 37-65.

–. "Virgin Land and Savage People." In *Indians and Europeans: Selected Articles on Indian-White Relations in Colonial North America,* edited by Peter Hoffer, 100-22. New York: Garland, 1988.

Jennings, Francis, William N. Fenton, Mary A. Druke, and David R. Miller. "The Earliest Recorded Description: The Mohawk Treaty with New France at Three Rivers, 1645." In Jennings et al., *The History and Culture of Iroquois Diplomacy,* 127-53.

–, eds. *The History and Culture of Iroquois Diplomacy: An Interdisciplinary Guide to the Treaties of the Six Nations and Their League.* Syracuse, NY: Syracuse University Press, 1985.

Jennings, Francis, William N. Fenton, Mary Druke Becker, and D'Arcy McNickle Center for the History of the American Indian, eds. *Iroquois Indians: A Documentary History of the Diplomacy of the Six Nations and Their League.* Microfilm collection. Woodbridge, CT: Research Publications, 1984.

Johnson, William. *The Papers of Sir William Johnson.* Various editors. 13 vols. Albany: University of the State of New York, 1951.

King, Robert J. "Terra Australis: Terra Nullius Aut Terra Aboriginum?" *Journal of the Royal Australian Historical Society* 72, 2 (1986): 75-91.

Krech, Shepard, III. *The Ecological Indian: Myth and History.* New York: W.W. Norton and Co., 1999.

Kymlicka, Will. "American Multi-Culturalism and the 'Nations Within.'" In *Political Theory and the Rights of Indigenous Peoples,* edited by Duncan Ivison, Paul Patton, and Will Sanders, 216-36. Cambridge: Cambridge University Press, 2000.

–. *Liberalism, Community and Culture.* Oxford: Oxford University Press, 1989.

Leder, Lawrence H., ed. *The Livingston Indian Records, 1666-1723.* Gettysburg: Pennsylvania Historical Association, 1956.

Leibniz, Gottfried Wilhelm. *Monadology, and Other Philosophical Essays.* Translated by Paul Schrecker and Anne Martin Schrecker. Indianapolis: Bobbs-Merrill Co., 1965.

Liszka, James Jakób. *Moral Competence: An Integrated Approach to the Study of Ethics.* 2nd ed. Upper Saddle River, NJ: Pearson Education, 2002.

Locke, John. *Two Treatises of Government*. Edited by Peter Laslett. 2 vols. New York: Cambridge University Press, 1960.

Long, John. *Voyages and Travels of an Indian Interpreter and Trader*. 1791. Reprint, Toronto: Coles, 1971.

MacIntyre, Alisdair. *After Virtue*. Notre Dame, IN: University of Notre Dame Press, 1981.

Merrell, James H. *Into the American Woods: Negotiators on the Pennsylvania Frontier*. New York: W.W. Norton, 1999.

–. "Their Very Bones Shall Fight: The Catawba-Iroquois Wars." In Richter and Merrell, *Beyond the Covenant Chain*, 115-33.

Michelson, Gunther. "The Covenant Chain in Colonial History." *Man in the Northeast* 21 (1981): 115-26.

Morison, Samuel Eliot, ed. *The Francis Parkman Reader*. Cambridge, MA: Da Capo Press, 1998.

Morito, Bruce. *Thinking Ecologically: Environmental Thought, Values and Policy*. Halifax, NS: Fernwood, 2002.

Moss, Robert. *The Firekeeper: A Narrative of the Eastern Frontier*. New York: Tom Doherty Associates, 1995.

Nabakov, Peter. "Native Views of History." In *The Cambridge History of the Native Peoples of the Americas*, Vol. 1, *North America*, edited by Bruce G. Trigger and Wilcomb E. Washburn, 1-59. New York: Cambridge University Press, 1996.

Nagel, Thomas. *Ruthlessness in Public Life*. Edited by Stuart Hampshire. New York: Cambridge University Press, 1978.

O'Callaghan, E.B., and John Romeyn Brodhead, eds. *Documents Relative to the Colonial History of the State of New-York* ... 15 vols. Albany: Weed, Parsons, and Company, 1853-57.

O'Callaghan, E.B., and Christopher Morgan, eds. *The Documentary History of the State of New-York*. 5 vols. Albany: Weed, Parsons, 1850.

Parmenter, Jon William. "Pontiac's War: Forging New Links in the Anglo-Iroquois Covenant Chain." *Ethnohistory* 44, 4 (1997): 617-54.

Peña, Elizabeth S. "The Role of Wampum Production at the Albany Almshouse." *International Journal of Historical Archeology* 5, 2 (2001): 155-74.

Pomedli, Michael. "Eighteenth-Century Treaties." *American Indian Quarterly* 19, 3 (1995): 319-39.

Rachels, James. "Moral Philosophy as a Subversive Activity." In *Applied Ethics: A Reader*, edited by Earl R. Winkler, 110-29. Cambridge, MA: Blackwell Publishers, 1990.

Richter, Daniel K. "Indian-Colonist Conflicts and Alliances." In *Encyclopedia of the North American Colonies*, edited by Jacob Ernest Cooke, 223-36. New York: Charles Scribner's Sons, 1993.

–. "Ordeals of the Longhouse: The Five Nations in Early American History." In Richter and Merrell, *Beyond the Covenant Chain*, 11-27.

Richter, Daniel K., and James H. Merrell, eds. *Beyond the Covenant Chain: The Iroquois and Their Neighbors in Indian North America*. Syracuse: Syracuse University Press, 1987.

Rose, J. Holland, Arthur Percival Newton, and E.A. Benians, eds. *The Cambridge History of the British Empire*. Vol. 1, *The Old Empire from the Beginnings to 1763*. London: Cambridge University Press, 1929.

Rousseau, Jean-Jacques. "Discourse on the Origin and Foundations of Inequality." In *The First and Second Discourses: Jean-Jacques Rousseau*, edited by Roger D. Masters, 77-181. New York: St. Martin's Press, 1964.

Scientific Panel for Sustainable Forest Practices in Clayoquot Sound. *First Nations' Perspective: Relating to Forest Practices Standards in Clayoquot Sound*. Victoria: Government of British Columbia, 1995.

Searle, John. "Minds, Brains, and Programs." *Behavioral and Brain Sciences* 3 (1980): 417-24.

Sheehan, Bernard W. "Indian-White Relations in Early America: A Review Essay." *William and Mary Quarterly*, 3rd series, 26 (1969): 267-86.

Shewell, Hugh *"Enough to Keep Them Alive": Indian Welfare in Canada, 1873-1965*. Toronto: University of Toronto Press, 2004.

Sioui, Georges E. *For an Amerindian Autohistory*. Translated by Sheila Fischman. Montreal and Kingston: McGill-Queen's University Press, 1992.

Skye, Raymond. *The Great Peace ... The Gathering of Good Minds*. Brantford, ON: Working World Training Centre, 1998. CD-ROM.

Snyderman, George S. "The Function of Wampum in Iroquois Religion." *American Philosophical Society Proceedings* 105 (1961): 571-608.

Speck, Frank G. *The Penn Wampum Belts*. New York: Museum of the American Indian, 1925.

Stock, Leo Francis, ed. *Proceedings and Debates of the British Parliaments Respecting North America*. Vol. 2. Washington, DC: Carnegie Institution, 1924.

Taylor, Charles. *Sources of the Self: The Making of the Modern Identity*. Cambridge, MA: Harvard University Press, 1989.

Tehanetorens. *Wampum Belts*. Ohsweken, ON: Iroqrafts, 1983.

Thwaites, Reuben G. *The Jesuit Relations and Allied Documents: Travels and Explorations of the Jesuit Missionaries in New France, 1610-1791*. 73 vols. Translated by Reuben G. Thwaites. Cleveland: Burrows Brothers, 1896.

Trelease, Allen W. *Indian Affairs in Colonial New York: The Seventeenth Century*. Ithaca, NY: Cornell University Press, 1960.

Trigger, Bruce G. "Brecht and Ethnohistory." *Ethnohistory* 22, 1 (1975): 51-56.

–. *Children of Aetaentsic: A History of the Huron People to 1660*. Carleton Library Series 195. Montreal and Kingston: McGill-Queen's University Press, 1976.

Trigger, Bruce G., and Wilcomb E. Washburn, eds. *The Cambridge History of the Native Peoples of the Americas*. Vol. 1, *North America*. New York: Cambridge University Press, 1996.

Tully, James. *Strange Multiplicity: Constitutionalism in an Age of Diversity*. New York: Cambridge University Press, 1995.

Turner, Dale. *This Is Not a Peace Pipe: Towards a Critical Indigenous Philosophy*. Toronto: University of Toronto Press, 2006.

Van Laer, A.J.F. "Documents Related to Arent Van Curler's Death." In *Yearbook*, edited by A.J.F Van Laer, 30-34. Albany, NY: Dutch Settlers Society of Albany, 1927-28.

Van Loon, L.G. "Tawagonshi, Beginning of Treaty Era." *Indian Historian* 1, 3 (1968): 23-26.

Wallace, Paul A.W. *Conrad Weiser: Friend of Colonist and Mohawk, 1696-1760*. New York: Russell and Russell, 1945.

Walters, Mark D. "Brightening the Covenant Chain: Aboriginal Treaty Meanings in Law and History after *Marshall*." *Dalhousie Law Journal* 24, 2 (2001): 75-138.

Warren, William W. *History of the Ojibway People*. St. Paul: Minnesota Historical Society Press, 1984.

Washburn, Wilcomb E., and Bruce G. Trigger. "Native Peoples in Euro-American Historiography." In *The Cambridge History of the Native Peoples of the Americas*, Vol. 1, *North America*, edited by Bruce G. Trigger and Wilcomb E. Washburn, 61-124. New York: Cambridge University Press, 1996.

Webb, Stephen Saunders. *1676: The End of American Independence*. New York: Alfred A. Knopf, 1984.

Webber, Jeremy. "Relations of Force and Relations of Justice: The Emergence of Normative Community between Colonists and Aboriginal Peoples." *Osgoode Hall Law Journal* 33, 4 (1995): 623-60.

White, Richard. *The Middle Ground: Indians, Empires and Republics in the Great Lakes Region, 1650-1815*. Cambridge: Cambridge University Press, 1991.

Whitmore, W.H., ed. *The Andros Tracts: Being a Collection of Pamphlets and Official Papers ...* 3 vols. New York: Burt Franklin, 1971.

Williams, Paul. "The Chain." Master's thesis, Osgoode Hall Law School, 1982.

Williams, Robert A., Jr. *Linking Arms Together: American Indian Treaty Visions of Law and Peace, 1600-1800*. New York: Oxford University Press, 1997.

–. "Linking Arms Together: Multicultural Constitutionalism in a North American Indigenous Vision of Law and Peace." *California Law Review* 82, 4 (1994): 981-1049.

Winthrop, John. "General Considerations for Planting New England." In *Chronicles of the First Planters of the Colony of Massachusetts Bay, 1623-1636*, edited by Alexander Young, 270-78. Boston: C.C. Little and J. Brown, 1846.

Wraxall, Peter. *An Abridgment of the Indian Affairs, Contained in Four Folio Volumes, Transacted in the Colony of New York, from the Year 1678 to the Year 1751*. Edited by Charles Howard McIlwain. Cambridge: Harvard University Press, 1915. Reprint, New York: Benjamin Bloom, 1968.

Wroth, Lawrence C. "The Indian Treaty as Literature." *Yale Review* 17 (1928): 749-66.

Zwicky, Jan. *Wisdom and Metaphor*. Kentville, NS: Gaspereau Press, 2003.

Index

Printed and bound in Canada by Friesens

Set in Stone by Artegraphica Design Co. Ltd.

Copy editor: Lesley Erickson

Proofreader: Jenna Newman

Cartographer: Eric Leinberger